First published in October 2006

A catalogue record for this book is available from the British Library

ISBN 1 84425 309 0

Library of Congress catalog card no 2006924132

Published by Haynes Publishing,
Sparkford, Yeovil, Somerset BA22 7JJ, UK
Tel: 01963 442030 Fax: 01963 440001
Int. tel: +44 1963 442030 Int. fax: +44 1963 440001
E-mail: sales@haynes.co.uk
Website: www.haynes.co.uk

Haynes North America Inc,
861 Lawrence Drive, Newbury Park,
California 91320, USA.

Designed by Richard Parsons

Printed and bound in Great Britain by J. H. Haynes & Co. Ltd, Sparkford

ILLUSTRATIONS

Unless otherwise stated, all photos are from LAT Photographic, and are
mainly taken from the archives of *The Autocar* (latterly *Autocar*), *The
Motor* (latterly *Motor*), and *Classic & Sports Car*. The author is grateful
to Kevin Wood of LAT for his warm welcome and his help in
assembling the necessary material. For details of the archive's services,
write to LAT Photographic, Teddington Studios, Broom Road,
Teddington, Middlesex TW11 9BE, visit website www.latphoto.co.uk,
or phone 0208 251 3000.

Classic BRITISH SPORTS CARS

JON PRESSNELL

CONTENTS

PREFACE

As I sit writing this, my 42-year-old MG is parked outside, hood-down, with another few hundred miles of summertime motoring under its belt. Soon it will be taking me back to my home in the south-west of France, hood-down all the way, so long as it's not raining – or at least not raining *too* hard.

If you've read this far, chances are that this will be your sort of book. Because it's about cars that aren't the average tin box, cars that don't just put the wind in your hair but also have the character, the performance and the road behaviour to put a smile on your face.

For those who are new to the classic-car scene, the pages that follow contain a review of the most interesting and historically significant sports cars Britain has made – and you should know that the two don't necessarily go together.

Some of these cars have had entire books – sometimes many books – devoted to them. Others have received less attention, and sometimes even been the subject of less than favourable comment over the years. I have tried to put each car in its context and give an idea of its appeal, and what it is like to drive – as well as endeavouring to incorporate as many fascinating tit-bits of information as possible.

Having spent the past 20 years writing for *Classic & Sports Car* magazine, I have researched the history of a great many of the cars featured in these pages, driven a fair proportion of them, and spent time talking to many of those who designed the cars or played an important part in their history. So this is a short cut, if you like, to an understanding of the models featured.

If you're already a knowledgeable enthusiast, *Classic British Sports Cars* should thus prove a handy and I hope reliable work of reference and synopsis. It is all too common – and so frustrating – to plough through a serious marque history and yet not find basic technical information or the exact date an important change took place, or when a model was introduced or deleted. Aware of this, I have tried to make the 'Specification' and 'Evolution' sections as accurate as possible. This has often entailed much back-and-forth telephoning and e-mailing to experts on the model in question.

Despite this, it has sometimes not been possible to pinpoint a date more than approximately. Changes were often phased in, without any announcement, just as models were quietly dropped from production but continued to be listed for many months – sometimes years, even – after their manufacture had ceased.

The same challenges arise when seeking technical information. In pre-war years it was quite common for manufacturers not to cite the horsepower their engines developed – or if they did, not to quote at what rpm maximum power was achieved. Nor was it always the case – astonishing though this might seem today – that a magazine road test invariably furnished a maximum speed or an acceleration figure, let alone a reliable guide to the car's kerb weight, fuelled-up and ready to go.

In my wish to provide the most complete and accurate information possible, I have occasionally had to admit defeat. That such instances have been rare is due to the support I have received from friends and acquaintances – old and new – in the classic-car world. Some of these people have been unstinting in their help, and in some instances have also vetted what I have written. My sincere thanks go to them all: their names are given in the acknowledgements section.

In closing, it is perhaps appropriate to say that when I reached the age of 30 and realised that I hadn't at that stage owned a sports car, I went out and bought one – not quite straightaway, not quite impulsively, but certainly with determination. I've never regretted it, and throughout my 20-odd years of sports-car ownership I've had fun, made friends, and – I hope – stayed a little younger than might otherwise have been the case.

You can do the same – whether with a superb vintage Bentley or Lagonda or the crumbling remains of an old Austin-Healey bought for a few hundred pounds. If this book encourages you to take the plunge, I'll be delighted. You won't regret it, I promise.

Happy reading...and *bonne route*!

Jon Pressnell
September 2006

OPPOSITE The Triumph Spitfire in its original low-bumper form. It needn't cost you much to buy a popular post-war sports car such as this.

BELOW To the fore in this group of vintage Bentleys is the emblematic supercharged 4½-litre model. Coveted from their very earliest days, pre-1931 Bentleys command substantial prices today, so this is the other end of the spectrum.

INTRODUCTION

Of all the corny questions, what constitutes a sports car has to be the corniest of all – not least as what a casual observer might call a sports car can quite often be rejected as such, with derision, by an informed enthusiast. Sometimes, of course, it cuts the other way. Arriving once at a bed-and-breakfast in his tuned MG, the author was greeted with an 'Oh I do like your car – it's really cute' from the lady proprietor. Sports cars aren't supposed to be cute. But then again, how else could you describe, for example, a Frogeye Sprite or a little sprat of a Berkeley?

The basic ground rule followed in this book is that a sports car is a two-seater open car of better than average performance and road behaviour for its size; having a certain competition record is a bonus, although virtually everything this side of a Hillman Super Minx can claim some sporting silverware. But advancing the definition above is of course to make oneself a hostage to fortune.

In the era pre-war when most cars were open, many recognised sports cars carried four-seater tourer coachwork. Yet their performance and their achievements in motor sport leave no doubt as to their status: it is plainly ridiculous

to say that a supercharged Bentley 4½-litre is not a sports car simply because it carries open tourer bodywork. Yet the preconception that four seats are incompatible with the genre almost had the author omit the Vauxhall 30/98 from his selection, an omission that on reflection really would have been idiotic. At the same time, though, one somehow knows that an MG TD is a sports car but that a Singer Roadster, with its four seats, is not...

One is on safer ground in stipulating that a sports car should be open, and the author has rigidly adhered to this criterion. A reasonable rule of thumb is that if a sporting two-seater or close-coupled four-seater is closed, it's a grand tourer. Such a definition fits an Aston Martin DB4 as comfortably as it does a fixed-head Jaguar E-type.

But doesn't the term grand tourer – GT in accepted shorthand – presuppose that the car possess the comfort and refinement to make it suitable for the grand tour? On that basis you can count out the noisy and harsh Lotus Elite, the cramped greenhouse-effect MGA coupé, and the relatively uncouth TVRs of the 1960s. So are such vehicles sports cars? In saying 'no', one casts them into a label-less

OPPOSITE At speed in a Jaguar XK120: the finely-slatted grille and slim bumpers distinguish it from the later XK140, which incorporates a number of mechanical refinements, not least the fitment of rack-and-pinion steering.

BELOW The MG TD (foreground) is clearly a sports car, while the Singer Roadster behind is not; but is this an emotional judgement rather than a logical one?

no-man's land. So be it: the virtues and charms of such cars – along with their vices – give them an appeal that transcends arbitrary categorisation.

Proof, however, that one is skating on thin ice comes when one considers that the demands of competition motoring and of engineering advancement make a closed vehicle more effective as a sports car. A closed structure is more rigid, allowing for lighter weight and better suspension control, and is in addition more aerodynamically efficient, allowing greater speed for a given power output. So why deny the status of sports car to lightweight efficient performance vehicles such as the Lotus Europa, the Clan Crusader, or such enticing rarities as the knee-high mid-engined Unipower? Not for nothing, after all, did pundits refer to the Clan and its great rival the Ginetta G15 as being modern-day Spridgets.

But we'll stick to our definition – give or take a pair of rear seats. This is, after all, a personal selection – which means that you won't find every British sports car within these pages, but merely those the author deems significant and/or interesting.

The predictable 'greats' are present – whether one is talking of the E-type or of such pre-war landmarks as the

ABOVE There's not much finesse to the engineering of this Triumph TR – the egg-crate grille identifies it as a TR3 – but it's every inch what people understand by a sports car.

MIDDLE RIGHT The convertible Elan is manifestly a sports car. This is a Sprint, with the 126bhp Big Valve engine and the characteristic – although not universal – Sprint two-tone finish.

MIDDLE LEFT Too uncouth to be a true grand tourer, the 1960s TVR is a stimulating drive but falls into a no-man's land between sports car and GT. Built on a tubular chassis, it can be found with a variety of engines, including the Ford V8; this example dates from 1965 and has an 1800cc MGB power unit.

RIGHT Based on Standard-Triumph parts, the Fairthorpe Electron Minor was a somewhat crude device sold in component form from the end of the 1950s until the early 1970s.

Invicta. There are also, of course, the well-loved old favourites from Austin-Healey, MG and Triumph. But alongside such machinery are less well-known cars.

Some will cause raised eyebrows at the very least – and possibly even have the odd vintage purist snorting with outrage into his Single Malt. But the author makes no apologies for including such cars as the Vale and the Wolseley Hornet Special in his selection. They were regarded as sports cars in their time, have as much of a sports character as more readily accepted vehicles, and sin primarily for having tried just a little too hard in their presentation; more to the point, their story is interesting, and they provide a counterpoint to the extravagantly priced Bentleys, Lagondas and Aston Martins of the era.

Why then, does this book not include such specialist oddballs as the Fairthorpe or the Turner, while taking in, for example, the Swallow Doretti? Call it arbitrary if you like, but quite simply the author regards the Doretti as being of greater interest. Similarly, why is the exquisite pre-war Squire not given its place in the spotlight? The story of former Bentley and MG man Adrian Squire's mission to create the best sports car in the world is a fascinating one, certainly; but ultimately he only built seven cars. As blips on the screen go, the gorgeous supercharged Squire barely lights a diode, hence its exclusion from these pages.

Not that commercial success or otherwise enters into the equation. Only 15 of the Rover-based Marauder were made before the small firm closed its doors, while barely 70 of the exalted Bristol-powered post-war Frazer Nashes trickled out of the company's Middlesex works in a nine-year period. There is something fascinating, too, about heroic failure, whether we're talking of the Daimler Dart or the catastrophe of the Triumph TR7.

Nor is technical excellence a criterion for selection – despite highlights such as the 16-valve Bentley engine,

RIGHT Delicious! The twin-cam XK-series Jaguar engine, here in an E-type. Company boss William Lyons knew the appeal of an engine that was striking to look at as well as capable of strong performance.

BELOW Equipped with a supercharged Anzani engine, the 1½-litre Squire was made between 1934 and 1936, but only seven cars were completed in this period.

Lotus's spaceframes, or Jaguar's splendid XK twin-cam. How could it be, when so many of the cars featured are concoctions – inspired or otherwise – of mass-production saloon components?

Fond though the author is of Austin-Healeys, for instance, he would be the first to admit that some of their Austin-derived mechanicals are pretty horrible. Nor is there anything hugely clever about the MG TC's whippy chassis, or the Jowett Jupiter's tendency – in its day – to destroy its engine and gearbox. It is an easily sustainable position to maintain that a banal Traction Avant Citroën saloon has more engineering worth than many of the cars in these pages – and will out-corner them into the bargain. But that's not the point, is it?

ABOVE RIGHT The Aston Martin DB4: a grand tourer, and no argument about it.

RIGHT Built around Austin components, BMC's Austin-Healey sports cars are hardly cutting-edge in technical terms – but does that really matter? This photo shows a 3000 MkII (left) and the MkII Sprite.

ACKNOWLEDGEMENTS

I am grateful to the people listed below for their help:

HRG expert Ian Dussek; Chris Booth, proprietor of the Rolvenden Motor Museum and expert on Morgan three-wheelers; Ian Glass of the Marauder Register; MG historian Malcolm Green of Magna Press; Ian Blackburn and Dave Hardwick of the Singer Owners' Club; Ken Painter and Arnold Davey of the Lagonda Club; Lea-Francis expert Barrie Price of AB Price Ltd; AC Cobra historian Rinsey Mills; Bruce Dowell, Clive Millar and Ben Yates of the Sunbeam Talbot Darracq Register; Ian Rendall of the Invicta Car Club; Leon Gibbs and Guy Woodhams of the Sunbeam Talbot Alpine Register (special thanks to the former for ploughing through production statistics for me); Jim Harvey of the Dellow Register; Charles Helps, Lotus Six registrar at the Historic Lotus Register; Riley specialists Barrie Gillies and Ian Gladstone; Keith Brading, formerly of the Frogeye Car Company; Richard Cownden; my father Professor LS Pressnell for – as ever – his economic insights; Graham Skillen of the Marendaz Special Register; pre-war MG specialists Barry Walker, Andy King and Mike Allison; Dave Williams, Martin Eyre and Chris Gould, for their advice on Austin Sevens; Dave Cox, a wealth of knowledge on Vale Specials; Andy Bell of Ecurie Bertelli, for his advice on pre-war Aston Martins; Dick Serjeantson of the Wolseley Hornet Special Club; Tony Marshall of the Register of Unusual Microcars; Gavin Allard of the Allard Owners' Club; Lotus Seven expert Tony Weale; Frazer Nash specialists Martin Stretton and John Marsh; Vauxhall 30/98 historian Nic Portway; John Burnell of the Alvis Owner Club; Roger Dunbar of Elva Racing. My apologies if I have omitted anyone's name. All errors, it goes without saying, remain the responsibility of the author.

TOP Is the fixed-head Triumph TR7 a sports car? Arguably not – but criteria are personal, and do change.

MIDDLE Put a top on the E-type and it becomes a GT. This is a Series I car.

RIGHT The Sunbeam Alpine (here a Series V) is based on Hillman Minx components and built on an underpan derived from the Husky utility estate car; but at the time this was less damaging to its sports-car credentials – daftly, one has to admit – than the fact that it had wind-up windows and a decent hood.

AC ACE

Max Speed	117mph*
0–60mph	9.1sec*
	*Ace-Bristol

ABOVE The narrow air intake identifies this Ace as one of the 37 to have the Ford engine; in contrast, 223 left Thames Ditton with the AC engine and 463 with the Bristol unit.

BELOW This Aceca was originally one of 151 with the AC engine, but its owner, recordbreaker Donald Campbell, had it re-equipped with the Bristol straight-six.

The AC Ace was the aristocrat of 1950s British sports cars. Hand-crafted, elegant, of relatively advanced engineering, it stood a clear distance above the MG or the Austin-Healey, and had a quiet distinction lacking in the bigger and more flamboyant XK Jaguars. It seemed perfectly in tune with the small Surrey firm's old adage that it was the Savile Row of motor-car manufacture; as with a fine suit, though, such quality had to be paid for, and in 1955 an Ace cost £1651, a smattering less than an XK140 roadster but a full £525 more than an Austin-Healey 100.

As with the Cobra and the ME3000, the Ace was not conceived in Thames Ditton. By 1952 AC's antique 2-litre model was largely unsaleable, and the company lacked funds to develop a replacement. When it was suggested that it might usefully look at the sports-racers being built by John Tojeiro,

company boss William Hurlock didn't take much persuading that these could provide the basis for a new model.

Based around a simple round-tube ladder chassis, the Tojeiro specials had transverse-leaf all-independent suspension and carried Ferrari-like aluminium barchetta bodywork over a lightweight tube-steel frame. AC bought rights to the design, had the AC 2-litre engine and its Moss gearbox installed, and exhibited the resultant AC Ace at the 1953 Earls Court Motor Show.

Although AC's long-stroke 90bhp overhead-cam straight-six – dating from 1919 – didn't endow the Ace with hugely strong performance, the new sports car handled well; after a few well-judged tweaks to the front end it had the good looks, too, to match its fine manners. The performance to suit came in 1956, when the Ace became available with

THE AC ACECA AND GREYHOUND

In 1954 AC announced a fastback coupé version of the Ace. The wood-framed doors had wind-up glass (as opposed to the sidescreens of the Ace), and cockpit noise was reduced with the help of a glassfibre bulkhead. Weighing 2cwt more than an Ace, the Aceca had a lower-ratio back axle to compensate, but really only came into its own with the arrival of the optional Bristol engine in 1956. In all, 328 Acecas were made, the last in 1963: 151 were AC-engined, 169 had the Bristol unit, and just eight the Ford straight-six. Contrary to what might be expected, big brother the 2+2 Greyhound (1959–63) was not based on the Ace/Aceca, having a square-tube chassis with coil-and-wishbone front suspension and a trailing-arm independent rear. Most of the 83 Greyhounds made used either the 1971cc or 2216cc Bristol engine, but a handful had the AC unit and two or three the Ford straight-six.

Bristol's delicious BMW-derived 'six' and its accompanying gearbox; offering 125bhp in its most favoured form, this added £360 to the car's cost. In 1961, however, Bristol switched to the Chrysler V8, and AC had to look elsewhere for an engine. The result, launched at the 1961 Motor Show, was a short run of Aces powered by the 2.6-litre Ford Zephyr/Zodiac engine, offered either in standard 85bhp form or in five different stages of tune. The new model – recognisable by a lower bonnet line and shallower radiator grille – was cheaper, in 85bhp form, than the AC-engined car, and during 1962 this faded from the price lists; the Bristol-powered Ace continued to be available until the Ace was discontinued in August 1963.

Common to all Aces is poised, nicely-adustable handling, accurate and well-weighted steering, and a surprisingly resilient ride; with the arrival of disc front brakes (intitially as an option) in 1957, the braking became equally impressive. Where the variants differ is in their power and its delivery. The AC engine is smooth and torquey, the Bristol unit peppily rev-happy and with a gearbox every bit as sweet, and the Ford 'six' – at least in tuned form – full-blooded and gutsy without losing its essential refinement. Whichever Ace you were lucky enough to choose, your investment bought you a truly fine motor car; it's no surprise that today the cars are so sought-after, and command such high sums.

I DIDN'T KNOW THAT...

- The transverse-leaf suspension of the Ace was inspired by that of the original 500cc Cooper racing cars – which used at back and front the independent front suspension of the Fiat Topolino. Thus the AC's suspension can be traced back to a 1936 Italian runabout.
- A special Ace-Bristol with a revised front body and a low-cut windscreen competed in the 1957 Le Mans 24-hour race. It finished an honourable tenth overall – and was driven home to England afterwards. For 1958 AC commissioned a full-blown racer, with a Tojeiro-designed chassis with coil-spring suspension and an elegant new body. Despite the chassis breaking up, the AC finished eighth, just ahead of a Swiss duo in a near-standard Ace.
- Stablemate to the Ace in the 1950s was a very different beast: a 350cc three-wheeler known as the AC Petite. Between 1951 and 1958 roughly 2000 were made.
- Light engineering work keep AC afloat, including making golfbag trolleys – it was said that the Ace made no money. The company also dabbled in narrow-gauge railways, re-bodying the carriages for the trains that took holidaymakers along Southend pier.
- A long-term money-spinner was making government-sponsored invalid cars. The first model appeared in 1951, and was replaced by a more car-like offering six years later. In 1967 this in turn gave way to the glassfibre-bodied pale-blue vehicles that for many years were a familiar sight on British roads. The ending of this lucrative contract in the mid 1970s did much to hasten AC's decline.

SPECIFICATION

Engine:	1991cc (AC), 1971cc (Bristol) or 2553cc (Ford) water-cooled straight-six; sohc (AC) or ohv (Bristol/Ford)
Power:	85bhp at 4500rpm/90bhp at 4500rpm/102bhp at 5000rpm (AC); 105bhp–130bhp depending on specification (Bristol); 85bhp–170bhp depending on specification (Ford)
Transmission:	four-speed gearbox; optional overdrive (Ford and AC engines only)
Construction:	tubular chassis, tubular steel body frame, aluminium panels
Front suspension:	independent by upper transverse leaf and lower wishbone; telescopic dampers
Rear suspension:	independent by upper transverse leaf and lower wishbone; telescopic dampers
Steering:	cam-and-peg
Brakes:	all-drum; optional front discs from 1957, standardised in 1960
Kerb weight:	16.5cwt (Ace-Bristol)

EVOLUTION

October 1953	Ace launched
October 1954	Aceca announced
February 1956	Bristol engine available
October 1957	Optional front disc brakes
October 1959	Greyhound prototype shown
October 1960	Definitive Greyhound shown
May 1960	Disc front brakes standard
October 1961	Ford engine available
August 1963	Ace and Greyhound discontinued

BELOW The old-fashioned interior of the Ace barely changed over the years; this is a Bristol-powered car. Note the robust fly-off handbrake, and the overdrive switch to the left of the rev-counter.

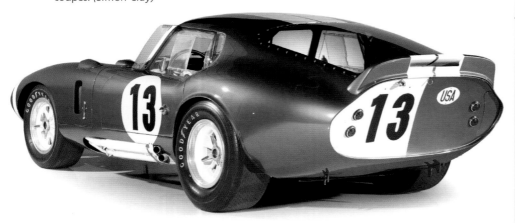

ABOVE This 1964 Cobra has only the mildest of flared arches – and an eggbox grille and side vents – to distinguish it from the Ace. Of the 979 Cobras and AC 289s made, 75 small-arch cars had the 260ci engine and 571the 289ci unit; in contrast, only 27 wide-arch AC 289s left Thames Ditton. *(Simon Clay)*

BELOW In all, seven leaf-sprung Daytona coupés were built. This is car CSX 2299, the most successful of the coupés. *(Simon Clay)*

Few cars have become such a cult as the AC Cobra. The reasons are obvious: muscular good looks and raw power in an open trad-Brit sports car make for a high-octane brew...especially when mastering this cocktail demands skill and dedication.

Back in 1962 it seemed a somewhat unlikely project, bringing together as it did the flamboyant Texan racer Carroll Shelby and the genteel family-run AC Cars. But Shelby wanted to create a sports car of his own, and could see the appeal both of Ford's new compact V8, with its clever thin-wall block casting, and of AC's tubular-chassis Ace, with its simple but robust construction. The final element was an accident of good timing: AC's antique straight-six was on its last legs and the alternative Bristol engine was going out of production, leaving AC

to fall back on a Ford Zodiac power unit of embarrassingly banal origins.

So a deal was soon stitched up: cars would be shipped less engine and gearbox to Shelby in the States, who would drop in the Ford V8 and appropriate gearbox before selling the result as the Shelby Cobra. British and European cars would be fully built by AC, and carry the Thames Ditton firm's name.

The first cars used the V8 in its original 260ci 4.2-litre form, and retained the Ace's box-type steering, but soon the 289ci 4.7-litre engine was standardised, along with rack steering. The chassis was largely unchanged from that of the Ace, as was the body: this was the sleeker-fronted Ace-Ford item, given a lift by an egg-crate grille and lightly flared wheelarches, plus side vents on all but the earliest cars.

THE 'DAYTONA' RACING COUPÉS

For long-distance events such as Daytona and Le Mans the Cobra had one fundamental problem: lousy aerodynamics. Accordingly Shelby lieutenant Peter Brock designed a slippery coupé body to fit over a largely unmodified tubular frame. One car was built by Shelby and five by an Italian bodyshop; when British race entrant John Willment wanted one, a further example, to a slightly different shape, was constructed – with Shelby input – in his workshops. Additionally, AC built a coupé (see opposite) to its own design. These eight were all leaf-sprung cars; Harold Radford was commissioned to build two coil-sprung coupés, but his efforts were deemed unsatisfactory, with one car being scrapped. The best results for the coupés were class wins in the 1964 and 1965 Sebring 12-hour events and a fourth overall in 1964's Le Mans; despite this, the cars secured Shelby the 1965 GT World Championship.

Shelby was soon overseeing a racing programme for the Cobra, and as well as leading to the Daytona coupés this prompted thoughts of fitting the competition-bred 'High Performance' 427ci Ford engine. It didn't take a genius to realise, however, that dropping the 7-litre unit straight into the 1950s AC chassis – complete with transverse-leaf suspension inspired by that of the Fiat Topolino – would be a recipe for disaster. With help from Ford in the States, AC therefore created a new chassis, still tubular but much more beefy and with coil-over-damper suspension. This was clad in a wider body with aggressively flared arches. Meanwhile, AC in Britain offered the new chassis with less extreme flares and the 4.7-litre engine, as the AC 289. Strange as it might seem, neither in the US nor in Britain did this second-generation Cobra sell in great numbers, and production ended in 1968. An adaptation of the chassis was used, with Ford's mainstream 428ci 7-litre powerpack, for AC's subsequent 428 fastback and convertible.

But this was not the end for the Cobra. Restorer Brian Angliss ended up taking over some of the body bucks and chassis tooling from AC, put the Cobra back into production, and ultimately bought the rights to the AC name; Shelby, recognising a good thing, also began manufacture of a small series of cars in the States.

ABOVE All bulges and menace, this is a 427 Cobra, with the 7-litre Ford engine; a roll-hoop was a popular period accessory.

I DIDN'T KNOW THAT...

- The most newsworthy Cobra in its day was the racing coupé built by AC for 1964's Le Mans. In testing, it was clocked by the police at 180mph on the M1 motorway, in the small hours of one morning. Much tabloid foaming at the mouth possibly helped hasten the arrival of Britain's 70mph speed limit.

- The 7-litre coil-sprung cars were intended primarily as homologation specials for racing – but insufficient were made to meet the 100-car requirements for 1965. After sitting outside Shelby's premises, 31 unsold race-spec cars were spruced up and sold as hardcore road cars called the 427 S/C (or 'Semi-Competition'); features included a glassfibre bonnet scoop, side exhausts, rear-wing lips, and reinforcing bonnet rivets. Engines were of special 'side-oiler' type, but tune varied.

- One of the more extraordinary Cobras was the 1964 Mercer-Cobra designed by former Chrysler stylist Virgil Exner, and finished with copper and brass trimmings; it was built in Turin by Sibona-Basano.

- A fair number of coil-spring Cobras were fitted with the much cheaper and more mildly tuned 428ci (7014cc) Special Police Interceptor engine.

- Two coil-spring Cobras were bodied as sharp-edged convertibles by Italian stylist Ghia.

- Five coil-spring chassis, their wheelbase extended, were supplied to Paramount for use in the film *Monte Carlo or Bust*, in which they were dressed up as fake vintage cars.

- AC Cars is still in existence, but no longer owned by Brian Angliss; at the time of writing it is beginning manufacture of the Cobra in Malta.

SPECIFICATION

Engine:	4261cc/4727cc/6997cc/7016cc water-cooled V8; ohv
Power:	350bhp (gross) at 5750rpm (Cobra 289); 271bhp (gross) at 6000rpm (AC 289); 390bhp (gross) at 5200rpm (Cobra 427)
Transmission:	four-speed gearbox; optional automatic (really!) on later 289ci Cobras
Construction:	tubular chassis; tubular body frame with aluminium panels
Front suspension:	independent by upper transverse leaf and lower wishbone; telescopic dampers (narrow-body cars). Independent coil-and-wishbone; telescopic dampers; anti-roll bar on S/C (wide-body MkII cars)
Rear suspension:	independent by upper transverse leaf and lower wishbone; telescopic dampers (narrow-body cars). Independent coil-and-wishbone; telescopic dampers; anti-roll bar on S/C (wide-body MkII cars)
Steering:	cam-and-peg, then rack-and-pinion
Brakes:	discs all-round
Kerb weight:	21.0cwt (AC 289)

EVOLUTION

February 1962	First Cobra laid down
July 1962	First customer cars
January 1963	289ci engine standardised; rack-and-pinion steering
July 1963	Wing vents introduced
October 1964	First coil-spring car
July 1966	Last leaf-spring car
December 1966	Final coil-spring cars to Shelby
July 1968	Last AC 289 leaves Thames Ditton

ALLARD

Max Speed	110mph*
0–60mph	7.4sec*

*Cadillac-engined J2

ABOVE The K3 offers three-abreast seating, facilitated by a right-hand gearchange; the body is in aluminium, and sits on a chrome-moly tubular frame. This car has a Cadillac engine.

BELOW Essentially the same body – only narrower – was used on the first series of Palm Beach; this is a launch-time photo of this uninspiring Ford-powered model. The MkII was more attractive, but still a sales no-hoper.

Big, brawny, unsophisticated: you could say that the Allard car mirrored the character of its creator, Sydney Allard. Down-to-earth London garage-owner Allard earnt his bread-and-butter selling Fords, making his name before the Second World War as a fearless and successful trials driver, latterly with the Ford-based Allard Specials of which he manufactured a small run.

Post-war he became a fully-fledged manufacturer, making a surprisingly extensive variety of models built around the bulletproof mechanicals of the V8 Ford. Most are largely forgotten these days, but one, the stark competition J2, has always enjoyed a certain cult status as a bare-fist bruiser in the best tradition of tame-me-if-you-dare performance sports cars.

The first post-war Allards were seen in 1946, and used the 3.6-litre flathead Ford V8 and all its associated mechanicals,

fitted in a chassis using mass-production sidemembers provided by John Thompson Motor Pressings. The engine was mounted far back in the chassis, to put plenty of weight over the rear wheels for trials use, and as on pre-war Allard Specials the transverse-leaf Ford front suspension was given a Ballamy split-beam independent conversion with abnormally generous wheel travel.

Body styles – all with a bulbous waterfall-grille front – were a two-seater (retrospectively called J1, or K2 in later longer-wheelbase form), an open tourer (L-type), and a drophead (M1); a two-door saloon (P1) followed, along with a related drophead (M2X), both with a fresh style of coachwork and with coil springs for the split-beam front axle. This latter feature also appeared on a restyled two-seater known as the K2.

THE PALM BEACH

The Palm Beach was announced in 1952, intended largely for the US. Built around the new tubular chassis, it was offered with the 1508cc Consul engine or the 2267cc Zephyr 'six'; swing-axle coil-spring front suspension was used, and the live rear axle, again on coils, was located by twin radius arms each side and a Panhard rod. The Palm Beach simply couldn't compete with the TR2 and the Austin-Healey – price and lacklustre looks apart, its handling and roadholding were enough to leave journalist-racer John Bolster 'frankly horrified', as he later recounted. Even when restyled and given unusual sliding-pillar torsion-bar front suspension and the choice of either Zephyr or Jaguar engines, the car was a no-hoper, although two final cars with coupé bodywork and a de Dion back axle – one with a Chrysler V8 – looked tempting. In all, 84 Palm Beaches were built, of which only seven were the MkII.

The coil-spring front was also used on the 1949 J2, which in addition had a coil-sprung de Dion rear. Specifically aimed at the US market, the J2 was a stripped-down competition model, and as with the K2 could be exported to the States less engine and gearbox, allowing fitment of a Cadillac, Lincoln or Chrysler V8; home-market cars tended to use a bored and stroked 4.4-litre alloy-head adaptation of the Mercury flathead or else a Ford/Mercury unit with the Ardun overhead-valve conversion. By all accounts the J2 was a pretty frightening device to drive fast – although that didn't stop Sydney Allard from taking one to third place in 1950's Le Mans – and it was soon developed into the revised J2X, which moved the engine forward to give slightly more benign handling.

Allard next designed his own tubular chassis, that could be standardised across his entire range. This encompassed the coil-sprung swing-axle front and the de Dion rear and underpinned the P2 Monte Carlo saloon, the bizarre 'woody' Safari estate, the K3 sports car – all these V8-powered – and, suitably adapted, the more modest Palm Beach. As with the J2, British buyers of the V8s had to content themselves with Ford/Mercury flatheads: Americans could specify Cadillac, Chrysler or Lincoln engines.

But it was all pretty academic. In a more open market such ungainly oddballs weren't saleable, while the Palm Beach, in theory an intelligent re-positioning of the marque, simply couldn't compete with the TRs and Healeys. By 1958 it was all over.

I DIDN'T KNOW THAT...

■ A P1 saloon was driven to victory in the 1952 Monte Carlo Rally by Sydney Allard – the only time the rally has been won by a car driven by its designer and builder. As a hillclimbing and trials champion, and as the pilot of the third-placed finisher of 1950's Le Mans 24-hours, Allard counts as one of the most versatile of competition drivers.

■ As a last bid to stay in motor-manufacturing, Allard attempted to sell a revolting little three-wheeler known as the Clipper; only a dozen or so were made.

■ Another scheme was to give the 100E Ford Anglia a tuned engine, a wraparound rear window and rear tail-fins; a single one of these Allardettes was made in 1958. The name was revived in 1966 for a series of re-engined and/or supercharged 105E Anglias – including a 1500GTS that had a Shorrock-supercharged 1500cc Cortina engine.

■ After abandoning car manufacture, Allard was a key figure in introducing drag racing to Britain, and built various dragsters.

■ Although the J2/J2X (173 made) is the best-remembered Allard, the mainstays were the M1 tourer (500 made) and the P1 saloon (559 made); that only 25 of the M2X drophead and 11 of the Monte Carlo saloon were made shows how unsaleable were these later cars.

■ The K3, which was mainly sold in the US with a Cadillac engine, was more successful, with 62 finding buyers in the 1952–54 period. In essence it shared its body and chassis design with the Palm Beach.

SPECIFICATION (J2 FORD/CADILLAC)

Engine:	4375cc/5440cc water-cooled in-line V8; sidevalve/ohv
Power:	120bhp at 3800rpm (alloy-head Ford); 160bhp (approx) at 4000rpm (Cadillac)
Transmission:	three-speed gearbox
Construction:	separate chassis; tubular body frame; aluminium body
Front suspension:	independent, with split (swing) axle and coil springs; location by radius arms; telescopic dampers
Rear suspension:	de Dion axle with coil springs co-axial with telescopic dampers; location by diagonal radius rods and torque tube
Steering:	Marles worm-and-roller
Brakes:	all-drum, inboard at rear
Kerb weight:	21cwt (Cadillac-engined)

EVOLUTION

March 1936	Competition debut of first Allard Special
July 1937	First 'production' Allard Special
January 1946	Post-war range announced
Summer 1946	First examples of J1 swb 2-seater and L-type tourer
October 1946	First K1 two-seater
Summer 1947	M-type drophead available
August 1949	P1 saloon and J2 announced
April 1950	K2 replaces K1
March 1951	M2X drophead launched
October 1951	J2X unveiled
April 1952	Safari estate introduced
July 1952	Palm Beach announced
October 1952	P2 Monte Carlo saloon and K3 announced
April 1953	J2R sports-racer unveiled
October 1956	Palm Beach MkII introduced; Monte Carlo, K3 and Safari no longer listed; J2R available to order
Early 1958	Last Palm Beach registered

BELOW Two J2Xs: closest to camera is a car with a Chrysler engine, while behind is a Cadillac-powered example. At the wheel are *Classic & Sports Car* colleagues of the author.

ALVIS 12/50

Max Speed	70mph
0–60mph	n/a

ABOVE A late model, from 1930, this 'Beetle Back' is on the 12/60 chassis and the car is capable of a happy 60–70mph; the body is by Carbodies of Coventry.

BELOW A delightful 1929 shot of a front-wheel-drive Alvis in four-seat tourer format, characteristically low-slung, and with the radiator relatively far forward. The car carries the famous Alvis hare mascot.

The Alvis 12/50 is one of those 'reference' vintage cars: consistently well-regarded, it has never had to justify its place in any review of the 1920s motoring scene and has always been a respected component of bodies such as the VSCC. Admittedly he is an interested party, but Alvis historian Kenneth Day refers to the 12/50 as being in many people's eyes 'the finest British light car of the vintage period'.

Yet the 12/50, if you analyse it, is in fact a fairly unexceptional device, rigorously conventional in most of its details and distinguished only by its use of a pushrod overhead-valve engine in an era of leaden sidevalves. But the Alvis, like the MGB of 40 years later, used well-executed orthodoxy to good effect – in particular through high levels of workmanship and the use of good-quality materials. The

result was a car that offered sturdy performance and good roadholding and handling and which in sports format had bodywork that was distinctively eye-catching. Further icing on the cake was a solid portfolio of competition successes.

The 12/50 was in essence a development of the first Alvis car, the sidevalve 10/30 announced in 1920, with the 10/30's 1460cc engine replaced by an ohv unit of the same capacity, using the same bottom end. Launched in June 1923 as the 10/30 sports, it became the 12/50 with the arrival of a 1496cc engine for the Motor Show that same year.

Various bodies were available, but the most charismatic was an alloy-bodied two-seater sports type with a sharply tucked-in tail, on the underside of which the spare wheel was mounted. This model was invariably – if unofficially –

THE FRONT-WHEEL-DRIVE ALVIS

Alvis was a pioneer of front-wheel drive, anticipating both DKW and Citroën. Initially seen in 1925, the fwd Alvises were at first purely for racing, and used a supercharged 12/50 engine turned through 180 degrees, in conjunction with a reversed de Dion axle and paired quarter-elliptic springs at the front and Bugatti-style reversed quarter-elliptics at the rear. This led to a straight-eight fwd racer, initially with horizontal valves but soon with ohv in a twin-cam head; one of these cars came sixth in 1928's Le Mans and first in class. In 1928 a front-wheel-drive roadgoing model was introduced, with an ohc 1482cc four-cylinder engine, blown or unblown, transverse-leaf independent front suspension, and an independent rear using quarter-elliptic springs; in theory the straight-eight was also to be available in road trim, but this never materialised. Only 142 fwd 'fours' were made, all but five in 1928, and a mere ten eight-cylinder cars.

referred to as the 'Duck's Back' Alvis, and generally had a polished rather than painted finish. For 1927 the 'Duck's Back' was replaced by a two-seater with a more rounded tail, this being known as the 'Beetle Back'.

Changes to the 12/50 over the years were unspectacular, with the 1926 models seeing the most significant raft of improvements: the chassis was strengthened, a plate clutch replaced the previous leather-cone item, and front brakes became standard. Additionally, a longer-stroke 1645cc engine became available, but this less revvy unit was generally fitted to touring rather than sports 12/50s. The sports engine, meanwhile, received a big-port head the following year.

In 1927 Alvis introduced the 14/75, which was in effect a six-cylinder 12/50. Sales of the 12/50 fell away, and at the end of 1929 it briefly ceased to be listed. However, in September 1930 it was reintroduced, with an uprated coil-ignition version of the long-stroke engine. To give a bit more pep to this now heavier car, in early 1931 a twin-carb sports model called the 12/60 was introduced, developing a healthy 56bhp at the flywheel.

Both the 12/50 and the 12/60 were finally discontinued at the end of the 1932 model year; these modest vintage 1½-litres together constitute the best-selling Alvis type in the company's long history.

I DIDN'T KNOW THAT...

- The Alvis mascot of the time, standard on all 12/50s, was a hare.
- The 'Duck's Back' body was not exclusive to the 12/50: it was first seen on the 10/30, and was latterly available on the 1598cc sidevalve 12/40 of 1922–25.
- 'It is a car for the artistic driver, and responds blithely to proper handling,' wrote *The Autocar* in a 1925 road test of the 12/50.
- Competition successes include winning the 1923 200-Mile Race at Brooklands, a third place in the 1925 Boillot Cup in France, and a first and a class award in the 1927 Brooklands Six-Hour Race.
- In all, an impressive 3753 of the 12/50 were made, plus 287 of the 12/60; the best years were 1926, with 862 cars built, and 1927, when 923 examples left the Coventry works. By 1929 output had fallen to 140, and only briefly picked up in 1931 with the arrival of the final-generation 12/50 and 12/60 models.
- Bodies available included a lightweight fabric saloon built on Weymann principles; called the Alvista, this weighed 22cwt, against 28cwt or so for a steel saloon.
- The 12/50 and 12/60 always retained a separate gearbox, Alvis being scathing about the disadvantages of having a gearbox in unit with the engine.
- Alvis carried on making cars until 1967, latterly with small numbers of 3-litre models with bodies by Park Ward to a design by Graber of Switzerland. The company survives, as a producer of specialist military vehicles, and is now part of the BAE Systems group, having previously taken over Sweden's Hägglunds and Vickers Defence Systems, the latter being the maker of the Challenger tank.

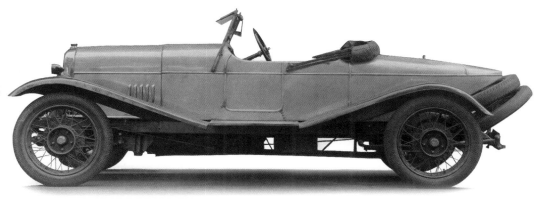

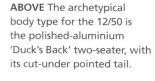

ABOVE The archetypical body type for the 12/50 is the polished-aluminium 'Duck's Back' two-seater, with its cut-under pointed tail.

SPECIFICATION

Engine:	1496cc/1645cc water-cooled in-line 4-cyl; ohv
Power:	50bhp (12/50)/56bhp (12/60); rpm not quoted
Transmission:	four-speed unsynchronised
Construction:	separate chassis; body construction varies
Front suspension:	beam axle with semi-elliptic leaf springs; friction dampers
Rear suspension:	live axle with semi-elliptic leaf springs; friction dampers
Steering:	worm-and-wheel; worm-and-roller from 1928
Brakes:	drum, mechanically operated; standard on all four wheels from 1926
Kerb weight:	18cwt (12/50 tourer); 21.5cwt (12/60 2-seater)

EVOLUTION

March 1920	Launch of 10/30
June 1923	Overhead-valve sports 10/30 introduced
Late 1923	Capacity increased to 1496cc, thereby creating 12/50
September 1924	Optional front-wheel brakes
September 1925	Sidevalve cars discontinued; front-wheel brakes standard; improved chassis
October 1929	12/50 ceases to be listed
September 1930	12/50 reintroduced
March 1931	12/60 introduced
October 1932	12/50 and 12/60 no longer listed

LEFT This rear view of the 12/60 clearly shows how the 'Beetle Back' got its name. These later cars were heavier, so the extra power of the 12/60 engine was surely welcome.

ASTON MARTIN 1½-LITRE

Max Speed	85mph*
0–60mph	24.6sec*

*1933 Le Mans

ABOVE Sitting on the long-wheeelbase chassis, this is a MkII tourer. Clearly visible at the front are the Hartford friction dampers and the cables operating the braking system.

RIGHT The C-type had somewhat ungainly streamlined styling. The relatively long tail is not apparent in this shot. Based on the 2-litre Speed Model, only seven C-types were made.

For those who associate the marque with big V8-powered grand tourers swathed in cream leather, it is a valuable corrective to realise that Aston Martin made its name, in the inter-war period, with small-capacity models that were every inch a sports car.

Under the direction of marque founder Lionel Martin roughly 60 cars were laboriously assembled in the 1921–25 period, production models having a 1½-litre sidevalve engine.

Following a change in ownership, a new Aston Martin was launched at the 1927 London Motor Show. Created by Italian-born Augustus Cesare Bertelli, the car featured an overhead-cam 'four' of 1495cc. The worm-drive rear axle was a weak point, but the engine and Bertelli-designed gearbox were robust and the shaft-operated big-drummed Perrott brakes notably effective.

After winning the Rudge-Whitworth Cup at 1928's Le Mans, for the fastest lap by a 1½-litre car, Aston Martin phased in dry-sump lubrication for 1929, and at the Motor Show that year announced the classic underslung-chassis 2/4-seater International model – as well as a bob-tailed 2-seater International of which only six were made. Both cars cost £598 – which certainly put them at the opposite end of the spectrum from a £185 M-type MG Midget.

Too well-built and heavy to be hugely fast, the International rewarded its owner with well-honed handling and unquestionable durability – Aston offered a lifetime guarantee to the initial purchaser. The model continued until 1932, the last examples having a Moss gearbox (now in unit with the engine), cable brakes, and a more durable ENV back axle.

THE 2-LITRE 15/98

The 15/98 was announced as a long-wheelbase four-door saloon or as a slightly bulky open tourer; a short-wheelbase 2/4-seater sports model and a swb drophead arrived for 1938. With bigger full-winged coachwork on a wider and more softly sprung chassis, the new Aston was a less sporting car, yet while the larger – and now wet-sumped – power unit gave more torque it didn't provide more performance, as the cars were now heavier. Worse, the engine was wretchedly rough in its original form, and plans to build most 15/98s as saloons had to be abandoned on account of the excessive noise generated. A dry-sump super-sports version – the Speed Model – was offered, but struggled to find purchasers, whether traditionally-bodied or as the long-tailed streamlined C-type. In all, 150 of the 15/98 were made, along with an estimated 20 of the Speed Model – seven of these being the C-type.

Replacing the International was a 2/4-seater version of the Le Mans 2-seater announced at the 1931 show. With its slab tank, outside exhaust, dual-cowl scuttle and cycle wings, this low-slung model had a sparse elegance that made it a great success; also available was a long-wheelbase tourer, the Le Mans Special, but only 15–16 were built.

Meanwhile, Aston continued to do well in competition, where the cars' durability compensated for their lack of outright speed: at 1932's Le Mans Bertelli's car finished seventh and the following year Astons ended up fifth and seventh overall.

During 1934 came the MkII model, with a stiffer chassis, better front axle location, and a counterbalanced crank – while costs were shaved by moving to a flat scuttle. With 70bhp at its disposal, the MkII was good for 85mph flat-out; the racing Ulster model was guaranteed to achieve 100mph.

Alas, the cars were simply too expensive and the company, under new ownership since 1933, decided that if it were going to charge high prices it had better offer a more powerful and less spartan motor car. The result was the new 2-litre 15/98 model launched for 1937.

With this, Aston moved away from its original constituency. But the company had enjoyed its moment of glory with the 1½-litres, regarded by many as the finest – if not the fastest – of pre-war medium-sized British sports cars.

SPECIFICATION

Engine:	1493cc water-cooled in-line 4-cyl; ohc
Power:	70bhp at 4750rpm (MkII)
Transmission:	four-speed unsynchronised gearbox
Construction:	alloy panelling over ash frame
Front suspension:	rigid axle with leaf springs; Hartford friction dampers
Rear suspension:	underslung live axle with leaf springs; Hartford friction dampers
Steering:	worm-and-roller
Brakes:	drum, cable-operated from late 1932
Kerb weight:	19cwt (1933 2/4-seater)

EVOLUTION

September 1927	Aston Martin 1½-litre announced
October 1928	Dry-sump engine shown; improved steering
October 1929	International announced
Early 1930	Underslung chassis standardised
October 1931	'Beetleback' Le Mans replaces 2-seater International. Long-wheelbase 2-door and 4-door saloons and four-seat tourer announced; only handful made
February 1932	'New International' introduced
October 1932	Le Mans 2/4-seater replaces 'New International'
October 1933	Long-wheelbase Le Mans Special tourer introduced
January 1934	MkII available: 2/4-seater, lwb tourer, lwb saloon
June 1934	Ulster model available
October 1936	2-litre 15/98 launched – lwb tourer and lwb saloon
October 1937	Swb 2/4-seater and drophead introduced
August 1940	Last 15/98 made

I DIDN'T KNOW THAT...

- The Aston Martin marque was created in 1914 by Lionel Martin, who made his money in tin-mining and quarrying. There was no Mr Aston: this part of the name derives from the Aston Clinton hillclimb in Buckinghamshire, where Martin had successfully competed in a modified Singer.
- Sadly, if inappropriately, Lionel Martin died in 1945 after an accident when he was riding a pedal tricycle.
- The winged Aston Martin badge in its third – 1932-on – form, as still used today, was designed by racing driver, journalist and accomplished artist SCH 'Sammy' Davis.
- Many significant names criss-cross the history of the pre-war Aston Martin. Drivers of racing Astons include Richard Seaman, Pat Driscoll and Richard Shuttleworth, while Harry Grylls, the future Rolls-Royce engineer behind the Silver Shadow, owned a works racer, as briefly did Reginald Slay of the Squire Motor Company.
- The only pre-war Aston to carry continental coachwork was a two-seater MkII built by Gläser of Dresden.
- The pre-war prime-movers of Aston Martin went very different ways: AC Bertelli became a pig-farmer, Claude Hill joined Ferguson Research to work on 4wd systems, and Gordon Sutherland took over coachbuilder Abbotts of Farnham – best-known for its estate conversions of post-war big Fords.
- An experimental 2-litre saloon was built in 1938, using a box-section body frame made from electrical conduit. Known as 'Donald Duck', this ungainly four-door led to the Atom prototype of 1939, which had a combined body/chassis frame made of rectangular steel tubing, and independent front suspension.

ABOVE The Ulster was the racing version of the 1½-litre Aston Martin; this particular car finished 12th at Le Mans in 1935. Not visible is the unusual position of the spare wheel, laid flat in the bell-shaped tail.

AUSTIN SEVEN ULSTER & NIPPY

Max Speed 66mph*
0–60mph n/a*
* Unblown Ulster

ABOVE The elegant 'door-less' Ulster always has a high-set exhaust, adorned with a fishtail endpiece. Cars were supplied with a full-width windscreen and full wings.

BELOW Bert Hadley, the well-known Austin works driver, wringing the best out of one of the three twin-cam racers, during the Coronation Trophy at Donington Park in 1938.

The Seven might seem an unlikely base for a sports car, but Herbert Austin's baby spawned a whole family of sports models, as well as some extraordinary Seven-derived racers.

Introduced in 1922, the Seven had the signal virtue of being a big car in miniature, with four (water-cooled) cylinders, four wheels, and four-wheel brakes. With its simple A-shaped chassis, there was nothing complicated about the Seven, but it was made of the best-quality materials – which is one reason why people (including the author) are still recycling bits of ancient Austins into specials of one sort or another.

The first sporting variant was the Sports model of 1924. Sitting high on a normal Seven chassis, it had a slender high-set pointed tail and racily-flared wings; with a standard engine, it was light enough for it to be proudly advertised as good for 50mph. More seriously sporting was the Brooklands Super Sports introduced the same year, with its sleek aluminium body and uprated engine. Relatively few were made, however, as its creator, the coachbuilder and racer Gordon England, concentrated instead on the Austin-endorsed manufacture of the delightful bob-tailed fabric-bodied Gordon England Cup model of 1925–28.

But the cult sports Seven is the Ulster – to the point where replicas are hugely popular. Indeed, with only 200 or so Ulsters made, between 1930 and 1932, it is almost certain that if you encounter a car it will be a reproduction. The Ulster – which was only ever informally so called – began life in 1928 as a supercharged works racer, and one finished third in the 1929

FROM 'RUBBER DUCK' TO TWIN-CAM

By the early 1930s racing Sevens were faced by ever-stronger opposition from the highly-tuned ohc MGs. Austin responded by building a series of specialised single-seater racers. The first were three stumpy-tailed supercharged cars known as the 'Rubber Ducks'. These were only moderately successful, and in 1932 Austin secured the services of Murray Jamieson, then working with supercharger specialist Amherst Villiers. The following year a new design of streamlined racer emerged, powered by a blown alloy-head sidevalve engine with two plugs per cylinder. Developing nearly 70bhp, it was good for just over 120mph, but it soon became clear that for ultimate power better breathing was required. The result was Jamieson's extraordinary twin-cam single-seater of 1936, which had an all-new engine with twin gear-driven overhead camshafts and an output of 116bhp. Three money-no-object cars were built, with the sidevalve car's split-beam semi-independent front suspension, and piled up an impressive array of silverware.

Ulster TT, giving rise to the Ulster label. Production versions, supercharged or normally-aspirated, arrived in 1930, and featured lowered suspension, with a bowed front axle, and a sparse 'door-less' pointed-tail body.

The Ulster was priced in 1931 at £225 in 33bhp supercharged form or £185 as a 24bhp unblown car, which made it quite expensive, so in 1933 Austin came up with a more affordable sports Seven, the Type 65, intended exclusively as a road car. With its long-wheelbase chassis lowered in the same way as that of the Ulster, an elegant down-swept tail, and a 21bhp engine, the alloy-bodied Type 65 was a sensible compromise, and at a launch price of £148 it sold well; in 1934 it was given a steel body and subsequently re-named the Nippy. Meanwhile, for those wanting something more overtly sporting – if only in looks – during 1934–35 Austin offered the Sports 75 or Speedy, which had a cowled cockpit and a marginally more powerful 23bhp engine; few were made.

With the discontinuing of the Nippy in early 1937 the sports Seven was no more, but in the intervening 70 years enthusiasts have continued to build their own sporting Sevens and to construct – in particular – their own replica Ulsters, for which bodies and fittings are available off-the-peg. Challenging to drive fast, with all sorts of quirks in their roadholding, handling and braking, such cars are a wonderful dose of affordable vintage-era fun. A big smile comes as standard with a sports Seven.

I DIDN'T KNOW THAT...

- The Ulster had pressure lubrication of the big ends rather than the 'spit-and-hope' system of regular Sevens; a similar system was used on the 75/Speedy, but not on the 65/Nippy. This did, however, have the Ulster's more robust crankshaft. From late 1936 the Nippy became optionally available with the former Speedy engine, with pressure-fed big ends for its two-main-bearing crank; from December 1936 a fully pressure-fed two-main-bearing unit was offered, again as an alternative to the normal splash-fed engine, which was now with three main bearings.
- Roughly 275 of the 65s were made, and c.800 of the Nippy; it is thought only 50–60 of the Speedy were made.
- As well as replica Ulster bodies, it is also possible to obtain repro Brooklands Super Sports and Gordon England Cup shells. You can't build any of these onto the long-wheelbase chassis introduced in 1931, unless you convert this to swb form; however, sports bodies are available for the lwb frame.
- Seven brakes were always mechanical rather than hydraulic, and have long been a butt of jokes. All sports models had cable-operated brakes, and early Ulsters had uncoupled front and rear systems. From August 1936 all Sevens gained adjustment at each wheel and full compensation, but it was only in July 1938 – by which time the Nippy had been discontinued – that rod-operated rear brakes were fitted. It is possible to make the Seven's brakes work efficiently, but it is no surprise that many cars have been converted to hydraulics.

SPECIFICATION

Engine:	747cc water-cooled in-line 4-cyl; sidevalve
Power:	24bhp at 5000rpm (Ulster)/33bhp at 5000rpm (supercharged Ulster)/21bhp at 4000rpm (65/Nippy)/23bhp at 4400rpm (late Nippy)/23bhp at 4800rpm (Speedy)
Transmission:	three-speed close-ratio, unsynchronised (Ulster); four-speed close-ratio, unsynchronised (early Type 65); synchromesh on third/fourth from 1934 model year, and on second from 1935 model year
Construction:	separate chassis; body aluminium (Ulster/Speedy/65) or steel (Nippy)
Front suspension:	bowed beam axle with transverse leaf spring; single friction damper
Rear suspension:	live axle with quarter-elliptic leaf springs; torque tube; friction dampers
Steering:	worm-and-wheel
Brakes:	four-wheel drum, mechanically operated; semi-Girling system from August 1936
Kerb weight:	8.5cwt (unblown Ulster)

EVOLUTION

July 1922	First Austin Seven
January 1924	Austin Seven Sports announced
June 1924	Brooklands Super Sports available
August 1925	Gordon England Cup Model introduced
July 1928	Super Sports Model (supercharged) announced
Late 1928	Gordon England Stadium replaces Cup Model
February 1930	Sports Model (Ulster) available
Early 1932	Final Ulsters built
June 1933	Type 65
April 1934	Sports 75 ('Speedy') available
June 1934	Steel body for last Type 65s
August 1935	Speedy discontinued
February 1937	Nippy discontinued

BELOW The Nippy is a more mainstream sports Seven. The rounded rear is distinctive, but structurally weak. Proof of the Seven's usability, this particular car is a veteran of many overseas trips.

AUSTIN-HEALEY 100

Max Speed	111mph
0–60mph	10.3sec

ABOVE The classic original: 14,612 of the Austin-Healey 100 were made, of which 3924 were BN2s with the four-speed gearbox. Uniquely, the windscreen folds flat rearwards.

BELOW The two coupés. The red car was a favourite of Donald Healey's and still has his special radio. The blue car has been restored after having at one stage lost its roof. *(Author)*

The Austin-Healey 100 represents one of those great moments when industrial, engineering and aesthetic considerations melded to create a landmark vehicle. A new marque was established, a struggling small enterprise was saved from extinction, and a long line of commercially and competitively successful sports cars was initiated.

Rally-driver and engineer Donald Healey felt he was throwing the dice for the last time when he commissioned the creation of a new cheap Healey to take over from the less-than-moneyspinning Riley-engined cars. Knowing that Austin was looking for a use for the mechanical components of the catastrophic Austin Atlantic, the new design was based exclusively around Atlantic running gear, built into a Healey-created underslung chassis topped by a sleek body drawn up by Healey body man Gerry Coker.

Donald Healey, unhappy with the grille and depressed by what he saw as the slim prospects for his Warwick firm's continued survival, only grudgingly allowed the 100 to be displayed at the 1952 Motor Show – on the condition that the nose be positioned facing a pillar on the stand. But the press loved the 100, and so did BMC boss Leonard Lord, who on the spot decided that the car would be made by his company, under the Austin-Healey name.

Production began in 1953, and continued until the end of the 1956 model year, when the new six-cylinder 100-Six was introduced. In this time the only significant change was a move from a three-speed gearbox to a four-speeder, along with a stronger back axle, for the 1956-season BN2.

The 100 was soon active in racing – the rallying came later, with the six-cylinder cars – and in 1955 a series of 55 special

THE 100 COUPÉS

A brace of 1953-manufactured 100s were given coupé bodywork – and by a stroke of fortune both survive. With lines by Gerry Coker, they were used as personal cars by Donald and Geoffrey Healey and at the same time as development vehicles. The red car – originally with a black roof – is executed with more finesse and has a glasshouse with an integral front screen; Donald Healey's favourite car for many years, and only disposed of in 1962, it ended up with 100S mechanicals. The blue-and-silver sister vehicle, meanwhile, received the six-cylinder engine of the 100-Six along with 100S all-disc brakes. With the demand in the Healey's principal market, the US, being for open cars, the idea of a 100 coupé was never followed through; this is probably just as well, since cockpit heat, especially in the blue car, turns the interior into a Turkish bath on a hot day.

racing 100S models was made. These had a fully-balanced testbed-run 132bhp engine with an alloy eight-port head and a nitrided crankshaft, along with a raft of detail upratings, and incorporated a close-ratio gearbox, a racing clutch, and four-wheel disc brakes. The all-alloy body featured an oval grille, a louvred bonnet, and a full-width Perspex aeroscreen. Hand-assembled at Warwick, each car was tested by Geoffrey Healey or chief development engineer Roger Menadue.

Less radical was the 100M. Announced at the 1955 Motor Show, this was a BN2 fitted with the Le Mans tuning kit Healey had been offering since 1954; output was 100bhp, or 110bhp if high-compression pistons were specified, and a recognition point was a louvred bonnet with leather straps.

With its less weighty 'four', the 100 has sweeter handling than the later six-cylinder cars, and is also the least heavy of the breed. Its performance is thus well up with the six-pack, and for those who don't mind a more spartan driving environment (including a notoriously lousy hood), the original Austin-Healey may well be the best. It's a dual-mode sports car, one you can either grab by the scruff of the neck or else just treat as a lazy torque-rich grand tourer. The only real downside – other than limited ground clearance – is the excessive cockpit heat. The author still has fond memories of touring Wales in a nicely-prepared example...

I DIDN'T KNOW THAT...

- The BN1 three-speed gearbox, mated to a Laycock overdrive, is an adaptation of the four-speed column-change Austin gearbox, only with first gear blanked off; being a conversion from a column mechanism, side selectors mean the gearlever emerges from the left-hand side of the transmission tunnel, this arrangement lasting on 'Big Healeys' until 1961.
- The first 20 cars were built at Healey's Warwick works, and had all-aluminium bodies by Jensen. The Longbridge-assembled cars, as with all subsequent 'Big Healeys', had Jensen-supplied bodies with the front and rear shrouds (the key panels surrounding the bonnet and boot apertures) in aluminium, with the rest of the body in steel – other than very early cars, which also had aluminium bonnet and boot lids.
- Many cars have in recent years been given a louvred bonnet, as fitted to the 100M; as it was also possible at the time to buy such a bonnet from Warwick, it should be stressed that the presence of a louvred bonnet does not perforce indicate a 100M. Geoffrey Healey has given a figure of 1159 genuine 100Ms, and research suggests that 640 were built as such at Longbridge and the remainder were converted at Warwick.
- A genuine 'M' should have a rectangular cold-air box attached to the carbs, carrying a plaque reading: *This car has been fitted with a 'Le Mans' modification kit.*
- Tickford, who built the 100 prototype, constructed a one-off drophead.
- In a 100S-based streamliner Donald Healey achieved a speed of 192.74mph on the Bonneville Salt Flats in 1954.

SPECIFICATION

Engine:	2660cc water-cooled in-line 4-cyl; ohv
Power:	90bhp at 4000rpm (100)/132bhp at 4700rpm (100S)
Transmission:	three-speed gearbox with overdrive (BN1); four-speed gearbox with overdrive (BN2); four-speed gearbox without overdrive (100S)
Construction:	separate chassis, underslung at rear; alloy and steel bodywork (100S all-alloy)
Front suspension:	independent coil-and-wishbone; anti-roll bar; lever-arm dampers
Rear suspension:	live axle with leaf springs, located by Panhard rod; lever-arm dampers
Steering:	cam-and peg
Brakes:	all-drum (100); all-disc (100S)
Kerb weight:	18.75cwt (100)

EVOLUTION

October 1952	Show debut of 'Healey 100'
May 1953	Austin-Healey 100 (BN1) enters production at Longbridge
February 1955	First 100S completed
August 1955	BN2 production begins
November 1955	Last 100S made
July 1956	Last BN2 manufactured

BELOW The 100S generally had a full-width Perspex screen, but this car has the regular fold-flat item. Each 'S' was tested either by Healey's chief development engineer or by Donald Healey's son and chief collaborator Geoffrey Healey.

AUSTIN-HEALEY 100-SIX & 3000

Max Speed	121mph*
0–60mph	9.8sec*
	* 3000 MkIII

ABOVE The drum front brakes and crinkle-cut grille identify this as a 100-Six rather than a 3000 MkI; the screen no longer folds, and the car has gained door handles, but the sidescreens remain.

BELOW The still-born 4000 (foreground) has BMC 1800 bumpers and Minor rear lights; this car has an auto gearbox. Behind is a late 3000 MkIII, with paired front indicators and sidelights.

You can't escape the laws of economics. In the world of sports cars that's doubly true, as the only way to make the sums add up is to share as many components as possible with mainstream vehicles. Thus, when BMC moved over to the new C-series 'six' for its big saloons, the Austin-Healey clearly had to follow suit, rather than remain with a four-cylinder engine that survived only in de-tuned commercial-vehicle format.

The Healeys weren't overjoyed, as the 2639cc 'six' was heavier and barely more powerful, with a dreadful head design, and so its main contribution to the car was to spoil its handling. But they had no choice, and in 1956 the 100-Six was born, in a new 2+2 format with a cut-back rear deck and two tiny rear seats; the two-seater returned to the price lists in 1958. Other than a wheelbase extended by 2in

the Healey was largely unchanged, retaining the 100 dashboard and its side gearchange. There was, however, a new front grille, and the windscreen no longer folded.

The 100-Six wasn't a hugely clever car, its softer character summed up by some of the pimpish two-tone colours offered to the seemingly taste-blind US market to which most were despatched. But the six-cylinder 'Big Healey' soon became a copybook example of how painstaking development can improve the breed – as evidenced by the car's prowess in international rallying.

First the cylinder head was redesigned in 1957 to give individual inlet and exhaust ports for each cylinder. Then in 1959 came the 3000 MkI, physically identical but with a 2912cc engine and much-needed disc front brakes. More power – courtesy of a 132bhp triple-carb engine – arrived

THE AUSTIN-HEALEY 4000

Had the Healey family had its way the Big Healey would not have died with the 3000 but would have been re-engineered to take the IoE Rolls-Royce engine of the Vanden Plas 4-Litre R. Lighter than the C-series, the 175bhp alloy Rolls unit was fitted in a bodyshell widened by 6in. BMC was impressed, commissioned six development cars, and pencilled in early-1968 production. Then it changed its mind. Crucially, the tooling for the engine had been disposed of; but also BMC was running out of money, while new partner Jaguar didn't want a potential E-type rival. With two of the development cars part-built, the project was cancelled. Having driven one of the three prototypes, the author can report that the 4000 would have been a fast, torquey and relaxed car, riding more comfortably than a 3000, having more internal space, and lacking the Big Healey's traditional scuttle-shake.

with the 3000 MkII of 1961, identifiable by a vertical-slat grille, while 1962 saw the car catch up with the competition by being given wind-up windows and a fold-down integral hood. The car also lost its triple carbs in favour of an easier-to-tune twin-SU set-up, at the cost of a mere 2bhp.

In 1964 came the ultimate 3000, the 150bhp MkIII with its wood-veneer dashboard, and in this form the Healey continued until 1968. Other than the arrival of separate indicators in April 1965 (accompanied by larger sidelights and rear lights), the only change during this period was a revised chassis in May 1964, slightly improving the Healey's famously wretched ground clearance.

The six-cylinder Healey has the reputation of being a man's sport car. It's certainly a demanding car to drive hard on give-and-take roads, especially in the wet, as it's not difficult to have the tail step out – and then at this crucial moment you find your movements restricted by the too-close steering wheel. But adopt a more relaxed approach, and you'll find that the Big Healey is a wonderful grand tourer, effortlessly swallowing up the miles in overdrive top. Nobody has ever pretended that the vintage-style Healey is perfection on wheels, but it has basin-loads of character and looks that are seductive enough to make one willingly forgive its failings.

I DIDN'T KNOW THAT...

- Assembly of the Austin-Healey moved to MG's factory in Abingdon in 1957, but bodies continued to be built and painted at Jensen. Geoffrey Healey told the author that the quality of Abingdon-built cars was better than that of those made at Longbridge – and additionally each car was road-tested after completion.
- In 1964 the Healeys created a fastback 3000, panelled by Jensen around an alloy-tube frame. BMC boss George Harriman liked the car and asked his styling department to come up with a revised proposal that would be less costly to produce. This was duly built, but logic prevailed: with the MGB GT imminent and an MGC GT on the horizon, the project was abandoned.
- In 1956 the 1954 streamlined 100 record-breaker was given a revised body and a supercharged 100-Six engine and exceeded 200mph in the hands of Donald Healey, at the Bonneville salt flats – this despite the engine blowing up on the second run.
- The MkII engine was given triple carbs principally so that a three-carb installation could be homologated for competition, allowing the use of triple Webers – in conjunction with an alloy cylinder head.
- The most celebrated 'Big Healey' rally victory was that of Pat Moss and Ann Wisdom in 1960's gruelling Liège–Rome–Liège – the first time an all-female crew had won a major European rally.
- The rarest six-cylinder Healey is the 3000 MkII two-seater, of which only 355 were made; the most common is the final Phase 3 MkIII, of which 11,691 left Abingdon.

ABOVE The interior of a 3000 MkI: the 100-style dashboard only disappeared with the arrival of the MkIII, but on six-cylinder cars it was leathercloth-covered rather than painted.

SPECIFICATION

Engine:	2639cc/2912cc water-cooled in-line 6-cyl; ohv
Power:	102bhp at 4600rpm (early 100-Six)/ 117bhp at 4750rpm (later 100-Six)/ 124bhp at 4600rpm (3000 MkI)/132bhp at 4760rpm (3000 MkII)/130bhp at 4750rpm (3000 MkIIa); 148bhp at 5250rpm (3000 MkIII)
Transmission:	four-speed gearbox with optional overdrive
Construction:	separate chassis, underslung at rear; alloy and steel bodywork
Front suspension:	independent coil-and-wishbone; anti-roll bar; lever-arm dampers
Rear suspension:	live axle with leaf springs, located by Panhard rod or (BJ8 Phase 2/3) by twin radius arms; lever-arm dampers
Steering:	cam-and-peg
Brakes:	all-drum (100-Six); front discs and rear drum (3000)
Kerb weight:	22.0cwt (100-Six); 23.5cwt (3000 MkIII PhI)

EVOLUTION

August 1956	100-Six (BN4) enters production
November 1957	Production moves to Abingdon Uprated six-port 117bhp engine
March 1958	Two-seater 100-Six (BN6) introduced
March 1959	3000 (BN7 and 2+2 BT7) introduced
May 1961	3000 MkII (BN7 and 2+2 BT7) introduced
November 1961	Centre gearlever
June 1962	3000 MkIIa (BJ7) introduced – convertible hood and wind-up windows
February 1964	3000 MkIII (BJ8) announced
May 1964	3000 MkIII Phase 2 – revised chassis
April 1965	3000 MkIII Phase 3 – revised lighting
November 1967	Series production ends
March 1968	Last 3000 leaves Abingdon

AUSTIN-HEALEY SPRITE 'FROGEYE'

Max Speed	83mph
0–60mph	20.5sec

ABOVE The Frogeye is a perfect exercise in minimalist design. It was a huge commercial success, with 48,987 made between 1958 and 1961 – more than any subsequent variant except the 1500 Midget.

BELOW Spot the difference! This is actually an all-glassfibre Frogeye Car Company 'Frog'; roughly 130 'restoration assemblies' and complete cars were made, the last in 1998.

Cooked up by Donald Healey and BMC boss Sir Leonard Lord, the Frogeye Sprite was one of those strokes of genius: a reinvention, nothing less, of the bargain-basement sports car previously incarnated by the original MG Midget and the sports Austin Sevens.

To make the recipe work, the structure had to be simple, and the mechanicals had to be taken out of the BMC parts bins. A monocoque tub made largely of straightforward folded sections achieved the former, with the help of a stripped-to-the-bone body: no bootlid, a one-piece bonnet, simple sidescreens rather than winding windows, and an absence of such fripperies as door handles or a front bumper. As for the mechanicals, they were pure Austin A35 – from the 948cc engine to the coil-and-wishbone front suspension and the back axle – but with all-round hydraulic brakes and the

deliciously quick and accurate Morris Minor steering rack. The only departure was in the use of quarter-elliptic rear suspension, with additional axle location by two radius arms. It's tempting to think this resulted from both Geoffrey Healey and his chassis designer Barry Bilbie being former Austin Seven owners, but apparently the idea was Donald Healey's, and intended to avoid the spring wind-up that could occur with normal semi-elliptics.

Having only a modest 42.5bhp twin-SU version of the eminently tunable A-series engine under the bonnet, it was inevitable that hotter Sprites would soon became a mainstay of the British tuning industry, and Healey in Warwick helped the process along by offering items such as Shorrocks superchargers, disc brakes, and wire wheels; it should be noted that BMC itself never offered the latter two options.

THE FROGEYE CAR COMPANY HEALEY FROGEYE

There are plenty of replicas around, but few that have received the approval of the original car's creators. One of those exceptions is the reproduction Frogeye launched in 1986 by Keith Brading: built on the Isle of Wight and latterly marketed under the Healey name, it had the approval of Donald Healey and benefited from engineering development work by son Geoffrey. The glassfibre-bodied Frogeye was built around a galvanised square-tube frame and was initially intended as a way of recycling Sprite/Midget mechanicals, including those of the 1500: everything but the rear suspension, which used caravan-type rubber springing, was ex-Spridget. Later cars, sold fully-built to Japan, moved to home-brewed coil-spring set-ups front and rear, abandoned the Spridget rear axle, and used a Maestro engine mated to either a Ford or FSO (ex-Fiat) five-speed gearbox. The final cars of 1998 had a K-series engine.

Taking the process a stage further, Healey also experimented with a 'Super Sprite', building three such cars, under the 'XQHS' code. Latterly equipped with a Coventry Climax engine, they had modified bodies and it was envisaged they would enter limited production at Warwick, using a glassfibre shell; but BMC signalled its disapproval, and the project stopped there. Meanwhile, one of the most developed Sprites was that of rally driver John Sprinzel, who ended up making a series of special-bodied cars with a glassfibre bonnet and an integral hardtop; these were latterly known as Sebring Sprites, and replicas are available today. Sundry glassfibre bonnets were also available, finally, for those who found the bug-eyed look not to their taste.

Soon nicknamed the Frogeye – or 'Bugeye' in the States – the Sprite delivered all that was asked of it: adequate performance, nimble handling, safe roadholding, and a big smile on the face of its driver. Nor was the Frogeye impractical, for all its spartanism. As well as saving weight and complication, the sidescreens allowed hollowed-out doors which gave extra elbow room and enabled capacious door pockets to be provided; the bootlid-less rear, meanwhile, could swallow an enormous amount of luggage, even if extracting the spare was something of an exercise. Later generations of Sprite and Midget might have become more civilised, but they lost the charming and functional minimalism of the original.

I DIDN'T KNOW THAT...

- All Frogeyes made in the UK were assembled at Abingdon, bodies arriving at the MG factory having been painted at the Morris works in Cowley. Cars were also built in Mexico, South Africa, Belgium, Holland, Eire and Australia, from CKD kits of parts.
- The original thought was to have symmetrical front and rear body sections – an idea taken up by Pininfarina's Peugette concept car two decades later; the prototype came close to this, with the headlamps folding down, 928-style, into the bonnet.
- To keep costs down, even the rev-counter was in theory an option on home-market cars. The author has never seen a car without a rev-counter, and doubts if any Sprites left Abingdon with such a denuded dashboard. US buyers got the rev-counter as standard, along with the front bumper, the heater/demister, the windscreen washer and the laminated windscreen for which British customers had to pay extra.
- For 1960's Le Mans, Healey re-bodied a Frogeye using a Falcon kit-car glassfibre shell; the car won its class and finished 20th overall.
- In 1959 a series of records fell at Bonneville to a streamlined 'Austin-Healey Sprite' with a supercharged 948cc engine; in fact the car – given the Abingdon code EX219 – wasn't an Austin-Healey at all, but MG's EX179 recordbreaker of 1954, re-engined for the occasion.
- In 1960 tuning specialist Speedwell built a Frogeye streamliner – to a design by leading aerodynamicist Frank Costin – and achieved a 132.2mph flying kilometre with the car.

ABOVE The cockpit is simple but well conceived – and surprisingly roomy. The car would originally have had rubber floor matting rather than carpets, and in theory the rev-counter was optional.

SPECIFICATION

Engine:	948cc water-cooled in-line 4-cyl; ohv
Power:	42.5bhp at 5200rpm
Transmission:	four-speed gearbox
Construction:	steel monocoque
Front suspension:	independent coil-and-wishbone; lever-arm dampers
Rear suspension:	live axle with quarter-elliptic leaf springs; location by radius arms; lever-arm dampers
Steering:	rack-and-pinion
Brakes:	drum (front discs available from Healey)
Kerb weight:	12.75cwt

EVOLUTION

March 1958	First Frogeye produced
May 1958	Press launch
October 1958	Lift-the-dot forward hood fixing replaced by slot-in steel strip
April 1959	White hood, tonneau and sidescreens optional
March 1960	Sliding-pane sidescreens phased in
November 1960	Last Frogeye made
February 1961	Last chassis number allocated: semi-CKD for Innocenti Spider

LEFT Wire wheels were never a BMC option, but were offered by Healey at Warwick, along with front disc brakes and other tuning items – including a Shorrock supercharger.

AUSTIN-HEALEY SPRITE II-IV & MG MIDGET

Max Speed	94mph*
0–60mph	14.1sec*

1275cc Midget

ABOVE One of the last pre-facelift Sprite MkIVs. For the 1970 model year the cars were given slimline bumpers, matt-black detailing, and a revised interior with heat-formed seats and trim.

BELOW Their shape honed in the wind-tunnel, three of these elegant Midget coupés were built, two being campaigned by Dick Jacobs; the cars weighed nearly 3cwt less than a regular Midget.

Not everyone liked the Frogeye's looks, and when sales took a blip, BMC initiated a re-style. Legend has it that Healey in Warwick was tasked to create the front and Abingdon the rear: this is broadly true, but the two parties realised what was going on, and pooled their efforts. The result was the Sprite MkII of 1961, a car that retained the basic Frogeye monocoque but had new front and rear ends incorporating a conventional bonnet and a bootlid in the rear deck. Not only that, but an MG version, the Midget, was introduced, giving MG dealers a car to sell as well as short-circuiting the agreement whereby Donald Healey received a royalty on each Sprite.

With the same 948cc power unit as before, the 'Spridget' was heavier, slower, and surely more costly to build. It is tempting to think that it was thus a typical example of a

brilliant idea screwed up by an idiot management; but taking the longer view, the Abingdon duo put BMC in a better position to compete with the forthcoming Triumph Spitfire, and offered a platform that could be further developed throughout the 1960s, during which time the Frogeye would surely have fallen from favour had it been kept in production. It also allowed the MG version to continue until the end of the following decade, even if by then the design was hopelessly outdated.

A 1098cc engine arrived for 1963, along with disc front brakes, and then at the beginning of 1964 the cars received wind-up windows and conventional semi-elliptic springs that gave less nervous handling and a better-controlled ride; the purgatorial build-it-yourself hood remained, however, until the 1275cc engine arrived in 1966 with the Midget MkIII and

THE SPRIDGET COUPÉS

Both MG and Healey built special hardtop racing Spridgets. The Abingdon cars were elegant fastbacks, with alloy panelwork glued and riveted to a Midget platform. Created on the suggestion of Dick Jacobs of MG specialist Mill Garage, who raced two of the cars, their lines were inspired by those of the Aston Martin DB4. At Warwick, Healey built various coupé Sprites, beginning with a Frogeye-based car for 1961's Le Mans. Further cars were constructed for 1963 and 1964, but it was only after wind-tunnel testing led to a revised fastback body style that the cars came good, one of these streamlined alloy-bodied cars – capable of approaching 150mph – being the first British car home and 15th overall in the 1967 and 1968 events, the latter year with an injected engine. One of the coupés was later trimmed as a road car, and there was briefly talk of a small production run.

Sprite MkIV. These models were the definitive 'Spridget', with a zippy 65bhp engine, a quick-to-erect integral hood, and pleasant BMC interior trim. Fast enough to be enjoyable, with deliciously quick steering, a delightful gearchange and fail-safe adjustable handling, the Sprite and Midget were the perfect starter sports car, less spacious than their Triumph rival but with better road behaviour.

Thereafter it was downhill. The British Leyland cost-cutters moved in and for 1970 the interior trim was downgraded and the exterior given slimline bumpers and a crass matt-black facelift. Worse was to come: to stay in the crucial US market the Midget – the Sprite had by then been discontinued – was given the Triumph 1500cc engine for 1975, along with hefty plastic-covered bumpers and raised suspension. The last-named was necessary to meet US bumper-height regulations, and destroyed the car's delicate handling, while the front bumper restricted airflow to the engine and could cause overheating.

The Midget 1500 was by now emphatically a poor relation to the Spitfire, and pretty much a laughing stock, not least in de-toxed 50bhp US-market form – 'This thing is trash', wrote one *Car & Driver* journalist. But the MG had low price and some residual cuteness on its side, and so carried on selling, a rolling testimony to BL's financial and managerial bankruptcy.

I DIDN'T KNOW THAT...

■ The MG Midget was mechanically identical to the Sprite, but until 1969 was sold at a slight premium. This was supposedly accounted for by better trim: a padded dash-top roll, more piping on the seats, carpet on the bottom of the backrests, better-calibrated instruments, and waistline and bonnet strips. By the time of the MkIII Sprite and MkII Midget only the exterior brightwork and grille distinguished the MG from the Healey – and the bonnet strip disappeared in 1968.

■ Healey experimented with a B-series engine in the Sprite, extending the wheelbase by 3in to preserve the car's handling. The BMC Competitions Department later considered such a hybrid for rallying.

■ Jack Brabham fitted the Coventy-Climax engine to some cars. Additionally a series of 'Spridgets' was fitted with the 1600cc Ford 'Kent' engine as an aftermarket conversion; the cars were called the Atlantis.

■ A series of 11 Sprites received elegant WSM fastback coupé bodywork created by Doug Wilson-Spratt. Most were all-aluminium, but two had alloy doors and a grp body.

■ The Sprite was made in Italy by Innocenti – with a body designed by Tom Tjaarda of Ghia, later to be responsible for the line of the De Tomaso Pantera. Most of the 7651 built between 1961 and 1968 were the open 'S' spider, but 794 of a coupé 'C' model were also made. All were 948cc or 1098cc, and the rear suspension was Innocenti's own semi-elliptic design, in conjunction with telescopic dampers.

■ From November 1967 US-market cars had a different design of (padded) dashboard.

SPECIFICATION

Engine:	948cc/1098cc/1275cc/1493cc water-cooled in-line 4-cyl; ohv
Power:	46.5bhp at 5500rpm (948cc)
	55bhp at 5750rpm (Sprite II/Midget I)
	59bhp at 5750rpm (Sprite III/Midget II)
	65bhp at 6000rpm (1275cc)
	66bhp at 5500rpm (Midget 1500)
Transmission:	four-speed gearbox; synchro first gear only on 1500
Construction:	steel monocoque
Front suspension:	independent coil-and-wishbone; optional anti-roll bar from 1964 (standard from 1973); lever-arm dampers
Rear suspension:	live axle with quarter-elliptic leaf springs; location by radius arms (Midget MkI and Sprite MkII); thereafter semi-elliptic springs with no additional location; lever-arm dampers
Steering:	rack-and-pinion
Brakes:	all-drum until October 1962; thereafter front discs
Kerb weight:	13.9cwt (Midget MkI); 15.4cwt (1500)

EVOLUTION

May 1961	Austin-Healey Sprite MkII announced
June 1961	MG Midget (MkI) announced
October 1962	1098cc engine and disc front brakes
March 1964	Sprite MkIII and Midget MkII: wind-up windows, semi-elliptic rear, uprated engine
October 1966	Sprite MkIV and Midget MkIII: 1275cc engine, integral hood
November 1967	Specific padded dashboard for North America
December 1968	Midget loses bonnet strip; horizontal-flute seats
October 1969	Matt-black facelift: slimline bumpers, revised interior
January 1971	Healey name deleted
July 1971	Last 'Austin Sprite'
October 1971	Round rear wheelarches (export Midget)
January 1972	Round rear wheelarches (home-market Midget)
August 1973	Front anti-roll bar standard on home-market cars
October 1974	Midget 1500 introduced
October 1979	Final run of 500 UK-market cars begins, all black
December 1979	Last Midget produced

LEFT A pre-facelift MkIII Midget, with the MG's extra chrome trim. The author helped rebuild this particular car, using one of the very first new bodyshells from British Motor Heritage.

BENTLEY 3-LITRE/4½-LITRE & SPEED SIX

Max Speed	92mph*
0–60mph	n/a*

*4½-litre (unblown)

ABOVE This 3-litre is a replica of 1927's Le Mans winner – which was in fact a 4½-litre rather than a 3-litre. In all, 1622 3-litres were made, against 655 un-blown 4½-litres and 545 6½-litres – of which 181 were Speed Sixes.

BELOW Not a normal 8-litre, this is the short-wheelbase racing special created by Bentley Drivers' Club stalwart Forrest Lycett. In ultimate 340bhp form it has been clocked at over 140mph.

What can one say of the vintage Bentley? Firstly, that its reputation is inextricably enmeshed with motor racing, thanks to five wins at Le Mans; without these successes the marque would have been nothing, admitted its creator, Walter Owen Bentley. Secondly, that despite that famous jibe by Ettore Bugatti that Bentleys were nothing more than high-speed lorries, the cars might have been heavyweights (in fact the 3-litre was relatively light) but they certainly weren't crude in their engineering. Thirdly, that Bentleys weren't only open tourers with fabric-covered Vanden Plas bodies, and that all too many closed Bentleys have been resurrected as bogus Le Mans racers when they haven't been any closer to the famous circuit than the author's Morris Eight.

The original 3-litre model of 1919 had a four-cylinder engine with a gear-driven single overhead camshaft and the advanced feature for the time of four valves per cylinder. Engineered with a fine attention to detail, the 3-litre was a multi-faceted sports car for the connoisseur, proving its mettle with its 1924 Le Mans victory; wins in 1927 and 1928 by the bigger – but still four-cylinder – 4½-litre cemented the marque's reputation. Most mythical of all was the 'Blower Bentley', a 4½-litre with a twin-rotor supercharger between the dumb irons. This was the brainchild of Bentley racer Sir Henry Birkin: 'WO' was unconvinced of the merits of supercharging. Five racers and 50 road cars were built, and 'WO' felt he'd made his point when normally-aspirated Speed Sixes won at Le Mans in 1929 and 1930.

In 1925 the first six-cylinder Bentley was introduced, intended as a quieter and more touring-orientated model,

THE 4-LITRE AND 8-LITRE

At a time when building a more expensive Bentley was seen as a means of financial salvation, September 1930 saw the launch of the 8-litre, Britain's largest car, with a price deliberately a whisker above that of the Rolls-Royce Phantom II, to mark out its territory as the ultimate luxury car. But the 8-litre was also capable of massive performance, being good for a disdainful 100mph thanks to the 230bhp delivered by its straight-six, an evolution of the 6½-litre unit. Initially the money came rolling in, but then the slump bit, and sales evaporated. Bentley's response was to scale down the 8-litre and fit it with a new inlet-over-exhaust 'six'. But the resultant somewhat heavyweight 4-litre had none of the performance expected of the marque, and found few friends – least of all 'WO' himself, who called it 'curious and little-lamented'. Just 50 were built – against 100 of the 8-litre.

more suitable for closed bodies than the relatively raucous four-cylinder cars. It was also an important money-spinner for the firm, as it cost little more to make than the 'fours' but could be sold at a much higher price. The Big Six, as it was called, had a 6597cc engine with the same ohc four-valve-per-cylinder configuration as the four-cylinder cars, and offered such massive torque that it could be trickled around London without changing out of top gear. A sports version, the Speed Six, followed.

Contrary to what might be thought, it wasn't an extravagant racing programme that brought Bentley down; 'WO' calculated the entire effort cost £3500 annually – say £140,000 in today's money. Rather it was that the slump caused sales of the cars not just to fall but effectively to dry up. The situation was compounded by the introduction in September 1930 of the 8-litre, which was hardly the ideal car to launch into the teeth of a biting recession.

In July 1931 Bentley went into receivership. Rolls-Royce bought the company, retaining the services of 'WO', and in 1933 the Bentley was relaunched as the Rolls-based 3½-litre, under the slogan 'The Silent Sports Car'. In all, just over 3000 vintage Bentleys were made, over a ten-year period. That approximately 1,600 are known to survive speaks for itself.

I DIDN'T KNOW THAT...

- 'WO' once said that he had no trouble keeping the supposedly boisterous 'Bentley Boys' of his racing team under control; his problem was more in stopping squabbles between their wives and girlfriends.
- In the mid-1920s WO Bentley attempted – without success – to persuade William Morris to take an interest in Bentley Motors. In later years 'WO' became an enthusiastic user of the post-war Morris Minor.
- The body of the first Bentley was drawn up by *The Autocar* artist F Gordon Crosby – as was the famous winged badge.
- The six-cylinder Bentley engines had their overhead camshaft actuated via a set of connecting rods mounted on eccentrics, rather than using gears or a chain. This unusual layout was revived several decades later on the vertical-twin NSU Prinz engine – and a device operating on the same principle was offered as an aftermarket accessory for the Citroën Traction Avant.
- During the period when Bentley was in receivership and seemed certain to be bought by Napier, 'WO' worked on a Napier-Bentley that was in effect a scaled-down 6¼-litre development of the 8-litre Bentley.
- Bentley moved to Lagonda in 1935, further developing the 4½-litre (see pages 62–63) before creating the Lagonda V12. Post-war he was responsible for the all-independent-suspension twin-cam Lagonda 2½-litre, whose engine was used in pre-DB4 Aston Martins. Later consultancy work included designing a stillborn new car for Armstrong-Siddeley.
- WO Bentley – in common with Jowett Javelin creator Gerald Palmer and Citroën stylist Flaminio Bertoni – designed his own house.

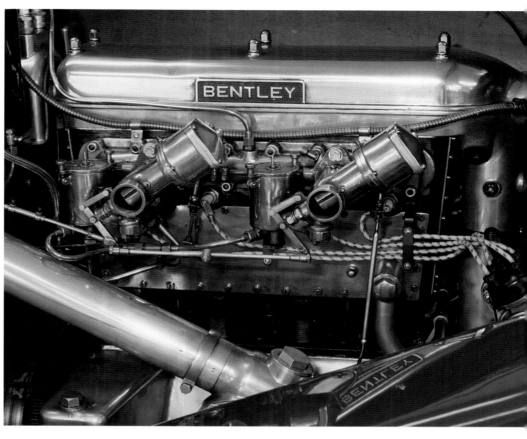

ABOVE High-grade engineering: a 3-litre engine, complete with early 'sloper' SU carburettors. The overhead camshaft and sixteen valves were advanced features for the day, but then WO Bentley had previously worked on aero-engine design.

SPECIFICATION

Engine:	2996cc/4398cc water-cooled in-line 16-valve 4-cyl; gear-driven sohc 6597cc water-cooled in-line six-cylinder; conrod-driven sohc
Power:	87bhp at 3500rpm (final 3-litre)/100bhp or 110bhp at 3500rpm (std 4½-litre)/160bhp or 180bhp at 3500rpm (Speed Six)
Transmission:	four-speed unsynchronised
Construction:	separate chassis; body construction varies
Front suspension:	beam axle with semi-elliptic leaf springs; friction dampers
Rear suspension:	live axle with leaf springs; friction dampers
Steering:	worm-and-wheel
Brakes:	drum, mechanically operated (four-wheel from 1923)
Kerb weight:	30.5cwt (4½-litre tourer)

EVOLUTION

November 1919	3-litre announced
August 1921	Production begins
September 1923	Front-wheel brakes
June 1925	Big Six announced
June 1927	4½-litre announced – for Le Mans
September 1928	Speed Six introduced
July 1929	Supercharged 4½-litre announced
September 1930	8-litre launched
May 1931	4-litre announced
July 1931	Bentley Motors enters receivership
August 1931	Talk of merger with Napier
November 1931	Rolls-Royce acquires Bentley assets

BERKELEY

| Max Speed | 80mph* |
| 0–60mph | 21.8sec* |

* Excelsior triple

ABOVE The squared-up bonnet indicates that this is a B95 (as is the case here) or a B105, with the Royal Enfield vertical-twin engine. The 'cake-tin' hubcaps are typical Berkeley.

BELOW Charles Panter (standing), with the Bandit; at the wheel is future rally star Tony Pond. Three prototypes were laid down, and two completed; one car is known to survive.

The unlikely progeny of a Biggleswade caravan manufacturer and an eccentric designer of three-wheel microcars, the Berkeley was created by Charles Panter of Berkeley Caravans and Lawrie Bond, the man behind the front-drive Bond Minicar.

The little sports car had a glassfibre monocoque with aluminium reinforcement, and was initially powered by a two-stroke 322cc Anzani vertical-twin, driving the front wheels; having proved troublesome, this was soon replaced by a 328cc Excelsior 'twin'. In this form the Berkeley weighed a mere 6.5cwt, so on 18bhp it was still good for just over 60mph, with a 0–50mph time of 30.6 seconds. Despite a swing-axle rear, roadholding and handling were praised, and the pocket-sized sports car – it was only 3ft 7½in high – was soon appearing in motor-sport events.

For 1958 the Berkeley gained a three-cylinder 492cc version of the Excelsior engine, developed for Berkeley by Lawrie Bond; in common with later SE328s it also had a four-speed gearbox with a floor lever in place of the original three-speeder with positive-stop column change. Fuelled by three Amal carburettors, the new engine delivered 30bhp and gave the Berkeley 80mph performance: testers were impressed at how it could out-gun saloons with engines five times bigger.

Available also as a four-seater 'Foursome', this was a short-lived variant, however, as the 'triple' had a tendency to overheat and seize, and 1959 saw yet another new engine, a beefy hemi-head Royal Enfield 'twin'. Still driving the front wheels by chain, this 692cc unit developed 40bhp in the B95 model or a rousing 50bhp in 'Constellation' tune as used in

THE BERKELEY BANDIT

With the motorcycle-engined Berkeley effectively killed by the Austin-Healey Sprite – as well as by its inherent failings – Charles Panter commissioned John Tojeiro (see AC Ace) to design a more mature vehicle, using Ford Anglia 105E components. The result was the Berkeley Bandit of 1960, a car uncannily similar in looks and concept to the original thoughts on what was to become the Lotus Elan. Under the grp body was a folded-steel chassis (again very Elan), and strut front suspension based on Armstrong coil-over-damper units; at the rear was an unusual swing-axle independent set-up arrived at by cut-and-shutting the Anglia rear axle but which unfortunately gave the car somewhat challenging handling. Weighing only 11cwt, the Bandit was sprightly enough even with a standard 997cc Anglia engine, but Berkeley collapsed before this potential life-saver could make it to production.

the B105. That was 7½bhp more than a Sprite could muster, and the 'Frogeye' weighed 4.75cwt more than the 8cwt or thereabouts of the B105, so a white-knuckle 100mph was in theory possible.

Berkeley also built a substantial number of a three-wheeler model, the T60, to cater for this peculiarly British market niche. It was available either as a two-seater (1780 made) or a four-seater (50 made), and was only ever powered by the Excelsior 'twin'. Latterly, this engine made a return on a cheaper version of the four-wheeler, called the B65, but it is thought fewer than a dozen of these last-ditch 1960–61 cars were made.

The Berkeley was an honourable effort, offering a big dose of fun at a modest price. Its inevitable crudenesses would surely have tired in the end, especially in the faster but rougher and more vibration-prone Royal Enfield cars: it's a shame the smooth and revvy Excelsior 'triple' was such a liability, as it gave the car the performance lacking in the original twin-cylinder cars.

But it was all academic. Not only did the much more mature Sprite deal the Berkeley a fatal blow, but Panter over-reached himself financially – not helped by having to pay compensation for faulty engines – and then lost a court case he had brought against body-materials supplier Bakelite. With caravan manufacture a seasonal activity, the burden was simply too much, and another small specialist manufacturer bit the dust.

I DIDN'T KNOW THAT...

- The first creations of Lawrie Bond (1907–74) were a pint-sized front-wheel-drive 500cc racing car and the 98cc Bond Minibyke, a bizarre miniature motorcycle based around a torpedo-like oval aluminium tube and having fully enclosed wheels. He was also responsible for the Opperman Unicar of 1956–59, a fwd Formula Junior racer of 1961, and the Bond Equipe and three-wheeled Bond 875.
- Unlikely as it may seem, top rally driver Pat Moss, better known for her exploits in Big Healeys, once rallied a Berkeley. While being briefed on the car she asked where the jack was – only to be shown a block of wood. If she needed to change a wheel, she was told, all she had to do was lift the car up and pop the block of wood underneath…
- In later life many Berkeleys were re-engined with Mini powerpacks.
- Berkeleys scored a 1–2 class win in the 1959 Mille Miglia and another class win (Gran Tourismo up to 500cc) in the same year's Monza 12-hour race.
- Although the wide-bodied longer-wheelbase four-seater shell was intended to be combined with the Royal Enfield engine, these proposed two-seater and four-seater variants never made it to production.
- Club sources suggest that 146 Anzani-engined cars were made, approximately 1272 of the SE 328 and 22 four-seaters, 666 of the 3-cylinder SE 492, roughly 200 of the B95/B105, and ten or so Excelsior-powered B65s. In addition a healthy 1780 two-seat three-wheelers were made, plus roughly 50 four-seat trikes.

SPECIFICATION

Engine:	322cc Anzani vertical-twin two-stroke
	328cc Excelsior vertical-twin two-stroke
	492cc in-line 3-cyl Excelsior two-stroke
	692cc ohv Royal Enfield vertical-twin
Power:	15bhp at 4800rpm/18bhp at 5000rpm/
	30bhp at 5000rpm/40bhp at 5500rpm
	(B105: 50bhp at 6250rpm)
Transmission:	three-speed (SA322 and early SA328) or four-speed gearbox, unsynchronised; front-wheel drive, by chain
Construction:	glassfibre monocoque with aluminium reinforcement; steel front subframe
Front suspension:	independent by twin wishbone; combined coil springs and telescopic dampers
Rear suspension:	independent by swing axles and combined coil springs and telescopic dampers
Steering:	worm-and-nut
Brakes:	all-drum
Kerb weight:	6.5cwt to 7.9cwt depending on model

EVOLUTION

September 1956	Original SA 322 model launched
Spring 1957	2-cyl Excelsior SE 328 introduced
October 1957	3-cyl Excelsior SE 492 announced
October 1958	Four-seater introduced
March 1959	Royal Enfield B95/B105 introduced; SE 492 phased out
August 1959	Three-wheel T60 announced
October 1960	2-cyl Excelsior B65 announced Bandit prototype shown
January 1961	Berkeley in voluntary liquidation

BELOW The cockpit of an Excelsior-powered SE492; the floor gearlever with its sequential motorcycle-style change takes a little practice, until you've mastered the art of matching the revs accurately.

DAIMLER SP250

Max Speed 124mph
0–60mph 8.9sec

ABOVE The author has fond memories of driving this SP250, on which the wide-rim chrome wire wheels are definitely non-standard. The fins are very much of the era.

RIGHT The Dart as cleaned up for Sir William Lyons. Neither the sums nor the industrial logic added up. The SP250 was, alas, always a no-hoper – a last desperate throw of the dice by an enfeebled Daimler.

The idea of Daimler producing a high-performance sports car is more than faintly ridiculous, the firm being better known for its portly saloons and for its stately limousines that were once the choice of the British royal family. But at the end of the 1950s the ineptly-run Coventry company was in a mess, and needed a saleable product – fast.

Looking at the lucrative US market, it decided that the answer was to gun for a slice of the American pie enjoyed by MG, Triumph, and Jaguar. The result was launched in April 1959 as the Dart – and promptly re-named the SP250 when Chrysler pointed out that it held rights to the Dart name.

Rushed into production, the Dart had an underslung chassis copied from that of the Triumph TR, a gearbox also cribbed from the Triumph, and a body of somewhat bizarre lines that was made of glassfibre: Daimler simply couldn't

justify the money – or the time – that would be needed to tool for a steel body. But there was one ace in this slightly dog-eared technical pack: a brand-new 2½-litre alloy-head V8 engine designed under the direction of Edward Turner, famous for having created the Triumph Speed Twin and Ariel Square Four motorcycle power units. Drawing on motorcycle practice, this hemi-head jewel gave the Daimler a strong performance that bettered that of its cheaper rivals.

Unfortunately that was about all that could be said of the Dart. Its roadholding and handling were regarded as mediocre, its styling as ungainly – ugly, even – and its quality as unacceptable. In particular, owners were horrified by structural rigidity so poor that the scuttle shook severely and the doors burst open.

In May 1960 Daimler was purchased by Jaguar. Although it was not impressed by the Dart, Jaguar decided to keep it

THE SP250 'MKII'

In 1962–63 two SP250s were given bodies restyled according to instructions from Jaguar boss Sir William Lyons – a man with a keen eye for a good line. Lyons was reportedly not impressed, and the cars – coded SP252 – were cannibalised, with one car being made out of the two; eventually sold, it survives in the hands of an enthusiast. Producing the 'MkII' would have been perfectly feasible, but it was calculated that the SP252 would cost more to manufacture than the E-type. In such circumstances, and regardless of whether or not such a car would have found a market, Lyons was not inclined to create an in-house rival to his own sports car. An interesting postscript is that it seems the car was dusted down in 1966 or thereabouts and presented to BMH brass as a potential alternative to the MGC, as a replacement for the Big Healey.

in production, and see how it could be improved without spending too much money. By 1961 a series of body reinforcements had been phased in, leading to the so-called 'B' specification, after which the Daimler continued without anything but the most piffling of changes until it was discontinued in 1964. Sales in the first three years had been projected as 7500 cars; in the end only 2645 cars left the Daimler lines, against roughly 25,000 Austin-Healey 3000s produced in the same period.

By any standards the Dart was a failure – a last desperate throw of the dice by a struggling and poorly managed company. It deserved better. Get behind the wheel and you'll find a surprisingly beguiling car. Above all, the engine is simply one of the loveliest of the period, offering crisp, muscular performance and a delicious soundtrack. The gearchange isn't as bad as some say (it's short-throw and TR-like in feel), the steering – another point of criticism – need not feel over-heavy if it's properly set up, and the admittedly unsophisticated roadholding is only challenging if you have neglected to fit modern radial-ply tyres. There's also the bonus of a nicely furnished interior, while body rigidity on the 1961-on cars is no longer a problem, although scuttle shake is still evident. You'll have to form your own opinion about the styling – some say it grows on you – but at least it's original and dramatic.

I DIDN'T KNOW THAT...

- The Dart helped give birth to the Reliant Scimitar. Design consultancy Ogle created a special coupé body on the Daimler chassis, on behalf of a director of cosmetics company Helena Rubenstein. Two cars were made, the first being exhibited at the 1962 London Motor Show, and the design was sold to Reliant, who used it to reclothe the Sabre 6 chassis to create the Scimitar.
- At Earls Court in 1959 Hooper showed an ungainly 2+2 coupé based on the Dart, and one or two – or maybe more – shells were made in grp by Daimler. William Lyons and his chief engineer Bill Heynes asked for a car to be built up, and Lyons was reportedly so appalled that he ordered the car to be scrapped immediately.
- In 1963–64 kit-car manufacturer Tornado built a one-off version of its Talisman GT on a shortened and strengthened Dart chassis; apparently the car was planned for production – Jaguar not being hostile to the idea – but Tornado folded before the idea progressed any further.
- During development of the V8, one engine was tried with eight Amal motorcycle carburettors: the result was an impressive output of 200bhp or so.
- Only 1200 cars were made with left-hand drive, and early US sales were so poor that 130 unsold cars were shipped back to England, where they were modified to improve body rigidity.
- One SP250 was fitted with E-type front suspension and a coil-sprung independent rear; there were also experiments with rack-and-pinion steering.

SPECIFICATION

Engine:	2548cc water-cooled V8; ohv 'hemi' with alloy heads
Power:	140bhp at 5800rpm
Transmission:	four-speed gearbox; optional automatic
Construction:	cruciform chassis, underslung at rear; glassfibre body
Front suspension:	independent by coil and wishbone; telescopic dampers
Rear suspension:	live axle, leaf springs; lever-arm dampers
Steering:	cam-and-peg
Brakes:	four-wheel disc
Kerb weight:	20cwt

EVOLUTION

April 1959	Dart announced
September 1959	UK launch, as SP250
October 1960	Hardtop available
February 1961	Automatic transmission available to private UK buyers; previously only for export and police
April 1961	'B specification'. Body and chassis reinforcements formally introduced; also revised interior, standard-fit bumpers
April 1963	'C specification': heater and cigarette lighter standard
September 1964	Discontinued

DELLOW

Max Speed 69mph*
0–60mph 20.3sec*
* Supercharged

ABOVE This Dellow MkII is typical of the breed. The wheels are standard Ford items, and clearly visible is the front suspension's transverse leaf spring, controlled by high-set friction dampers.

BELOW Why it was ever thought anyone would want to buy new proprietor Neville Nightingale's MkVI Dellow is lost in the mists of time. *(Jim Harvey)*

The Dellow was designed to do a specific job – and that job it did well. The job in question was to be an effective contender in trials, and Dellows became a prominent presence in this arm of motor sport; indeed, you'll still see examples competing to this day.

The Dellow was a collaboration between nuts-and-bolts and fastenings manufacturer Ken Delingpole and Ron Lowe, who worked at his company, Delson, as a development engineer – hence the name. The production Dellows were descended from a series of six trials cars built by Lowe and based on Ford parts – engine, gearbox and axles – in an Austin Seven chassis, this assemblage then being given a skimpy open aluminium body built over a framework made from gas piping.

After a while, Dellow Motors decided to make its own chassis. Steel was rationed, and small-time car manufacturers had to improvise. Dellow's stroke of genius was to acquire a stock of rocket bodies, made of high-grade chrome-molybdenum steel, from which it constructed tubular chassis of superior rigidity to the whippy Austin frame. By 1950 the cars were being built using new Ford parts, and a supercharger was available as an option – giving an output of about 46bhp from the 1172cc sidevalve engine. You could also order parts to build your own Dellow.

At first the chassis retained Austin-like quarter-elliptics at the rear, but from 1951 a revised MkII had a more rigid frame and went over to coil springs for the rear axle, with Ford's radius rods and torque tube providing location. The result of these endeavours was a high-riding car with a rearwards weight bias; performance was surprisingly zippy, and off-road agility marvellous, but on-road stability was never of the

THE VERSATILE *Dellow* SPORTS CAR

DELLOW ENGINEERING COMPANY LIMITED · OLDBURY · BIRMINGHAM · ENGLAND

THE DELLOW MkVI

With sales of traditional-bodied Dellows minimal, the new owners of the name came up with a more modern offering. Launched in 1957 as the MkVI, all it had in common with its predecessors was the use of Ford parts – in this instance mainly from the 100E range. The all-enveloping body (uncannily like the Fairlite grp shell for the Ford Eight/Ten chassis) was in aluminium, and underneath was a ladder chassis, a split-beam Ford front axle on coil springs, and an underslung rear axle on semi-elliptic springs. This dull-looking bitsa with its boat-anchor 36bhp sidevalve engine and three-speed gearbox was the answer to a question nobody seemed to be asking, and it is thought no more then six were made; one survives, plus a chassis carrying a proprietary Falcon body. It was a sad end to the Dellow story, albeit one hardly rare in the world of small-time motor manufacturers.

highest order, although somewhat improved over that of the original MkI cars.

The company's success proved a flash in the pan. The MkIII, a longer-wheelbase four-seater introduced in 1952, was more of a road car than a trials competitor, and only 18 or so were sold; meanwhile output of the MkII fell to a trickle. A Consul-engined MkIV remained a one-off, and a MkV with a more streamlined body, coil springing all-round, and an optional four-speed gearbox, found only a few buyers.

In 1956 Delingpole sold the Dellow car operations to a Midlands supplier of foundry equipment who continued manufacture, latterly with a cheapened version of the MkII called the MkIIC and a better-equipped MkIIE using the more advanced – but still sidevalve – engine of the Ford 100E Prefect/Anglia. More significantly, the new company went ahead with an all-new sports car (see box), a venture doomed to failure; in 1959 Dellow Engineering ceased production, after barely more than a dozen cars of various types had been made.

The Dellow's moment in the sun was brief. Despite exaggerated talk of a production of 400–500 cars, roughly 250 were made, most of them the archetypal MkI and MkII, and almost all still exist – a formidable survival rate that reflects the car's continuing use at the muddier end of British motor sport.

I DIDN'T KNOW THAT...

- A key feature of MkI Dellows, and some later cars, is a fiddle brake – an outside handbrake lever that operates the front brakes when pushed forward and the rear brakes when pulled back. This aids manoeuvrability in trials, as does the ultra-rapid steering, with its 1.5 turns lock-to-lock.

- Weight distribution, helped by a 17-gallon fuel tank and by the two rear-mounted spare wheels generally fitted, is 40:60 front-to-rear on a MkII.

- The supercharged Dellow could manage 0–50mph in 12.6 seconds, aided by the low ratio of the back axle and the three-speed gearbox.

- On some surviving Dellows it is still possible to see the WD stencil marks on the rocket tubes forming the chassis.

- Ron Lowe, co-founder of the marque, refused to recognise the products of successor company Dellow Engineering as genuine Dellows.

- Dellows weren't just purchased by trials motorists. Four were sold to a manufacturer of milk-bottle-capping machinery, for use on farm visits.

- Dellow bodies were made by Radpanels of Kidderminster: owner Lionel Evans had worked in the aircraft industry during the war, and was skilled in tubular-framing and alloy-skinning.

- Some Radpanels bodies were fitted to regular Ford chassis. Indeed, there is one Radpanels Ford Ten special known to the author that has a body that is a dead ringer for that of the Dellow MkIII.

- A single left-hand-drive Dellow – a MkIII – was completed in February 1956 for a tea-planter in Pakistan. This was in anticipation of Pakistan switching to drive on the right – which in the end never happened.

SPECIFICATION (MK II)

Engine:	1172cc water-cooled in-line 4-cyl; sidevalve
Power:	30bhp at 4000rpm (standard engine)
Transmission:	three-speed gearbox with synchromesh on second/third
Construction:	separate tubular chassis; tubular steel body frame welded to chassis; alloy panelling
Front suspension:	beam axle with transverse leaf spring; Panhard rod; telescopic or friction dampers
Rear suspension:	live axle with coil springs; location by torque tube and diagonal radius arms; telescopic dampers
Steering:	Burman cam–and–peg
Brakes:	drum, cable operated
Kerb weight:	15cwt (supercharged)

EVOLUTION

January 1950	Regular production underway
February 1951	MkII available – coil-sprung rear, doors
May 1951	Last MkI
May 1952	MkIII four-seater announced
May 1954	MkV Dellow has début at Prescott
September 1954	MkIII discontinued
February 1956	Last Alvechurch-produced car
April 1956	Rights sold to Neville Nightingale
September 1956	Production re-starts under new ownership
October 1957	MkVI Dellow announced
March 1959	Last Dellow made

BELOW Launch-time photo of the 1952 MkIII: the re-shaped four-seater rear is clearly visible. This is in fact Lionel Evans's own car, and is 6in shorter than production MkIIIs.

ELVA COURIER

Max Speed	105mph*
0–60mph	9.2sec*
	* Mk III

ABOVE Restored with no expense spared, this 1960 MkII has an MGA engine with an HRG alloy crossflow head; the boat-like split screen used on the first Couriers has thankfully disappeared.

BELOW Low-slung and still oh-so-gorgeous, the GT160 was sidelined by likely costs – and by changes to the GT racing regulations which would have entailed major design changes.

The glassfibre-bodied Courier was the creation of Sussex garage proprietor Frank Nichols, who in 1955 had built his own sports-racer, christened Elva, from the French *Elle va*, meaning 'She goes'. Nichols was soon producing replicas, many going to the States. This was the start of a long line of competition Elvas.

In early 1958 the first Courier was built, using a simple round-tube ladder chassis with a twin-wishbone front and a Riley 1.5 back axle on coil-overs, located by radius arms and a Panhard rod; steering was by Morris Minor rack. Power came from a 1489cc MGA engine, mated to the MG gearbox and mounted well back in the chassis. These early Couriers – most of which went to the States – were slightly odd-looking cars, but by the beginning of 1960 the design had been refined into the MkII, with a 1588cc MGA engine

and a lower one-piece screen, as well as a more rigid structure to eliminate chassis flex. A hardtop coupé was also announced. The styling was a little awkward, with a reversed-rake rear window, but under the skin was an independent rear end with inboard drum brakes – although ultimately the car entered production with the existing live rear axle.

Financial difficulties saw manufacturing rights to the Courier pass to the Trojan/Lambretta concern in 1962, and at the end of that year a new MkIII open sports car and coupé were introduced. Powered by a 1622cc MGA unit, the MkIII had a new Trojan-designed box-section chassis that was cheaper to make, and Triumph Herald/Vitesse front suspension, complete with front disc brakes.

Three MkIV coupés with a new fastback rear and independent rear suspension were built on old-style round-

THE ELVA-BMW GT160

Sometimes a design is so beautiful that it remains etched in the enthusiast conscience despite never making it to production. Just such a car is the GT160, a low-slung mid-engined coupé a mere 3ft 4in high. The idea had been to build a road-practical GT racer, and Italian coachbuilder Fissore was commissioned to create the body, farming out design to associate Fiore – variously described as Italian or Parisian, but in fact English-born Trevor Frost. Three aluminium-shelled cars were built, and the car was unveiled at the 1964 Turin motor show, powered by a tuned 2-litre BMW engine mated to a Hewland gearbox. But that was as far as things went: in particular, Fissore's price for providing further bodyshells turned out to be three times the original quote, and Elva called it a day. All three cars survive, one having had an unsuccessful foray to Le Mans in 1965 and one having a Rover V8 engine.

tube chassis at about this time, and anticipated the MkIV-T announced at the 1963 Motor Show in sports and coupé forms – the 'T' standing for 'Tru-Track' independent rear suspension, a set-up built around TVR uprights and wishbones. There was a restyled nose and tail, and the open car used an MGB screen, while its higher-cut doors were Triumph Spitfire assemblies, in steel. Power units were quoted as either the 1798cc MGB engine or the 1498cc Ford Cortina GT unit, but the odd early MkIV-T emerged with the MGA 1622cc engine.

The Elva was now a more presentable product, both better styled and more comfortable, and Trojan could proudly claim to offer the only 100mph under-£1000 sports car with all-independent suspension. But within a year the company decided to concentrate on producing McLaren-Elva sports-racing cars, and in 1965 a final batch of 38 part-finished Couriers was passed to a specialist in Hertfordshire for completion.

It was a sad end to a venture which had once shown such promise. Sure, the Elva was a bit rough at the edges. But it handled well, at the expense of a firm ride, went adequately fast, and was keenly priced. Had Trojan persisted, one can't help feeling that the marque could have achieved a successful maturity, offering in fully-built form a convincing bespoke alternative to the cheaper MGB and the more delicate Lotus Elan.

I DIDN'T KNOW THAT...

- The original Courier body was styled by Tim Fry, an engineer at the Rootes Group who with colleague Mike Parkes was responsible for the conception and development of the Hillman Imp.
- For the competition motorist there was a special MkII called the Spyder, with a modified chassis having adjustable suspension and Elva magnesium-alloy wheels.
- About 400 Couriers were produced by Frank Nichols, most being the open MkII – very few MkII coupés were made. Around 80 per cent went to the States, including most of the 50 MkIs made.
- Two 'Sebring' racing Courier MkIV-Ts were made, with a tuned MGB engine and a lightweight body and chassis; according to the Elva brochure the model was also offered with the Lotus twin-cam engine.
- Despite heady talk of making 500 Couriers a year, Trojan built only 210 cars – 25 MkIIs, 116 MkIIIs and live-axle MkIVs (of which only five or six were MkIII coupés), the three tubular-chassis IRS MkIV coupés, and a miserable 66 MkIV-Ts.
- Tony Ellis, the final person involved with the Courier, produced a one-off coupé, powered by a V6 Ford engine; it showed promise, but production never happened.
- Despite the arrival of the MkIV-T, the MkIII continued to be listed, in open form only, and some were certainly made in 1964, alongside the first MkIV-Ts. It seems that you could also order the MkIV with a beam rear axle, and although no beam-axle MkIV coupés are known, at least one open MkIV was built with a non-independent rear.

SPECIFICATION

Engine:	1489cc/1588cc/1622cc/1798cc water-cooled in-line 4-cyl; ohv
Power:	72bhp at 5500rpm/79.5bhp at 5600rpm/86bhp at 5500rpm/95bhp at 5400rpm
Transmission:	four-speed gearbox
Construction:	separate chassis; glassfibre body
Front suspension:	independent coil-and-wishbone; coil springs co-axial with telescopic dampers; optional anti-roll bar
Rear suspension:	underslung live axle with coil springs co-axial with telescopic dampers; location by radius arms and Panhard rod (MkI/II/III); independent by double wishbones and coils, with telescopic dampers (MkIV-T)
Steering:	rack-and-pinion
Brakes:	all-drum on MkI/II; thereafter generally front disc
Dry weight:	12.75cwt (Mk I)

EVOLUTION

May 1958	First Courier (1489cc)
April 1960	MkII – one-piece screen, 1588cc engine Hardtop coupé introduced
November 1962	MkIII – box-section chassis; 1622cc engine
March 1963	MkIV-T introduced – IRS; 1798cc engine
October 1965	Last Couriers despatched to Ken Sheppard Sports Cars for completion

BELOW Something of a hybrid, this Courier started life as the prototype coupé. Steel doors, from the Triumph Spitfire, came later – allowing the Elva to have wind-up windows.

FRAZER NASH (PRE-WAR)

Max Speed	87mph*
0–60mph	18sec*

* Meadows 1496cc TT Replica

ABOVE That perfect profile: the classic TT Replica model, with its bath-tub rear, was pretty much the standard later-day Isleworth style. This particular car has a four-cylinder Meadows engine.

RIGHT Racing legend John Surtees enjoying himself in another TT Rep. Clearly visible is the dipped tubular front axle, suspended on firm quarter-elliptic springs.

If in modern times the Caterham Seven has been regarded as a motorcycle on four wheels, in pre-war days the same could have been said of the Frazer Nash: shared by both cars are the virtues of light weight, extreme simplicity, and razor-sharp responses. With the 'Nash there is a closer connection with the motorcycling world, however, in that the drive to the rear wheels is by cogs and chains – a unique arrangement pioneered in its direct ancestor the GN cyclecar.

When GN creators HR Godfrey and Archie Frazer-Nash split up, Frazer-Nash immediately re-entered motor manufacture, his new car retaining the GN's chain drive and being almost invariably powered by the 1½-litre Anzani sidevalve engine. Perpetually under-financed, he made only 141 cars in the 1924–28 period, before selling out to the

dynamic Aldington brothers; thereafter he had nothing to do with the design of Frazer Nash cars, although he was nominally a technical advisor to the re-formed AFN Ltd and remained a shareholder.

The Aldingtons refined the basic design, switching to the well-known Meadows pushrod engine in ever more developed forms, and the car became a favourite among the well-heeled motor-sport fraternity: at £325 in 1931 the Frazer Nash might have been half the price of an Aston Martin, but it was still roughly double the cost of an MG Midget, which perforce restricted its market.

Later Frazer Nashes had an ohc evolution of the Meadows 'four', designed in-house and initially less than reliable, with eight cars – known as the Shelsley – having a twin-supercharged version. Additionally 27 cars were built

THE FRAZER NASH-BMWs

As an intended prelude to licence-manufacture, AFN imported its first BMWs at the end of 1934. Over the years the company sold the 1½-litre 315, the 2-litre 319, the later 320, 326 and 327 models, and – above all – the delicious 328 sports car. Although most were imported fully-built, British coachwork was available, and 37 (both 315s and 319s) were given coupé, drophead or pillarless saloon bodies by Abbott, 19 (all 319s) received Whittingham & Mitchel coachwork, and Wendover, Bertelli and Freestone & Webb each bodied a car. Further to this, three 319/40 sports two-seaters were built by Tanner Bros of Fulham. Immediately before the outbreak of war, Frazer Nash was about to start providing its own body styles on the 328 chassis, and six chassis impounded during hostilities were bodied after the war by AFN – two in differing styles and the rest as clones of the German original.

with a six-cylinder Blackburne engine of either 1498cc or 1660cc. Unchanged throughout the life of the cars was the simple channel-section chassis, with its rigid differential-less back axle and tubular front axle, both suspended on unyielding quarter-elliptic springs.

But by the mid-1930s the crudenesses of the Frazer Nash had become evident to the Aldingtons, who from the end of 1934 had begun importing BMWs from Germany to sell as Frazer Nash-BMWs. Thereafter production of 'chain gang' cars fell to a trickle, with 19 being made in 1935, eight in 1936, four in 1937, and just two in 1938, with one final car assembled at the beginning of 1939.

Given that total output of pre-war Frazer Nashes was only 326 examples, it is perhaps astonishing that the marque has such a high profile, but this has much to do with the intoxicating dynamics of the cars. The unusual transmission gives a surprisingly slick and easy gearchange, although you need a bit of beef to operate the heavy clutch, and performance is strong whatever the power unit – although the Meadows can be a bit of a rough old brute. With less than a turn lock-to-lock, the steering is ultra-quick, and an aid to the exuberant tail-out motoring beloved of 'chain-gangers'. Adding to the appeal is a certain sparse elegance: few sports cars are as good-looking as the low-slung TT Replica with its rounded tail, exposed fuel tank and outside exhausts.

SPECIFICATION

Engine:	1496cc water-cooled in-line 4-cyl; sidevalve (Anzani), ohv (Meadows) or ohc (Frazer Nash). 1498cc/1660cc water-cooled in-line 6-cyl; dohc (Blackburne)
Power:	51bhp at 4200rpm (Anzani); 52bhp at 4000rpm or 63bhp at 4750rpm (Meadows); 68bhp at 5000rpm (Frazer Nash); 70bhp at 5000rpm (1498cc Blackburne); 65bhp at 4500rpm (1660cc Blackburne)
Transmission:	three-speed/four-speed by chains and sprockets, via bevel box and cross-shaft
Construction:	separate chassis; aluminium or steel body over ash frame
Front suspension:	tubular beam axle with quarter-elliptic leaf springs; friction dampers
Rear suspension:	beam axle with quarter-elliptic leaf springs; friction dampers
Steering:	generally Frazer Nash quadrant pinion
Brakes:	drum with shaft or cable operation
Kerb weight:	16.5cwt (Meadows TT Replica)

EVOLUTION

June 1924	First Frazer Nash
October 1924	First car with Plus Power engine
February 1925	First Anzani-powered car
September 1929	First Meadows-powered car
July 1932	Last Anzani-engined car
June 1933	Six-cylinder model introduced
June 1934	First car with ohc Frazer Nash engine
January 1939	Last chain-drive Frazer Nash (Meadows engine)

I DIDN'T KNOW THAT...

- The marque 'Frazer Nash' is always written thus, with no hyphen. Confusing matters, Archie Frazer-Nash was born Archibald Goodman Frazer Nash, but in 1938 changed his surname by deed poll to Frazer-Nash. None of this helps with a satisfactory punctuation for the BMW cars imported by Frazer Nash, which are inelegantly known as 'Frazer Nash-BMWs'.

- Various body styles were offered over the years. In the Archie Frazer-Nash period (1924–28) most were of Fast Tourer, Super Sports or Boulogne type. Under the Aldingtons their fabric-covered Sportop and wider-bodied Falcon styles, along with a good many of the Boulogne type, gave way in 1932 to the near-standard-issue two-seat TT Replica, accompanied by the four-seat Colmore.

- For a short period a nominal share in AFN Ltd was held by none other than celebrated writer Evelyn Waugh. This was not out of any great passion for chain-driven sports cars on the part of the author of *Brideshead Revisited*, but was rather as a gesture of support to his friend Richard Plunket-Greene, who was briefly the majority shareholder and backer of the company.

- Two chain-drive 'Nashes were built from new as saloons, and a further three were subsequently given closed bodies to replace their original open coachwork.

- A single 'chain gang' Frazer Nash was fitted with a 2-litre BMW six-cylinder engine.

- Three chain-drive single-seaters were built by Frazer Nash in the 1934–36 period, following on from the sole single-seater built by Archie Frazer-Nash, a streamlined 1927 creation known as 'The Slug'.

ABOVE An earlier generation of 'chain-gang' Frazer Nash, this is a 1926 Speed Model, made in the days when Archie Frazer-Nash (with the hyphen!) was still running the company.

FRAZER NASH (POST-WAR)

Max Speed	114mph*
0–60mph	10.4sec*

* Targa Florio

ABOVE The Le Mans Replica. It is a salutary thought that only 34 were made: they may be a cult today, but at the time only a few rich enthusiasts could afford such an indulgence.

BELOW The sole 'factory' Continental. Despite being a one-off, the car was etched in the consciousness of a generation of schoolchildren through its inclusion in the *Ladybird Book of Motor Cars*.

The Second World War ensured that things would not continue as before at the Isleworth home of Frazer Nash. The planned assembly of British-bodied BMW 328s was as dead as the company's pre-war activity selling the various BMW models: not only was BMW buried in the wreckage of the Third Reich but its car factory was in the Russian zone of occupied Germany. However, AFN Ltd's steering family, the resourceful Aldingtons, picked a way forward.

One idea was that Frazer Nash would collaborate with Standard on the building of a range of Triumphs based on the 320 and 328 BMWs, but soon a better prospect appeared: joining forces with the Bristol Aeroplane Company, which was contemplating diversifying into motor manufacture. Bristol bought a majority share of AFN, and it

was agreed that a new Frazer-Nash-Bristol would be built, based on the pre-war BMW 327. Bristol versions would be complemented by a Frazer Nash sports derivative. This plan soon unravelled, and in April 1947 AFN regained its independence, while Bristol forged ahead with what became the 400; in the interim BMW chief designer Fritz Fiedler joined Isleworth for a three-year stint, overseeing production of a Frazer Nash sports car using the BMW-based Bristol mechanicals.

Constructed around a tubular chassis inspired by that of the BMW 328, this used 328-style transverse-leaf front suspension and a torsion-bar rigid-axle rear based on the BMW 326 set-up; in contrast, the Bristol used a 326-like platform chassis. Two models were offered: a stark Competition or High Speed cycle-winged roadster and an

THE FRAZER NASH CONTINENTAL

After making do with an updated 327 engine, in 1954 BMW introduced an all-alloy V8, initially of 2580cc. It was inevitable, even in the twilight years of Isleworth manufacture, that such a power unit would tempt the Aldingtons, and a display chassis duly appeared at the 1956 Motor Show equipped with the V8 – and with talk of it being given Pininfarina coachwork. This was a prelude to the unveiling of a smart coupé at the following year's show. Called the Continental, it had however been bodied not in Italy but by local coachbuilder Peels of Kingston, using a Porsche 356 centre section; with a steep pricetag, it remained a one-off. Meanwhile, the show chassis had been bodied to a design by amateur stylist Peter Kirwan-Taylor (see pages 68–69), with a view to its owner competing at Le Mans. Both cars survive, the 'Kirwan-Taylor' coupé rebodied as a Le Mans Replica.

all-enclosed Fast Tourer. Latterly these were renamed respectively the Le Mans Replica and the Mille Miglia, the former owing its name-change to a rousing third place achieved by such a car in the 1949 24-hour race.

The Frazer Nash was perforce a hand-built and extravagantly expensive car, a Le Mans Replica costing £3501 in 1949, when obvious rival the Healey Silverstone cost £1247. To put these prices in perspective, an MG TC then cost £527. This didn't stop the cars being a highly successful presence in 1940s and 1950s motor sport, campaigned by the likes of Stirling Moss, Mike Hawthorn, Tony Brooks and Anthony Crook. Unsurprisingly, though, only 34 Le Mans Replicas were made, latterly with a simpler if less rigid parallel-tube chassis and with a handful of final cars having a de Dion rear. The Mille Miglia was even more expensive, and a mere dozen were assembled.

Isleworth's last gasp was an all-enveloping roadster using the new parallel-tube chassis. Called the Targa Florio, in celebration of a Le Mans Rep winning the 1951 event, only 14 were made, between 1952 and 1954, plus nine of a fixed-head Le Mans Coupé derivative, the last despatched in 1956. Additionally, three Sebring roadsters were made, with a coil-spring front and a de Dion rear.

By this stage AFN was busy selling Porsches, as well as DKWs and a few BMWs, and the curtain was brought down on this aristocrat of early post-war British sports cars.

I DIDN'T KNOW THAT...

- HJ Aldington suggested the use in the new Frazer-Nash-Bristol of the 3.5-litre engine seen in the BMW 335 of 1939–41. It is interesting to speculate how history might have changed had this happened. Another possibility that was again discarded was an experimental 2.5-litre twin-cam version of the 328 engine.
- The car presented to the press as the prototype Frazer Nash was in fact a 1940 Mille Miglia BMW fitted with a Frazer Nash radiator grille.
- The first post-war Frazer Nash to be sold was a prototype chassis with Touring of Milan roadster bodywork, purchased by the Shah of Iran.
- Getting wind of what was in effect an informal design competition to create an Austin-based sports car, in 1952 Isleworth built a single Targa Florio with Austin A90 engine, gearbox and back axle; BMC boss Leonard Lord however preferred Donald Healey's 100 model.
- Special-bodied cars included a Le Mans Replica given coupé coachwork by Motto in Italy, a flamboyant – some would say vulgar – four-seater cabriolet built at Isleworth, and a drophead shown at the 1951 Motor Show; castigated as 'gormless' by marque historian Denis Jenkinson, the last-named has been rebodied as a Le Mans Replica. Additional to these, one Le Mans Rep was given an 8V Fiat shell.
- A series of reproduction Le Mans Replica bodies and matching tubular chassis was laid down in the 1980s by a UK-based enthusiast, enabling fake 'Nashes to be constructed around Bristol or BMW mechanicals. Properly built, these can be as good as the original.

SPECIFICATION

Engine:	1971cc water-cooled in-line 4-cyl; ohv with alloy 'hemi' head
Power:	90bhp at 4500rpm to 125bhp at 5500rpm, depending on model
Transmission:	four-speed gearbox
Construction:	tubular frame with aluminium body
Front suspension:	independent by transverse leaf spring and lower wishbones; anti-roll bar; lever-arm dampers
Rear suspension:	rigid axle and longitudinal torsion bars; location by triangular A-frame; lever-arm dampers
Steering:	rack-and-pinion
Brakes:	drum
Kerb weight:	17.25cwt (Targa Florio)

EVOLUTION

July 1945	Bristol Aeroplane Company buys majority share in AFN Ltd
April 1947	Bristol and AFN agree to separate
October 1948	First post-war Frazer Nash sold, to Shah of Iran. High Speed 'Competition' model (latterly Le Mans Replica) and Fast Tourer (latterly Mille Miglia) exhibited at Earls Court
May 1950	First Fast Tourer delivered
April 1952	Prototype Targa Florio; new parallel-tube frame
December 1952	Parallel-tube frame standardised
October 1952	Austin-engined prototype shown
April 1953	Prototype Le Mans Replica Mk2 fitted with de Dion rear
	First Le Mans Coupé built
August 1954	First Sebring
October 1956	Continental chassis displayed at Earls Court
	Last Bristol-engined car built (Le Mans Coupé)
October 1957	Completed Continental coupé shown at Earls Court

BELOW An early Mille Miglia: when the simpler twin-tube chassis was announced in August 1952 – ahead of being standardised in December that year – the body was restyled to give a wider cockpit.

HEALEY SILVERSTONE

Max Speed	105mph
0–60mph	13.2sec

ABOVE Distinctive features of the Silverstone are its headlamps behind the grille, Peugeot-style, and the windscreen that winds down into the scuttle; at the rear the spare wheel serves as a bumper.

BELOW This Nash-Healey carries Pinin Farina coachwork; a closed coupé was also available. Only sold in the US, the Nash-Healey gave Nash a prestige boost and saved Healey.

Think of the Silverstone as a poor man's Frazer Nash Le Mans Replica and you won't be far off the mark: rugged, stark, no-nonsense – a bit rough around the edges, perhaps – but capable of motoring fast and not falling off the road.

Today the 1949–50 Silverstone is the most valuable and most sought-after of Healeys. It was conceived, however, as a cut-price bargain-basement model, pared to the minimum so it could be sold in Britain for less than £1000, and thus not incur the double rate of purchase tax then imposed on cars with a basic list price of £1000 or more.

The running gear was as used on the Healey Elliot saloon and Westland open tourer, in other words the twin-cam 2443cc Riley four-cylinder engine and its matching gearbox, and all-round coil-spring suspension using Healey's unusual trailing-link front end, with location of the live rear axle by torque-tube, radius arms, and a Panhard rod. The crucial difference was that the engine was moved back 8in in the chassis, which retained its regular 8ft 6in wheelbase. Aesthetics were improved, and so was the car's handling, the weight distribution now being spot-on; also helping was the addition of a front anti-roll bar and the use of stiffer rear springs and wider wheels.

Onto the rally-proven and torsionally-stiff Healey cruciform chassis was mounted a lightweight stressed single-skin alloy body, constructed over a steel frame rather than a traditional timber structure. Ingenious features were a retractable windscreen and the use of the spare tyre, protruding through

THE NASH-HEALEY

Donald Healey wanted to go into production with the Cadillac-engined Silverstone (see opposite), for the US market. But when GM was unable to supply engines he took up an offer from Nash to use its 3.8-litre 'Dual Jet-fire' straight-six in a new Healey model to spice up the Nash range. This initially had an all-enveloping body by Panelcraft of Birmingham, but later versions received open or coupé coachwork designed and constructed by Pinin Farina. Meanwhile various Healey-built prototypes were successful in competition, most notably with a fourth place in 1950's Le Mans and a third in the 1952 event; this was despite Nash's primitive seven-main-bearing 'six' dating back to the 1920s. The Nash contract saved a penniless Healey company and bankrolled development of what became the Austin-Healey 100. In all, 506 Nash-Healeys were made, 104 British-built and 402 with the Farina body, while a further 28 Panelcraft cars received Alvis 3-litre engines.

the tail, as a rear bumper, while to aid streamlining the headlamps were mounted behind the radiator grille.

With a dry weight of only 18.5cwt, the Silverstone was good for over 100mph on its 104bhp, and – according to *The Autocar* – could cover the 0–60mph sprint in 13.2 seconds. With such performance, the Silverstone soon became popular in club racing and gained a high profile among the motor-sport fraternity, being campaigned by drivers as diverse as Betty Haig, Louis Chiron and Briggs Cunningham – not to mention Donald Healey himself, who took the prototype to second overall on the 1949 Alpine Rally. But manufacture was barely profitable, and was wound up in October 1950, after only 104 Silverstones had been built, so that Healey's small Warwick works could be given over to the more remunerative production of Nash-Healeys – or, latterly, just their rolling chassis.

Drive a survivor, and you'll find a good-natured car with deliciously beefy steam-engine pulling power, a slow-ish gearchange, and worm-and-roller steering that is heavy at low speeds but positive, quick, and devoid of any slop once you're on the move. The Healey corners accurately, flatly, and with no tyre-scrubbing understeer; punt the Silverstone fast round a roundabout and the tail stays planted down. Surprisingly, the ride is nicely absorbant, and the body doesn't shake, creak or judder. The Silverstone really is a friendly old thing, effective in what it delivers but in no way elegant in the manner of that delivery. It's easy to see why it inspires such fondness in its owners.

I DIDN'T KNOW THAT...

- The Riley engine – whose design dates back to the 1920s – is not an overhead-cam unit. Its two camshafts are set high in the block, and actuate the overhead valvegear by short and nicely rigid pushrods. With its hemispherical combustion chambers the engine is notably efficient, and its only shortcoming – other than its substantial weight – is its old-fashioned long stroke.
- In the States, racer Briggs Cunningham fitted a 5½-litre Cadillac V8 to a Silverstone. This prompted Healey to do the same, mating the Cadillac power unit to a Ford three-speed gearbox and a Ford back axle. Another attempt to give the Silverstone more performance saw a car being fitted with a Wade supercharger.
- In light of the original plan to install the Nash straight-six in the Silverstone, in April 1950 the car received a wider body and a bonnet air-scoop, along with other minor modifications; cars to this specification were known as the 'E' model.
- A friend of the author rebuilt an accident-damaged Silverstone, cutting off the damaged front of the chassis, straightening the chassis legs, and making up two sleeves to take the re-fashioned front sections. Measuring as he went, the repaired sections were provisionally tack-welded in place: a measurement across the diagonals revealed that the chassis was about an eighth of an inch out of true. He rang Healey at Warwick for advice – and was told that if they got to within ⅜in when making the Silverstone they thought they were doing really well.

ABOVE Strictly speaking called the 3-litre Sports Convertible, the Alvis-Healey uses the Panelcraft body of the original Nash-Healey; the sidelight/flasher units on this car are not original.

SPECIFICATION

Engine:	2443cc water-cooled in-line 4-cyl twin-cam; pushrod ohv
Power:	104bhp at 4500rpm
Transmission:	four-speed gearbox
Construction:	cruciform chassis, steel body frame, aluminium panels
Front suspension:	independent by coil springs and trailing arms, with anti-roll bar; lever-arm dampers
Rear suspension:	live back axle and coil springs, location by torque-tube, radius arms, Panhard rod; telescopic dampers
Steering:	worm-and-roller
Brakes:	all-drum
Dry weight:	18.5cwt

EVOLUTION

July 1949	Prototype completed
April 1950	'E' model introduced – wider body
October 1950	Production ends
	Nash-Healey announced
October 1951	Alvis-engined '3-litre Sports Convertible' announced
February 1952	Farina-bodied Nash-Healey announced
Summer/autumn 1953	Last Alvis-Healey
August 1954	Last Nash-Healey

HRG 1100/1500

Max Speed	83mph*
0–60mph	18.1sec*

* 1948 HRG 1500

ABOVE The styling of the traditional HRG never changed, even though bodies came from more than one supplier. This is a 1947 model with the 1500 Singer engine.

BELOW The prototype Twin-Cam: disc brakes – front and rear – are hidden behind those spider-type alloy wheels, and the suspension at both ends uses transverse leaf springs and coil-over-damper units.

It took 13 years for the other half of the GN partnership to return to car manufacture. Unlike Archie Frazer-Nash, Ron Godfrey discarded the GN's archaic chain-drive, but in other respects the HRG was true to the GN ethos, in that it was a lightweight and simple sports car of modest dimensions.

Contrary to what might be expected, the name HRG represents the initials of the marque's three founders rather than being an abbreviation of 'HR Godfrey'. The 'H' stood for Brooklands racer Major Ted Halford, who had briefly worked with the makers of the Vale Special, the 'R' for Guy Robins, another Brooklands figure who was previously a production engineer with Trojan, and the 'G' – naturally enough – for Ron Godfrey himself.

As announced in 1935, the HRG was a conservative assemblage of bought-in components, built around a simple ladder chassis and employing the old-fashioned feature of quarter-elliptic front springs to suspend the tubular front axle. The engine was a 1½-litre Meadows pushrod unit, the unsynchronised gearbox came from Moss, and the rear axle was provided by ENV; brakes were by cable and the steering was by an ultra-quick (barely more than a turn-and-a-half, lock-to-lock) Marles box. But the ally-over-ash HRG was greater than the sum of its parts, thanks to carefully considered engineering, and soon established a reputation as a quality sports car that offered excellent handling, strong performance and rugged construction, at a high but not outlandish price.

In 1938 HRG replaced the Meadows unit with a modified Singer overhead-cam engine, de-stroked to 1496cc, and at the

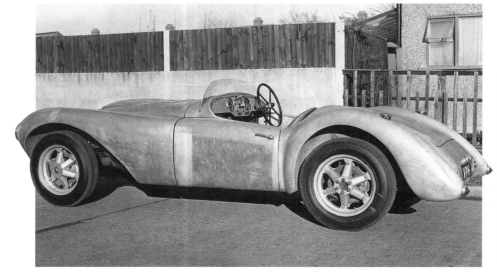

THE HRG TWIN-CAM

As a first step towards a new HRG, a twin-cam conversion of the long-stroke Singer engine was announced in 1953. In February 1955 a second version, now based on the short-stroke Singer SM unit, made its appearance in an all-new HRG. Totally of-the-minute, it had a tubular chassis, all-round independent suspension, and four-wheel disc brakes hidden behind mag-alloy wheels. The body was hardly the last word in elegance, but by the time a third car had been assembled HRG's newcomer was more than presentable – a sort of amalgam of Targa Florio Frazer Nash and AC Ace. It was hoped Singer would support the venture, and indeed a detuned version of the engine was offered in the Hunter saloon. But Singer was taken over by Rootes, and the project died. HRG focused on light engineering work – including a crossflow aluminium head for the BMC B-series engine – and ultimately closed its doors in 1966; a final prototype, Vauxhall-based, was built in the 1964–65 period.

same time introduced an 1100 model powered by a modified smaller-capacity Singer unit. With these engines came a synchronised Singer gearbox. Both these Singer-engined models were re-introduced after the war, but in 1950 the 1100 was discontinued. In 1953 the 1500 received Singer's new short-stroke engine, as used in the SM saloon, along with hydraulic brakes; always given twin carbs, the SM engine was at first modified by HRG, but the last cars received nothing more than a freer-flowing manifold.

It had been hoped to introduce an all-new HRG in the 1940s, complete with independent front suspension, hydraulic brakes, and a streamlined body. But the war intervened, and afterwards all that came to fruition was a so-called Aerodynamic model that combined an all-enveloping body with the old chassis and mechanicals. It wasn't a success, as the flexing of the chassis caused the body to break up, and production ended in 1949, after 34 cars and 11 chassis had been assembled.

Appreciably more expensive than the MG TC, the HRG struggled in the post-war years, and with the arrival of the MG TD the small Surrey-based company found purchasers thin on the ground. Production fell to a mere eight cars in 1951, and to four in 1953. General engineering work had become more important than car manufacture, but HRG felt it could bounce back with a fresh car of advanced design (see box); it wasn't to be, and the last of the 180-odd traditional-bodied 'square-rigger' HRGs left the Tolworth works in 1956.

I DIDN'T KNOW THAT...

■ There was only ever one closed trad-bodied HRG, a coupé with the body from an accident-damaged MG P-type Airline – and a Triumph engine. Chassis flex caused problems with the doors springing open, and thoughts of production were abandoned.

■ A single-seater HRG was built in 1949/50, for Formula 2 racing. It had a Standard Vanguard engine, complete with column gearchange, and was bodied by Cooper. Another post-war single-seater used a Lea-Francis engine.

■ Three lightweight HRGs with cigar-like bodies were built by Monaco Garage for 1949's Le Mans, and one came home eighth overall. Later that year the three cars, along with a one-off Aerodynamic coupé, achieved 1–2–3–4 in class in the Spa 24-hours.

■ In 1949 an experimental chassis was fitted with transverse-leaf independent front suspension, cantilever rear suspension, and a Bristol engine and gearbox; that same year a chassis was given a Maserati engine.

■ HRG played a key role in the affair of murderess Ruth Ellis, the last woman to be hanged in England. The man she killed, her lover David Blakely, owned one of the former 1949 Le Mans cars, and at one stage raced it with the prototype HRG twin-cam installed. He then commissioned the building of his own car, called the Emperor, and using the HRG twin-cam. It was after this blew up so he missed a race on Easter Monday 1955 that – on Easter Sunday – Ruth Ellis shot Blakely, as related in the film *Dance with a Stranger*.

SPECIFICATION

Engine:	1074cc/1496cc/1497cc four-cyl water-cooled in-line four; ohv (Meadows) or sohc (Singer)
Power:	61bhp at 4800rpm (1496cc Singer)
Transmission:	four-speed gearbox; synchromesh on top three gears (Singer)
Construction:	ladder chassis, wood body frame, aluminium panels
Front suspension:	tubular beam axle; quarter-elliptic springs; friction dampers
Rear suspension:	underslung live axle on semi-elliptic leaf springs; sliding trunnions; friction and Luvax hydraulic dampers (earliest cars friction only)
Steering:	worm-and-roller
Brakes:	all-drum, cable-operated until 1953
Kerb weight:	15.75cwt

EVOLUTION

November 1935	Meadows-engined HRG announced
September 1938	Singer engines phased in
Early 1946	Aerodynamic available
September 1947	Last UK-market Aerodynamic delivered
April 1949	Final Aerodynamic chassis despatched
August 1953	Short-stroke 1497cc SM engine fitted
February 1955	Twin-cam 'MkII' announced
August 1956	Last 'square-rigger' HRG despatched

BELOW The Aerodynamic was not a success; a final batch of chassis were despatched to Australia long after the last car had been assembled at HRG's works in Surrey.

INVICTA

Max Speed	90mph*
0–60mph	14.4sec*

* 4½-litre S-type

The Invicta is one of those Bulldog Drummond machines that the British do so well – but with a twist to the tale. The twist is that the hefty Invicta, often described as being a bit of a handful, was conceived expressly to be easy to drive, and gained much of its fame with women behind the wheel.

The car was created by Old Etonian Noel Macklin, who had previously been responsible for the sporting Eric-Campbell, and was made possibly thanks to backing from brothers Philip and Oliver Lyle, of the Tate & Lyle sugar family.

The idea behind the Invicta was to come up with a car so torque-rich that gearchanging was largely redundant; this was achieved through using a pushrod 2½-litre straight-six built by proprietary engine supplier Henry Meadows and subsequently supplanted by even more torquey 3-litre and 4½-litre Meadows units. The rest of the car was equally

composed of bought-in parts, and the completed chassis bodied by outside coachbuilders: it is said that all that was made at the works, in Cobham, Surrey, were the finned brake drums, the cast-aluminium dashboards, and various brackets.

To publicise the Invicta, Macklin employed his sister-in-law Violet Cordery. After a successful foray at Brooklands, Cordery broke 10,000-mile and 15,000-mile records at Monza during 1926, covered 5,000 miles non-stop at Montlhéry, and in 1927 drove a 3-litre Invicta around the world single-handed. Back on home turf, she and her sister Evelyn accomplished 30,000 miles in 30,000 minutes at Brooklands at an average speed of 61.57mph, before driving from London to Monte Carlo and back using only third gear. Another stunt was to go from London to John O'Groats and

ABOVE The low-chassis S-type: this is the classic Carbodies-built open tourer, but other coachwork was available. Tests proved that 6mph to over 90mph was feasible in top gear.

BELOW The relatively narrow cockpit is apparent in this shot, as is the height of the fold-flat windscreen. Note the outside handbrake and the adjustable armrest.

THE SMALL INVICTA

Big thundering high-priced motor cars were hardly the best thing to be selling in the early-'30s recession, and Invicta responded by introducing a 1274cc model in 1931. Powered by a Blackburne hemi-head ohc 'six', 50–100 of the 1498cc production version of the 12/45hp are thought to have been made, with open tourer or saloon coachwork by Carbodies; there are 22 or so known survivors. Stigmatised by Britain's top Invicta authority as being a 'gutless wonder', the heavyweight small Invicta was certainly no ball of fire, and some were subsequently fitted with SS-Jaguar or Triumph power units, or even with the 4½-litre Meadows engine. Invicta latterly offered the car in supercharged 12/90hp form, but engine problems led to most of the handful made being converted back to unblown specification. Nothing came of the twin-cam supercharged variant exhibited in chassis form at the 1932 Motor Show.

back in second gear, from London to Edinburgh and back in bottom gear, and finish off with eleven circuits of London in top; the plan to cap this with 25 laps of Brooklands in reverse was knocked on the head at the last minute.

Further publicity was garnered by famed rally-driver Donald Healey, who most notably took the ultimate low-chassis S-type 4½-litre to victory in the 1931 Monte Carlo Rally and to second place in the following year's event. In his memoirs Healey recalls how challenging was the Invicta's handling – 'despite claims to the contrary by some of today's historians' – and how heavy the clutch was: perhaps it was for the best that gearchanging was only infrequently required. Although the author cannot claim to have driven an Invicta, the owner of a 4½-litre he recently encountered vouches for the degree of muscle required to drive the car, so Miss Cordery – in her twenties at the time of her exploits – must have been a plucky young lady.

Macklin ceased production of the Invicta in 1933, passing the rights to his London service depot, who subsequently assembled a handful of 4½s, the last in 1935; his next project was the Railton, which was an Essex Terraplane chassis and engine clothed in bespoke British coachwork and incorporating a very Invicta-like front.

I DIDN'T KNOW THAT...

- Those who know the Surrey town may be amused to know that an initial requirement was for the Invicta to start off in top and climb Guildford High Street in that gear.
- Engineering for the Invicta was largely the responsibility of Willie Watson, who went on to work for Bentley before surfacing in the early 1950s at Aston Martin, where he played a key role in developing the V12 Lagonda racers and the DB3S. Before his death in 1927 at the wheel of his aero-engined recordbreaker 'Babs', JG Parry Thomas – previously behind the luxury Leyland Eight – was a consultant to the project.
- Roughly 1000 Invictas were built, of which perhaps only 50 were the low-chassis '100mph' S-type.
- Noel Macklin's claim to fame is less the Invicta than his work in creating Motor Torpedo Boats (or MTBs) to fight the submarine menace during the Second World War – and in organising their mass-production. He was also involved in the construction of the concrete flotation tanks that formed the basis of the mobile Mulberry Harbours used on D-Day. He was knighted in 1944, and went on to be a pioneer in the post-war development of pre-fabricated housing. His son Lance became a well-known racer, not least for former Invicta driver Donald Healey.
- The Invicta name was revived post-war with the 1946–50 Black Prince, an extravagant folly with a twin-cam Meadows engine, all-independent suspension, and a Brockhouse torque-converter transmission; the work of Willie Watson, a mere 16 were built.

ABOVE External exhaust down-pipes and louvred aprons add to the lines of the low-chassis model; Invicta tended to use somewhat heavy wings, without running boards.

SPECIFICATION

Engine:	2243cc/2973cc/4467cc water-cooled in-line 6-cyl; ohv
Power:	60bhp at 3000rpm (3-litre)
	105bhp at 3500rpm (4½-litre)
Transmission:	four-speed unsynchronised
Construction:	separate chassis; body construction varies
Front suspension:	beam axle with semi-elliptic leaf springs; friction or friction and hydraulic dampers
Rear suspension:	live axle with leaf springs, underslung on S-type; friction or hydraulic dampers
Steering:	worm-and-wheel
Brakes:	drum, mechanically operated
Kerb weight:	28.5cwt (4½-litre tourer)

EVOLUTION

April 1925	2½-litre Invicta announced
Early 1926	3-litre replaces 2½-litre
Late 1928	4½-litre announced
September 1930	Low-chassis S-type 4½-litre announced
July 1931	12-45hp 'Small Invicta' introduced
October 1932	5-litre announced, to replace 4½-litre – car never built
	Supercharged twin-cam shown
October 1933	Invicta company sold

BELOW Proof that not all Invictas were open tourers is this unusual close-coupled saloon S-type. Other styles encountered include the odd drophead coupé: remember that Invicta did not body the cars itself.

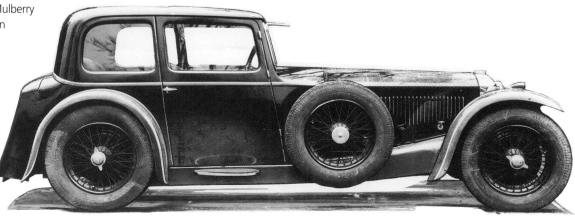

ABOVE Delicious and rare, this is an XK150 'S' roadster. In XK150 form the roadster has wind-up windows for the first time, in conjunction with a one-piece curved windscreen.

BELOW One for the road, one for the track: the XK-SS (foreground) is a converted D-type, while the C-type behind remains an out-and-out racer. Production of the XK-SS was halted by a disastrous fire at the works.

With the XK, Jaguar came of age as a manufacturer, signalling that it was to be taken seriously not just in Britain but internationally. The first of the line, the XK120, wasn't the star of the 1948 Motor Show just on account of its stunning good looks: it also attracted plaudits as the launchpad for the legendary 'XK' twin-cam, a power unit that was as effective as it was beautiful.

Indeed, the XK120 was principally intended as a showcase for the new six-cylinder engine, ahead of its use in the MkVII saloon. Series production was not envisaged: it was planned to build only 200 cars, further batches following if demand held up. Accordingly the car as announced was built around an ash body frame panelled in aluminium, while underneath was essentially a cut-and-shut MkV saloon chassis. But the XK's reception was such that William Lyons immediately

ordered tooling for an all-steel shell – although still with alloy doors, bonnet and boot-lid.

Initially offered only as a roadster, in March 1951 the XK120 became available as an elegant fixed-head coupé, and a drophead followed. Meanwhile, the car had demonstrated it was no 'Promenade Percy' by soon winning its competition spurs, beginning with a dramatic 1–2 in the August 1949 Silverstone production-car race and Ian Appleyard's celebrated victory in the 1950 Alpine Rally. Alongside these triumphs, the XK120 rapidly established itself as the most desirable sports car in the States, laying the cornerstone for Jaguar's US success.

In 1954 the XK120 gave way to the XK140. With its cowcatcher bumpers and clumsy coarse-slat cast grille, superficially the new model seemed nothing more than an

C-TYPE, D-TYPE AND XK-SS

Jaguar established its reputation for once and for all with a series of five wins at Le Mans with specialised racing cars. The 1951 and 1953 victories were with a car officially known as the XK120C. But the C-type was only tenuously related to the XK120: although it used all the XK's main mechanical components, there was rack-and-pinion steering, torsion-bar springing for the rear axle, and a tubular spaceframe replacing the separate body and chassis. The D-type was even more specialised, with a monoque body to which a square-tube front structure was attached. Jaguar's Le Mans victory in 1955 was followed by private team Ecurie Ecosse winning in 1956 and – with a stunning 1–2–3–4 – in 1957. In all, 87 D-types were made – they were considered a production car – and after Jaguar abandoned its racing programme in 1956, unwanted cars (16 in total) were converted into the roadgoing XK-SS.

uglified XK120. But under the skin there were important changes. The engine was moved forward, not only liberating more room in the cockpit but giving more stable understeer-biased handling, while the chassis gained rack-and-pinion steering and telescopic rear dampers and there was now the option of overdrive. Look beyond the aesthetics and the XK140 was a much better car.

The final evolution was the XK150 of 1957. Mechanically it was unchanged except for the welcome addition of four-wheel disc brakes, but the body was entirely remodelled: while bulkier, it nonetheless seemed both graceful and more modern, and the roadster still looked every inch a sports car, while gaining the convenience of wind-up windows. Dial in the availability first of a triple-carb 'S' version and latterly the option of a 3.8-litre engine – in either standard or 'S' tune – and the last of the line was certainly not past its sell-by date, even as it approached its 1961 replacement by the E-type.

By modern standards any XK still offers impressive performance. Drum-braked cars don't stop hugely well, and the XK120 can be a handful to drive fast, while later cars still demand a degree of muscle. But no other sports car of the era offered such a heady mix of performance, good looks and seductive appointments, at such a (relatively) affordable price. The XK was truly a landmark.

I DIDN'T KNOW THAT...

- It was originally intended to build a four-cylinder 1995cc XK100, and 50 or so power units were made. The engine was never used in a Jaguar, but one saw service in Goldie Gardner's MG record-breaker.
- The XK140 – and thus the XK150 – might never have come about, had Jaguar not been so successful in the early 1950s. The idea was to replace the XK120 with a completely restyled sports car that was longer, lower – and, yes, flashier. But the company had its hands full meeting demand for existing models, and so contented itself with facelifting the XK120 into the XK140.
- Special-bodied XKs were numerous, and included a Ferrari-like XK120 coupé by Belgian coachbuilder Oblin, a drophead XK120 by Swiss firm Beutler, an extraordinary XK140 built by Boano for flamboyant industrial designer Raymond Loewy, and XK150 coupés by Zagato (clumsy and contrived) and Bertone (predicatably elegant); most stunning, though, thanks to their high-camp rocket-era styling, have to be the three 'Supersonic' XK120 coupés built in 1954 by Ghia.
- Closer to home, ED Abbott came up with a four-seat open-tourer XK120, while in the 1960s Doug Wilson-Spratt, creator of the WSM Sprites, built a one-off 'woodie' XK150 estate.
- The XK120 was the most numerous XK, with 12,078 made. Next up was the XK150, with 9395 cars, just ahead of the 8884 XK140s built. The rarest XK variant is the 3.8-litre XK150 'S' roadster, of which only 36 were made, and the least rare the XK120 roadster, of which 7631 were built.

SPECIFICATION

Engine:	3442cc/3781cc water-cooled in-line 6-cyl; dohc
Power:	160bhp at 5000rpm (XK120); 190bhp at 5500rpm (XK120 drophead and all XK140s and 3.4 XK150s); 210bhp at 5750rpm (XK120 drophead SE and all XK140 SEs and 3.4 XK150 SEs); 250bhp at 5500rpm (3.4 XK150 S); 220bhp at 5500rpm (3.8 XK150); 265bhp at 5500rpm (3.8 XK150 S)
Transmission:	four-speed gearbox; overdrive optional (XK140/XK150) or standard (XK150 S)
Construction:	separate chassis; steel/aluminium bodywork (first XK120s all-alloy)
Front suspension:	independent, twin-wishbone and torsion bar; anti-roll bar; telescopic dampers
Rear suspension:	live axle with leaf springs; lever-arm dampers (XK120); telescopic dampers (XK140/XK150)
Steering:	recirculating ball (XK120); rack-and-pinion (XK140/XK150)
Brakes:	all-drum (XK120/XK140); all-disc (XK150)
Kerb weight:	26.1cwt (steel XK120 roadster); 28cwt (XK140 roadster); 28.2cwt (XK150 'S' roadster)

EVOLUTION

October 1948	XK120 unveiled
April 1950	First steel-bodied XK120 despatched
May 1950	Last alloy-bodied car despatched (240 made)
March 1951	Fixed-head coupé introduced
April 1953	Drophead announced
October 1954	XK140 introduced
May 1957	XK150 coupé and drophead annnounced
March 1958	XK150 and XK150 'S' roadster introduced
Feb 1959	'S' tune available on drophead and coupé
October 1959	XK150 3.8-litre introduced
October 1960	Drophead and roadster manufacture ends
October 1961	XK150 deleted

BELOW The cockpit of an XK – here an XK150 roadster – is always a delightful place to be, as William Lyons well understood the importance of such things; roadsters never had a wood dashboard.

JAGUAR E-TYPE

Max Speed	149mph*
0–60mph	7.1sec*

* 3.8-litre roadster

ABOVE Pure beauty: the E-type roadster in its original form, with cowled headlamps and delicate front and rear light units. Note how the twin exhausts kick up to follow the rear underpan.

BELOW A genuine Lightweight – there are plenty of fakes about. The raised vent panels in the roof and bootlid are characteristic, as are the alloy knock-on wheels.

As emblematic of the 1960s as the Mini, the Beatles and Mary Quant, it's all too tempting to regard the E-type with cliché-coloured cynicism. But the 'E' was an extraordinary vehicle. It was the sports car that had it all: racetrack breeding, sensational looks, blistering performance, first-class roadholding and handling, and a price-tag so low that more costly British and foreign competitors seemed an unjustifiable extravagance. The E-type was the car to be seen in, whether you were a pop-star, a TV presenter, or simply a sporting motorist who wanted to cut a dash. Never has a single car remained so durable a legend, either: today it is still the most lusted-after of classics.

The E-type was a productionalised and updated version of the D-type racer. Its lines, created by Jaguar aerodynamicist Malcolm Sayer, were a clear extrapolation of those of the graceful 'D', while its monocoque construction, with a square-tube front subframe, was pure D-type. But the 'E' also moved the game on, having fully-independent rear suspension that gave a ride/handling compromise only equalled by the Lotus Elan. Not only that, but it was available as a sleek fastback with superior aerodynamics to the roadster, sufficiently so that 150mph was claimed – a phenomenal speed for the time. Of course this had to be proved, and the press car that just attained this figure was in fact substantially modified, with a tuned engine, perspex windows, and the front over-riders removed to aid aerodynamic efficiency.

Alas, the E-type did not grow old gracefully. Few could complain about the 1964 move to a more torquey 4.2-litre engine and the accompanying abandonment of the awkward

THE E-TYPE 'LIGHTWEIGHTS'

The E-type was soon active in competition, with or without tacit 'works' support. But the truth is that the 'E' was too heavy to be successful against tailormade racers such as the Ferrari GTO. The result was a series of 12 special lightweight roadsters, constructed during 1963 and campaigned mainly in 1963 and 1964. Built around an aluminium monocoque, they were fully alloy-panelled (including an alloy rather than glassfibre hardtop), sat on knock-on alloy wheels, and had an alloy-block 3.8-litre engine with dry sump, D-type wide-angle head, and Lucas mechanical fuel injection. Weight was down by 500lb, and power boosted to 290–344bhp depending on specification. Other details included a ZF five-speed gearbox. Two 'Lightweights' subsequently received gorgeous flowing fastback bodies, one (the so-called Lindner/Nöcker car) works-built to a design by Malcolm Sayer, the other to a similar but long-nosed shape evolved by Dr Samir Klat of Imperial College.

and antique Moss gearbox with its 'crash' first. But in 1967 United States legislation meant the Jaguar lost its headlamp cowls, for the so-called 'Series 1½' model, as a prelude to a more comprehensive facelift into 1968's Series 2. These cars had clumsy new front indicator and rear light units, and a bonnet with a larger air intake, while the 2+2 model – introduced in 1966 – gained a re-raked front screen to make its higher roof less apparent.

Underneath, the E-type was unchanged, but the final version of the car was a radical transformation: the 'E' received Jaguar's new all-aluminium 5.3-litre V12, boosting power to 272bhp and maximum speed to an honest 142mph. At the same time the roadster went over to the 2+2's longer wheelbase and the regular coupé was deleted. The S3 E-type might have been the fastest of the line, but with a wider track, softer suspension, and standard power steering, it was also the least sporting – while the car's lines were further bastardised.

For some people the big-hearted comfortable grand-tourer character of the V12 has a strong appeal; for others only a tense, crisp 3.8 will do. But it is perhaps telling – or perhaps just inevitable? – that after peaking in 1969, sales of the E-type slumped badly, and continued to fall with the advent of the V12.

I DIDN'T KNOW THAT...

- Original thoughts for the E-type were for a slightly smaller car, to be powered by a 2.4-litre engine.
- The E-type was envisaged from the start as having a competition variant. Just such a car was completed in 1960, for US entrant Briggs Cunningham to campaign at that year's Le Mans; E2A, as it was called, did not complete the race.
- The very earliest E-types had the archaic feature of a bonnet opened using a T-bar, the lock being hidden behind a small hinged escutcheon.
- At one stage preliminary studies were carried out on a shorter bonnet for the E-type. These did the Jaguar's sensous looks no favours.
- Industrial designer Raymond Loewy, whose studios styled the post-war Studebakers, came up with an E-type coupé with a shortened squared-off bonnet and a reprofiled rear; the car was built by French firm Pichon-Parat. Italian styling house Frua displayed a less radically remodelled E-type at the 1966 Geneva show.
- The best-known E-type 'special' was 1967's Pirana, an E-type completely rebodied by Bertone. The work of Marcello Gandini, later to create the Lamborghini Countach, and commissioned by the *Daily Telegraph Magazine*, the Pirana's lines anticipated those of the Lamborghini Espada.
- The final 1974–75 US-market E-types had protruding rubber over-riders front and rear, to meet Federal legislation.

SPECIFICATION

Engine:	3781cc/4235cc water-cooled in-line 6-cyl; dohc (S1/S2). 5343cc water-cooled V12; sohc per bank (S3)
Power:	265bhp (gross) at 5500rpm (3.8); 265bhp (gross) at 5400rpm (4.2); 272bhp (DIN) at 5850rpm (V12)
Transmission:	four-speed gearbox; automatic optional from 1966 (2+2 and V12s only)
Construction:	monocoque with tubular steel front subframe; steel bodywork
Front suspension:	independent, twin-wishbone and torsion bar; anti-roll bar; telescopic dampers
Rear suspension:	independent by coil springs, with lower wishbone and upper driveshaft link, location by radius arms and anti-roll bar; twin telescopic dampers each side
Steering:	rack-and-pinion, power-assisted on V12
Brakes:	all-disc, servo-assisted
Kerb weight:	24cwt (3.8 roadster); 28.8cwt (V12 roadster)

EVOLUTION

March 1961	Announcement of E-type
October 1961	Internal-locking bonnet
June 1962	Last 'flat floor' model
October 1964	4.2-litre engine and Jaguar gearbox
March 1966	2+2 announced
December 1967	'Series 1½' introduced
October 1968	Series 2 introduced
March 1971	Series 3 V12 announced
October 1973	V12 coupé discontinued
September 1974	Final E-type roadster
February 1975	Official announcement of E-type's discontinuation

BELOW This 4.2 Series I shows the later cockpit style: earlier cars have an embossed aluminium finish to the centre of the instrument panel and the centre console.

JENSEN-HEALEY

Max Speed   119mph
0–60mph   7.8sec

ABOVE Never a car of great beauty, the Jensen-Healey was blighted in its final form by these ungainly impact bumpers. Underneath, there is a good car trying to get out.

BELOW Would the Jensen GT have been a success, had it stayed in production? One somehow doubts it – not least because of those dumb bumpers; in the end only 473 were made.

The Jensen-Healey promised so much. Yet in the end it failed to deliver, and retired from the scene barely four years after its introduction.

The idea seemed perfect: a new Healey based around uncomplicated off-the-shelf components, bankrolled by California's dominant importer of British sports cars, and made by Jensen at an affordable price.

After the last Big Healey had left the lines the Healey family didn't waste time in coming up with a replacement. Based around a simple monocoque made of numerous small pressings, it used Vauxhall Viva front and rear suspension – a well-conceived set-up with a properly located coil-sprung live axle. The project attracted the interest of Kjell Qvale, who had made his name importing MGs into California and who had sold vast numbers of Austin-Healeys, and the upshot was Qvale purchasing Jensen to use the West Bromwich concern to build the new car.

The various protagonists have differing versions of how events unfolded, but suffice it to say that the car ended up with a brand-new all-alloy Lotus 2-litre engine and with styling that was chopped around several times before emerging as a bland amalgam of Spitfire and TR6. The lacklustre lines of the Jensen-Healey were however the least of its problems. The quality of the early cars was abysmal – in sundry different areas – and in particular the 16-valve twin-cam Lotus 'four' was catastrophically unreliable. It was all a distressingly long way from the bulletproof robustness of the Big Healey.

A much-improved MkII version arrived in 1973, and was recognisable by its waistline strip, black-painted headlamp cowls, and wood interior detailing. By now the recession caused by the 1973–74 Fuel Crisis was biting, and Jensen, hobbled by the British three-day week, was in difficulty. Not improving matters, US regulations forced the

THE JENSEN GT

Where MG had successfully gone before, with the MGB GT, why not go there with the Jensen-Healey, and come up with a closed coupé variant? The idea was reasonable enough, especially if the resultant model could be trimmed to a more luxurious standard and sold at a higher price. Unfortunately the 2+2 Jensen GT, launched in July 1975, had none of the crisp elegance of the MG, and with its battering-ram impact bumpers and odd matt-black bonnet edge it looked frankly a bit gormless. With a smart burr-walnut dashboard, the uprated interior was a better place to be, but it was all academic, as only 473 cars were made, 202 of which stayed in Britain. Whether it would have been at least a modest success, had Jensen survived, remains one of those imponderables of history.

introduction of ugly impact bumpers at the end of 1974
– at which time the original crisp-to-use Sunbeam Rapier
gearbox was replaced by a less slick five-speed Getrag
unit. Faced with stagnant sales, production temporarily
stopped in December 1975 to allow for an uninterrupted
run of hopefully more profitable Jensen GTs to be made;
manufacture of the J-H never restarted, as in the spring
of 1976 Qvale ran out of patience and closed Jensen. A
mere 10,453 Healeys had been produced, all but 1914
going to export.

Sadness about the Healey's demise is not misplaced.
The 16-valve Lotus engine gives a strong if surprisingly
unrefined performance and the car has pleasantly vice-
free handling and a comfortable ride – although the
surprising lack of a front anti-roll bar does make its
presence felt. In its 1972 road test *Autocar* described
the Jensen-Healey as a 'future classic', which was both
prophetic and a judgement on how fundamentally right
the car was; but an equally telling commentary was
provided by the same magazine's reporting, a year later,
of its bitter disappointment at the shoddiness and
unreliability of its long-term test-car.

The tragedy of the Jensen-Healey was that it never
had time to establish itself and shake off its poor
reputation. One by one its many problems had been
solved, uninspiring styling excepted, but by then grim
external economic factors had pushed an already
enfeebled Jensen to breaking point.

I DIDN'T KNOW THAT...

- Contrary to what is sometimes said, William Towns, best
  known as the stylist of the Aston Martin DBS, was not
  responsible for the design of the Jensen-Healey. He
  presented proposals for the car, but these were not
  accepted. He was later recalled to restyle the front, and
  this and the J-H interior can be attributed to him – but
  nothing beyond this.
- It was originally intended to use the 2-litre (latterly
  2.3-litre) sohc Vauxhall engine in the Jensen-Healey. But
  when it was discovered that this was no longer available in
  de-toxed US specification, thoughts turned to the Ford
  'Pinto' and V6 engines and to the BMW overhead-cam
  'four'; indeed, the car was redesigned to accept the Ford
  V6. When discussions with these two companies failed,
  Jensen turned to Lotus. 'In the final analysis we said we've
  either got to buy the Lotus engine or forget the whole
  thing,' recalls Qvale.
- Notoriously, Jensen took the engines without any warranty
  from Lotus. 'The warranty Lotus was going to give us
  wasn't worth anything anyway,' Qvale told the author in
  justification of this decision.
- The Jensen-Healey never made any money for Jensen, and
  Qvale now feels that the whole project was a mistake.
- There were plans to supplement the Jensen-Healey with a
  daring gullwing-door GT. But when the project, dubbed the
  G-type, was costed out, it was hastily abandoned. The sole
  bodyshell survives, and was built into a complete car in the
  early 1990s.

ABOVE The MkII features
wood trim (both real and
fake) on the dashboard and
centre console; the armrests
are from a Vauxhall Victor
FD, just as the suspension is
from the Viva.

SPECIFICATION

Engine:	1973cc water-cooled in-line 4-cyl; all-alloy 16-valve dohc (belt-driven)
Power:	140bhp at 6500rpm
Transmission:	four-speed Chrysler UK gearbox; latterly five-speed Getrag
Construction:	all-steel monocoque
Front suspension:	independent by coil and wishbone; telescopic dampers
Rear suspension:	live back axle and coil springs; location by trailing and semi-trailing links; telescopic dampers
Steering:	rack-and-pinion
Brakes:	front discs and rear drums; servo
Kerb weight:	19.0cwt

EVOLUTION

March 1972	Jensen-Healey unveiled
July 1972	First cars leave factory
August 1973	MkII announced
November 1974	Impact bumpers and Getrag gearbox
July 1975	Jensen GT launched
December 1975	Jensen-Healey production ceases
April 1976	Last Jensen GT
August 1976	Sale of Jensen's assets

LEFT Chrome-detailed
bumpers, matt-black
headlamp scoops and a
waistline trim strip identify
– and disfigure? – a MkII
Jensen-Healey. These later
cars were much improved.

JOWETT JUPITER

Max Speed 85–90mph*
0–60mph 20.4sec*

* 19xx model

ABOVE The styling brief to Jowett's Reg Korner – later to work on the BMC 1800 – was supposedly to get as close to an XK120 in looks as he could, without Jowett getting sued; this is a MkI Jupiter.

BELOW Richard Mead bodied six Jupiters as convertibles; cars were available either with wind-up windows and a lined hood or with celluloid sidescreens and an unlined hood.

The Jowett Jupiter was one of the more improbable post-war British sports cars, being made by a small Yorkshire company better known for its pre-war two-cylinder economy cars and delivery vans. Yet despite this background the Jupiter not only has genuine sporting heritage but also won its class three times in a row – in 1950, 1951 and 1952 – at Le Mans.

Jowett reinvented itself after the Second World War with the sleek Javelin, a technically advanced saloon with a 1.5-litre flat-four engine and all-round torsion-bar suspension. Having seen the growing success of the MG in the United States, the company decided to make a sports car that could sell in the US and bring in much-needed foreign exchange. Former racing-car manufacturer ERA was engaged, and to do the design work brought in Robert Eberan von Eberhorst, the

famed German engineer who had helped create the pre-war Auto Union racers.

The result was a tubular-framed chassis (in chrome molybdenum) carrying Javelin mechanicals – with the welcome enhancement of positive rack-and-pinion steering. Unfortunately, the prototype body was a dumpy coupé that bordered on the ungainly, and so the production car was styled in-house, with more than a nod towards the Jaguar XK120.

What emerged was a drophead coupé that was not exactly sleek, but had a certain gawky elegance. Production was slow to begin, however – body panels were pressed down in Reading, by the former Miles Aircraft Company, and hand-finished by Jowett – and so the first Jupiters were sold in chassis form, ending up being bodied by an extraordinarily wide selection of British and foreign coachbuilders. Talk of 1000 cars

SPECIAL-BODIED JUPITERS

In all, 75 Jupiters received non-factory coachwork, over a third of the chassis being despatched in the first 12 months of the Jupiter's life, and with 48 being the work of British bodyshops. Most of these were relative small-fry, but six cars were built by Richard Mead, better known for bodying the Marauder (see pages 74–75), and four by Abbotts of Farnham. Of the foreign-built cars, four were bodied by Stabilimenti Farina in Italy, three by Ghia-Aigle in Switzerland, and Swiss firms Worblaufen and Beutler each clothed one car. Additionally a particularly elegant fastback was created by Danish importer Erik Sommer. One special Jupiter, by Adams & Robinson of Sunbury-on-Thames, only emerged fully-bodied in 1957 – more than five years after its chassis had been delivered – and a final car, on a 1951 chassis, was completed as a saloon by racing-car body specialist Maurice Gomm as late as 1964.

a year being sold in the US proved embarrassingly wide of the mark, and in all only 825 Jupiters were made.

It wasn't just that Jowett couldn't get the Jupiter into the showrooms fast enough: the engine, already unreliable in the Javelin, caused even more problems in tuned Jupiter form, while a decision by Jowett to build its own gearboxes was a catastrophe, with word soon getting out that the cars ate their transmissions. In a car-hungry market the Jupiter – already handicapped by a high price – simply became unsaleable.

The tragedy is that the sporting Jowett is a fine car to drive. Its 60bhp flat-four is not hugely zippy but it has plenty of mid-range pulling power, the column gearchange is one of the sportiest you're ever likely to encounter, and the suspension is soft enough to give a comfortable ride without compromising roadholding. More of a tourer than an out-and-out sports car, it has a terrier-like willingness that's rather endearing.

Expensive to make and dogged by reliability problems, the Jupiter was alas a lifeline that turned into another strand of the executioner's noose for Jowett, as it struggled to overcome the technical and financial problems that ultimately saw it close its doors in 1954. Plans for a simpler and lighter body never saw the light of day and the R4, an intended replacement with part-glassfibre bodywork, never made it past the prototype stage. One can't help feeling that Jowett's brave venture into sports cars deserved better.

I DIDN'T KNOW THAT...

- The Jupiter's seemingly rigid tubular chassis was in fact not strong enough, and the MkI cars had 6ft lengths of angle-iron welded onto the bottom of the main members to stop the cars sagging in the middle.
- The Le Mans class-winners of 1950 and 1951 were lightweight versions of the regular Jupiter, but the 1952 car was one of three spartan cycle-winged racers the company built. Called the R1, these had an engine quoted as delivering 70bhp. All three were dismantled and the chassis allegedly cut up, but one example was reconsituted from parts rescued from the factory scrapheap.
- The class-winning Le Mans Jupiter of 1952 only just made it. Having been driven back to the Jowett factory by mechanic Phill Green, the engine was stripped and its crankshaft – the weak point of the engine – put on a crack-detector. 'It was like a piece of Breton lace,' recalls Green. 'There wasn't more than ¼in between each hairline crack…'
- Kjell Qvale, the famous Californian sports-car importer, briefly handled the Jowett. 'We used to call it the Jumpiter, because the damn thing had a gearbox that lasted about a week,' he told the author. 'It was the most horrible damn thing. Just nothing worked.'
- Over the years Jupiters have been given many different engines, including MGA, Ford V4, Volvo and flat-four Porsche units, Ford straight-sixes, and Oldsmobile and Ford V8s – with a 7-litre Ford V8 surely being the most fearsome transplant.

ABOVE The front hinges up as one unit to reveal the water-cooled flat-four: the radiator sits behind the engine. Torquey but not hugely powerful, the Jowett 'boxer' was less than reliable.

SPECIFICATION

Engine:	1486cc four-cyl water-cooled flat-four; ohv
Power:	60bhp at 4750rpm/62.5bhp at 4500rpm
Transmission:	four-speed gearbox; column change
Construction:	tubular chassis, steel body frame, aluminium panels
Front suspension:	independent by double wishbones and longitudinal torsion bars; telescopic dampers
Rear suspension:	live axle with transverse torsion bars; location by four trailing arms and Panhard rod; telescopic dampers
Steering:	rack-and-pinion
Brakes:	all-drum, hydro-mechanical until January 1951
Kerb weight:	18.9cwt (MkIa)

EVOLUTION

October 1949	Jupiter unveiled – in chassis form
March 1950	First Jowett-bodied prototype
August 1950	First production chassis
November 1950	First complete production cars
January 1951	Hydraulic brakes replace hydro-mechanical
June/July 1951	Last rolling chassis delivered
January 1952	Power raised to 62.5bhp
October 1952	MkIa announced, with opening boot and metal dashboard
November 1954	Last Jupiter built

LAGONDA 2-LITRE TO 4½-LITRE

Max Speed	80mph*
0–60mph	27sec*
	* 3-litre Speed Model

ABOVE This Lagonda is a fabric-bodied 3-litre dating from 1930, built on the low chassis. The cycle wings and the diamond-pattern motif on the stoneguard are characteristic of the breed.

BELOW The Rapier was a flop for Lagonda. This 1934 car carries tourer coachwork by Abbott, with a somewhat severe door-line; a smart Abbott coupé was also available, described as 'an ideal woman's car'.

Lagonda was a maker of light cars when in 1925 it announced a bigger 2-litre model powered by an advanced twin-cam four-cylinder engine. In the ten years that followed – and which ended with the firm's bankruptcy – the small Staines-based company developed a range of cars that firmly established it as a purveyor of high-grade sporting and sports machinery. This position, achieved despite precarious finances and despite a competition record that was honourable rather than outstanding, was bolstered by victory in the 1935 Le Mans 24-hours race.

The original 2-litre model, called the 14/60, was – engine apart – a conventional but well-executed vehicle, and a sage way of putting clear blue water between Lagonda and the mass-produced cars of the big battalions. With the announcement of the 78bhp Speed Model, it took a step towards being a more sporting vehicle, and when in 1929 it

received a lowered chassis its sports character was affirmed, to be consecrated a year later by the arrival of a supercharged variant that offered impressive torque and drivability rather than high-strung ultra-performance. With sparse but well-proportioned tourer coachwork, generally cycle-winged in low-chassis form, these later 2-litres were too well made to be shatteringly fast, but provided a seductive alternative to those who found a Bentley too physically – or financially – intimidating.

A year after the first 14/60 came a 2.4-litre six-cylinder model, using an all-new pushrod ohv engine. The 16/65 had its engine first enlarged to 2.7-litres and then largely redesigned to give a displacement of 2931cc. This wasn't enough to make the resultant 3-litre a sports car, but moving the engine back in the frame and giving it a few tuning tweaks set it on the way, under the 3-litre Special label. A few months later came a low-chassis version, and the transformation was complete.

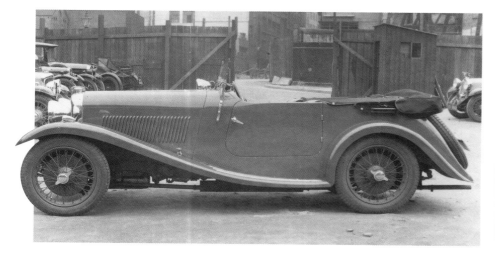

THE LAGONDA RAPIER

Sometimes the obviously logical course of action doesn't turn out to be so sensible after all. That was certainly the case with Lagonda's Rapier, an 1100cc twin-cam announced in 1933. Intended as a response to the straitened times of the early '30s, the 10hp Rapier with its pre-selector gearbox was supposed to be a high-quality small Lagonda for those who couldn't reach to a 4½-litre. That was all very well, but at £368 for a four-seat tourer you had to be rich enough not to have to penny-pinch in the first place. So too few bought the Rapier, exquisite engineering or not, and unsold chassis piled up at the works. After Lagonda's 1935 collapse the entire project was sold to a consortium led by its creator, Tim Ashcroft, who assembled cars from ex-Lagonda parts under the Rapier Cars Ltd name until 1938; a handful of these were supercharged.

Lagonda now had two ranges that offered everything from luxurious fabric-bodied saloons to businesslike sports tourers, all high-priced, and all well regarded – although the gearboxes had a reputation for being challenging to manipulate. But by the early 1930s the fashion was for six cylinders. The company's response was to create a new 2-litre model, the 16/80, by buying in a six-cylinder engine from Crossley. Lagonda stripped, rebuilt and tuned every engine, and the result was a car that outperformed its four-cylinder siblings and added a welcome dose of refinement; as for the 3-litre, in 1934 the engine was enlarged to 3½ litres.

The final pre-receivership model was a high-performance model that apologised to nobody: a 4½-litre car with the Meadows engine formerly used in the Invicta. After the company was revived under new ownership this was the sole model offered – in improved form – until newly-recruited chief designer WO Bentley came up with his V12 and related LG6 models. Most of the post-1935 4½s were saloons, dropheads or stately tourers, but the flashy LG45 Rapide with its outside exhausts and tuned engine was undoubtedly a sports car, and one with real cachet; alas, only 25 found buyers.

I DIDN'T KNOW THAT...

- The smaller models that preceded the 14/60 were pioneer unit-construction cars, with a combined body-cum-chassis hull made of tinned steel panels riveted onto an angle-iron frame.
- It is not strictly true to describe the 14/60 and 2-litre engine as an overhead-cam unit. Although high-set and operating directly on the rockers, the camshafts are in fact mounted on the side of the block rather than atop the cylinder head.
- From 1931 Lagonda offered a nine-year guarantee – dependent on the owner bringing the car back to the factory for inspection and rectification at three-year intervals. This was less generous than might appear, as likely costs risked exceeding the value of the car.
- Lagonda's response to complaints about its difficult gearbox – although old-stagers today say there's nothing wrong with it – was to fit the 3-litre with the Maybach vacuum-operated *doppelschnellgang* dual-range pre-selector gearbox. Complex and hideously heavy, this baffling-to-operate lump of German ironmongery necessitated a substantially strengthened chassis, which further added to the weight of the resultant 3-litre Selector model. Realising its mistake, in June 1933 Lagonda began to offer the simpler and gratifyingly effective ENV pre-selector. This was a prelude to the introduction of a freewheel transmission on the 4½-litre M45 Rapide; a synchromesh gearbox only arrived for 1936, on the revised LG45 introduced by the new owners of the firm.
- To ensure a truly parallel action, Lagonda devised a clutch using six driving pins operating in phosphor-bronze bushes, rather than a conventional splined mechanism.

SPECIFICATION

Engine:	1954cc water-cooled in-line 4-cyl; chain-driven dohc/2931cc water-cooled in-line six-cylinder; ohv/4453cc water-cooled in-line six-cylinder; ohv
Power:	60bhp at 4200rpm (early 14/60)/79bhp at 3800rpm/108bhp at 3100rpm
Transmission:	four-speed unsynchronised; four-speed double-overdrive pre-selector (3-litre Selector); ENV four-speed pre-selector (opt from 1933)
Construction:	separate chassis; body construction varies
Front suspension:	beam axle with semi-elliptic leaf springs; friction dampers
Rear suspension:	live axle with leaf springs; friction dampers
Steering:	worm-and-roller/cam-and-peg
Brakes:	drum, mechanically operated
Kerb weight:	31.9cwt (3-litre Special tourer)

EVOLUTION

September 1925	14/60 introduced
October 1926	16/65 six-cylinder introduced – 2389cc ohv
July 1927	2-litre Speed Model – tuned engine, mounted 9in further back
	16/65 receives 2692cc engine
September 1928	3-litre announced (high chassis)
March 1929	3-litre Special (high chassis; rearward engine position) announced
July 1929	First low-chassis 2-litre Speed Model; high-chassis Speeds continue until winter
September 1929	Low chassis standard on 3-litre Special
March 1930	Special engine fitted to all 3-litres
July 1930	Supercharged 2-litre announced
October 1931	3-litre Selector Model introduced; all 3-litres now in Special form
January 1932	Selector engine capacity increased to 3181cc
April 1932	Steel-bodied 2-litre Continental introduced (discontinued July)
August 1932	16/80 announced; 2-litre thereafter gradually phased out
June 1933	ENV pre-selector gearbox available
September 1933	Rapier and 4½-litre M45 announced
September 1934	3½-litre M35 and tuned 4½-litre M45 Rapide introduced; both swb 3-litre and 16/80 continue
August 1936	LG45 Rapide announced
March 1938	Final LG45

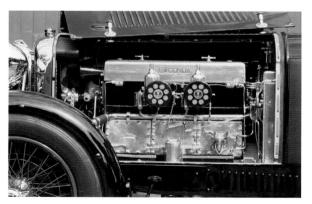

LEFT Fuelled by twin SU carbs, the tuned 'Special' engine of the 3-litre gives 80mph performance. The ohv unit is Lagonda's own, as opposed to the Crossley engine in the 16/80 and the Meadows in the 4½-litre.

LEA-FRANCIS HYPER

Max Speed 85mph
0–60mph n/a

ABOVE This Hyper carries the regular two-seater fabric coachwork. For the time, performance was dramatic for a 1½-litre vehicle, thanks to the use of a Cozette supercharger.

BELOW Slightly different in style, this is a later TT Replica Hyper with an aluminium body – still appropriately stark, as befits what was essentially a competition car.

Before the Hyper, Lea-Francis was pretty much just another Coventry-based small manufacturer, its products not even particularly sporting. With this new model, however, the company became a respected competitor in national and international motor sport, and gained a reputation that probably did much to help it survive in the motor business – albeit by the skin of its teeth – until the early 1950s.

Originally a maker of bicycles, Lea-Francis moved into motorcycles in 1912 and into cars in 1923. By 1927 most of the bugs had been ironed out, and it was selling respectable numbers of its mainstay Meadows-engined 12hp models. Successful forays at Brooklands then tempted the company to develop a special competition model with a supercharged engine.

Based on the regular touring chassis (the O-type), the S-type Hyper retained the 1½-litre pushrod 4ED Meadows engine but added a gear-driven French-made Cozette supercharger – along with a closer-ratio gearbox. Signalling this transformation there was a sportily raked-back radiator, and the only body initially offered was a two-doored fabric open tourer. The result was a car good for 85mph, possessed of genuinely impressive roadholding and handling, and capable of being enjoyed without the engine blowing itself to bits – although racing versions did at first have a tendency to destroy their pistons.

After a patchy first season racing the Hyper, lessons learnt resulted in an uprated competition version being offered for 1928, with stronger pistons and a built-up crankshaft in conjunction with roller-bearing big ends and

THE ACE OF SPADES

As it slid towards insolvency, Lea-Francis began the design of a new six-cylinder engine. Of 1991cc, it had a single overhead camshaft with needle-roller rockers and an unusual cylinder-head arrangement whereby the studs were attached to the lower face of the head and secured by nuts pocketed in the block. The engine made extensive use of Elektron magnesium alloy, not least for the timing cover, which was shaped like an Ace of Spades. This gave both the engine and the resultant car their name, the latter being launched in September 1930. With the company entering receivership in spring the following year, only 60 or so Ace of Spades models were made, some with a 2244cc engine that developed an impressive 70bhp – or 10bhp more than the 2-litre unit mustered. Well received by the press, the Ace of Spades could have been a great success, in happier circumstances.

tubular con-rods – serious stuff for the time. Carrying two-seat coachwork, again in fabric, it became known as the TT Replica. Other body styles on the Hyper chassis were a fabric saloon with an improbably low roofline, latterly called the Leafabric, and a Weymann coupé.

It would be tiresome to list the Hyper's many competition results, but the Lea-Francis was swift enough to come in third behind a Delage and a Bugatti in the 1928 Brooklands 200-mile race, and to win that year's Ulster TT, having lapped as fast as Birkin's 4½-litre Bentley. A private entrant, meanwhile, finished eighth in 1929's Le Mans and sixth in the following year's event.

By 1930, with two years of substantial losses behind it, Lea-Francis was heading for insolvency, at least in part as a result of over-spending on competition. The Hyper's moment in the limelight was also drawing to a close, and only 19 cars were built that year – of which eight were TT Replicas, these now having an aluminium body. At the 1930 Motor Show not a single order was taken for the Hyper, but this was a slightly academic full-stop to the model's career, as in March the following year Lea-Francis entered receivership.

In 1937 a new Lea-Francis company was established out of the remains of the old concern. The glory days of the Hyper were a good way in the past, but the laurels the zesty sports model had earnt for the Lea-Francis name surely stood the new enterprise in good stead.

I DIDN'T KNOW THAT...

- One of the first customers for a motorised Lea-Francis was celebrated writer George Bernard Shaw, who took delivery of one of the first motorcycles made by the company. It is said that his riding was somewhat erratic…
- The fourth Hyper made went to LT Delaney, the MD of Lea-Francis, and had a body in gold fabric, with matching wings and wheels.
- For 1929 a V-Type Lea-Francis was introduced, this in effect being a Hyper with fabric Weymann coupé coachwork but no supercharger.
- In 1928 Lea-Francis briefly held merger talks with Bentley Motors, but it soon became apparent that neither firm had the money to support the other.
- One Bentley director was challenged to a burn-up by LT Delaney – and found his '4½' outperformed by the 1½-litre LeaF on the roads of North London. A Hyper was subsequently sent to Cricklewood for examination by the Bentley engineers.
- Kept running under administration, Lea-Francis continued to make a small number of cars from parts in stock. A sole Hyper was sold in 1932 and it was only in 1934 – with the company still in receivership – that the 1930 Olympia show Hyper found a buyer.
- Lea-Francis designer Charles Van Eugen went on to collaborate with Victor Riley (of the Riley Motor Company) in the design of a large V8-powered luxury car called the Autovia. When this project folded in 1938, Van Eugen moved to Wolseley.

ABOVE In contrast, this Hyper has fabric four-seat tourer coachwork and full wings; there was also a fabric-bodied saloon. The 'CAV' torpedo sidelights are typical of the 1920s period.

SPECIFICATION

Engine:	1496cc water-cooled in-line 4-cyl; ohv
Power:	68–70bhp at 5000rpm (approx)
Transmission:	four-speed unsynchronised; right-hand change
Construction:	separate chassis; body construction varies
Front suspension:	beam axle with semi-elliptic leaf springs; friction dampers
Rear suspension:	live axle with semi-elliptic leaf springs; friction dampers
Steering:	worm-and-wheel
Brakes:	drum, mechanically operated
Kerb weight:	17cwt (approx)

EVOLUTION

July 1927	First Hyper completed
September 1927	Hyper announced
May 1928	Six cars laid down for TT – antecedents of TT Replica
October 1930	Final Hyper shown at Olympia
March 1931	Lea-Francis in receivership
June 1934	Last TT Replica Hyper sold

BELOW The sharply sloping tail is a characteristic feature of the regular two-seater Hyper bodywork; note how there is only one door, on the passenger's side of the car.

LEA-FRANCIS SPORTS

Max Speed 87mph*
0–60mph 19.2sec*
* 14hp

ABOVE As a 2½-litre, this car has triangular quarterlights, and wind-up windows in forward-hinged doors; the cockpit is more spacious, too, while the grille is narrower.

BELOW The first Lynx being finished; the ungainly screen was subsequently shortened. The eyebrow-raising styling was carried out according to the whims of the new boss of Lea-Francis.

The re-formed Lea-Francis was another of those small under-capitalised British firms that was doomed ultimately to disappear. But it had its last moment in the sun with its substantial but not inelegant sports models of the 1948–52 period.

When the re-established enterprise began production in 1938, it was with new 12hp and 14hp models based around a twin-cam four-cylinder engine designed by ex-Riley man Hugh Rose. As with the Riley unit, the twin camshafts were high-set, but still actuated by short pushrods – only in the case of the Lea-Francis the pushrods were even shorter, being a mere 2in long.

Post-war the 12hp and 14hp continued, but with bodies of fresh design, and in 1948 (by which time the 12hp had been abandoned) the two-seat 14 Sports was introduced.

Conceptually simple, in that it still had a beam front axle and mechanical brakes, the Sports was built the traditional way, with aluminium panels over an ash frame, and was an honourable contender at the quality end of the market: at launch it cost £1276 including purchase tax, which compares with £528 for an MG TC.

But if the 14 Sports was a well-handling and good-mannered machine – marque authority Barrie Price rates it 'arguably the best post-war Lea-Francis' – it was also no competitor to the new Jaguar XK120, being good for only 87mph on its 77bhp power unit. The answer came with a revised Sports introduced at the 1949 Motor Show.

This had the new 18hp Lea-Francis engine, a 2496cc twin-cam 'four' that in Sports form had twin SU carburettors and developed a muscular 100bhp. By the time manufacture

THE LEA-FRANCIS LYNX

Few failures have been more abject than that of the Lynx, which was launched to universal derision at the 1960 London Motor Show and failed to attract a single buyer. A vainglorious attempt to re-enter the motor industry by new owners of the company, it was an ugly cigar of a vehicle, painted an unfortunate lilac and priced way above even an XK150. Powered by a Ford Zodiac engine, it was so overweight it could hardly get out of its own way – although subsequent tuning of the engine remedied this – and the project was wound down with just three cars completed. Cobbled together in less than five months, the Lynx used a simple tubular ladder-frame chassis and the Lea-Francis torsion-bar front end; the rear axle was leaf-sprung and there were four-wheel disc brakes. A proposed saloon came to nothing, any more than plans to have the chassis more attractively bodied by a continental coachbuilder.

began there was also independent front suspension, this Citroën-inspired torsion-bar arrangement also being seen on the very last 14 Sports. Rounding out the package, the brakes were now hydro-mechanical – hydraulic at the front and mechanical at the rear – although the final cars boasted fully hydraulic braking. Physically the Sports was largely unchanged, but had a fixed three-piece windscreen, wind-up windows in front-hinged doors, and a more spacious cockpit with a small rear seat.

The bigger engine completely changed the character of the Sports, offering massive torque and effortless performance in third and top. With effective brakes, a tight-gated and slick gearchange, and a firmly-suspended sporting chassis, perhaps all it lacked was the precision of a steering rack, as offered by rival Riley.

Alas, by this time Lea-Francis was struggling to stay afloat. Output in 1951 fell by 15 per cent, and of the 579 cars made only 11 were 2½-litre Sports and a mere nine were 18hp saloons. The next year car manufacture wound down, and Lea-Francis turned primarily to the manufacture of gun trolleys for the Royal Navy.

In all, 118 of the 14 Sports had been made, and 77 of the 2½-litre Sports. At a 1951 price of £1775, the big-engined Sports was around £100 more expensive than a Jaguar XK120 roadster, complete with its gorgeous twin-cam straight-six: it wasn't much of a contest.

I DIDN'T KNOW THAT...

- The first prototype Sports had a tuned 12hp engine and independent front suspension – but the latter feature appeared only on the final 14 Sports, while only the odd early car was sold with the 12hp power unit.
- The 14 Sports formed the basis of the Connaught sports car, of which 14 were built between 1948 and 1951. Additionally the Formula 2 Connaught Type A used a derivative of the 14hp engine.
- The Sports models might have provided the glamour, but much of Lea-Francis's bread-and-butter was furnished by the sale of 'woodie' estate cars on the 14hp chassis. In 1949, for example, 243 of the total output of 482 Lea-Francis chassis were bodied as estates, against the manufacture of only 25 Sports.
- Hugh Rose's son Ken, who worked for a few years at Lea-Francis, went on to form Cosmic Car Accessories, later well-known for Mini add-ons and its black-and-silver alloy wheels.
- The 14hp engine was fitted to various racing specials, and one was installed in a chain-drive Frazer-Nash. Another home for the power unit was in a racing hydroplane.
- Two 2½-litre Sports were built as four-seat tourers by Westland of Hereford, better known for its open Healey bodies.
- Although assembly of the last Lea-Francis chassis took place in 1952, it was not until the following year that the final two 2½-litre Sports were completed, one being retained by Lea-Francis until 1959. The final cars trickled out of the works in 1954.

SPECIFICATION

Engine:	1767cc/2496cc water-cooled in-line 4-cyl twin-cam (pushrod ohv)
Power:	77bhp at 5100rpm/100bhp at 4000rpm
Transmission:	four-speed gearbox
Construction:	semi-cruciform underslung chassis, wood body frame, aluminium panels
Front suspension:	beam axle and semi-elliptic leaf springs; lever-arm dampers. Last 14hps and all 2½-litres: independent by torsion bars and twin wishbones; lever-arm dampers
Rear suspension:	live axle on leaf springs
Steering:	worm-and-nut (final cars recirculating-ball)
Brakes:	all-drum, hydro-mechanical/hydraulic
Kerb weight:	21.9cwt (14hp)

EVOLUTION

September 1947	First Sports completed
January 1948	Deliveries of 14hp Sports begin
October 1949	2½-litre Sports announced
February 1950	First 2½-litre Sports despatched
March 1950	Last 14hp Sports delivered
February 1953	Last 2½-litre Sports leaves works

ABOVE Superficially a 14hp, this is in fact the prototype 2½-litre Sports. The curved sill sections, merging into the wings, were deleted when the body was widened for the production 2½-litre.

BELOW Period catalogue for the Sports: clearly visible is the extra space in the cockpit, allowing a rear seat suitable for children. Fewer than a hundred of these cars were made.

The LEA-FRANCIS 2½ Litre Sports Model

A fast car that is fascinating to handle

LOTUS SIX

Max Speed	88mph*
0–60mph	12.6sec*

* tuned '1172'

ABOVE This Six uses sidevalve Ford power – which in such a light car assures surprisingly good performance. The body is all-alloy, over a tubular spaceframe.

RIGHT Peter Kirwan-Taylor in his all-enveloping Six, at Goodwood in June 1955. The body was built by Williams & Pritchard, and was intended to be as simple as possible to shape.

The Lotus Six might seem a slightly obscure choice of car for these pages. But think again. The Six was not only Lotus founder Colin Chapman's first production vehicle: it was also the engineering starting point for all subsequent Lotuses, laying down principles that are still invoked today by the company.

Until the Six, Chapman was nothing more than a spare-time builder of Austin Seven specials for trials events and 750 Motor Club racing. To his credit were three trials-cum-race specials and a brace of racers carrying the Lotus MkIII identity. The MkIIIs firmly established Chapman as the most innovative and successful competitor in 750MC circles, operating with a degree of calculated professionalism that out-performed and out-psyched his more amateur rivals – among them, incidentally, the original builder of the author's Austin Seven special.

But despite the clever tuning tweaks used on the MkIII's Austin engine, and despite his well-conceived strengthening of the Austin's whippy chassis, Chapman knew that he had to do away with the heavy channel-section Austin frame and the MkIII's separate body, and combine body and chassis in one lightweight structure. The result was the MkVI of 1952.

Instead of the fashionable twin-tube chassis and tubular superstructure favoured by people such as John Tojeiro, Chapman went for the more elegant and mathematically more rigid solution of a multi-tube spaceframe. Using a mix of 1in square and 1in and 1$\frac{7}{8}$in round tubing, every tube did a job, with the structure being further reinforced by aluminium floor, scuttle and side panels riveted in place. The outcome was a chassis/body – with ally 'loose' panels such

SPECIAL-BODIED SIXES

The Six conformed to the traditional exposed-wheel school of sports-car design, and as a consequence was aerodynamically far from good. Unsurprisingly, therefore, some enthusiasts gave their Six all-enveloping bodywork. One such individual was accountant Peter Kirwan-Taylor, who had Williams & Pritchard build a tautly-lined alloy-bodied barchetta to his design; Kirwan-Taylor hit it off with Colin Chapman, who helped with the design of the car, and as a result he went on to style the Elite. A less sculpted fully-enclosed open Six was the MG-powered car built by Ian and Alistair Kenyon; again this had a W&P body, drawn up by Ian Kenyon, and featured a de Dion back axle built by John Heath's HWM Motors. The car covered a mere 50 miles before being laid up, only emerging from storage in 1990. Further to these two cars, one Six spaceframe received a Falcon kit-car body and another a Mistral glassfibre shell.

as bonnet, wings and nose-cone – that weighed only 120lb; a telling comparison is that an all-steel Midget/Sprite monocoque with 'loose' panels weighs 408lb.

The idea was that the Six would be sold as a kit, for road and track use, and so it was designed around a single set of easy-to-source components – those of the Ford Eight/Ten, the design of which went back to 1932. This was a 'given', whether the customer decided to stick with the Ford sidevalve engine or to choose a more powerful and more modern unit; he didn't, however, have to suffer the Ford's rigid front axle, as Chapman used the split-beam independent front end he had perfected on the MkIIIs and which had been developed from Leslie Ballamy's LMB conversions. This was combined with long-stroke coil springs concentric with telescopic dampers – a set-up also used at the rear, where the Ford's torque tube was supplemented by a Panhard rod; some engine installations, though, demanded a conventional open propshaft, in which case axle location was by parallel radius arms plus the Panhard rod. Standard braking was by Ford's cable arrangement, but Lockheed hydraulics could be fitted.

The Six was immediately successful in racing, and was soon appearing with a variety of engines. By the time production ceased at the end of 1955 over a hundred had been made – and the template laid down for future Lotus spaceframe designs.

I DIDN'T KNOW THAT...

■ The first Six used a 1508cc Ford Consul engine reduced in capacity to slot into the under-1500cc racing class. Ford could not – or would not – supply an engine, so Chapman went from Ford dealer to Ford dealer, buying the engine part-by-part.

■ Other engines fitted include the TC-TD-TF MG engine, the alloy 1100cc Coventry Climax, the Bristol 'six', and – in a very early car – a supercharged 746cc MG unit as used in the pre-war J4. Most, though, retained the sidevalve Ford engine and matching gearbox: a 'medium-tuned' Ford Ten engine would give a 93mph maximum, said Lotus advertising, with a standing quarter-mile in 19 seconds.

■ Some Sixes used a de Dion rear axle, anticipating the use of this suspension in future Lotuses.

■ Colin Chapman was no mean driver himself, and in a Six powered by the modest Ford sidevalve he proved he could show much more exotic machinery the way home.

■ The Six's aluminium body was one of the first jobs undertaken by the Williams and Pritchard. They were determined to make their mark, and delivered bodywork of the very highest quality, so much so that there was no need to paint it – another reason why the Six was taken so seriously.

■ With the Six, Lotus established the practice of offering its cars in kit form; this only ceased following the 1973 imposition of VAT.

■ Kits to build an exact reproduction of the Six are currently available – just don't expect the operation to be much cheaper than buying the real thing.

SPECIFICATION

Engine:	1172cc water-cooled in-line 4-cyl, sidevalve (Ford; other engines to customer choice)
Power:	dependent on engine/tune
Transmission:	three-speed gearbox (Ford; otherwise four-speed)
Construction:	spaceframe combined chassis and body structure with aluminium panels
Front suspension:	independent by split beam axle; location by lateral radius arms; coil springs concentric with telescopic dampers
Rear suspension:	live axle; location by torque tube and Panhard rod; coil springs concentric with telescopic dampers
Steering:	cam-and-peg
Brakes:	drum, cable-operated; possibility of hydraulics
Kerb weight:	8.5cwt

EVOLUTION

July 1952	First appearance of Lotus MkVI, at MGCC Silverstone
February 1953	Lotus Engineering Co Ltd established, with loan of £25 from Chapman's girlfriend Hazel Williams Production of Six kits begins
October 1953	Hazel Williams wins 1172 Formula class in Six, Tarrant Rushton Speed Trial
January 1955	Chapman starts working full-time at Lotus Engineering
Late 1955	Lotus Six discontinued

BELOW The tail incorporates a small boot. Ford pressed-steel wheels are used on this example – making the car sit relatively high, even though coil-over-damper units have replaced the Ford rear axle's transverse leaf.

LOTUS SEVEN

Max Speed	102mph*
0–60mph	7.7sec*

* S2 Cosworth 1500

ABOVE As a Series I, this car has cycle wings and an alloy nose-cone; the power unit in this case is a tuned A-series, and the car is set off by wire wheels, a feature not invariably present on the S1.

Leaner and lower than the Six, the Lotus Seven was Colin Chapman's response to continuing demand for a clubman's racer and cheap road car; what he didn't appreciate, as he moved on to supposedly better things, was that this demand would remain sufficiently strong for the Seven still to be in production today, as the Caterham Seven.

The Seven's spaceframe was an evolution of that of the Six, using a combination of ¾in and 1in square and round tubing to which stressed aluminium panels were riveted; at this stage all the body was in aluminium. Gone was the sit-up-and-beg Ford running gear, however, the Seven using a coil-sprung Austin/Nash Metropolitan axle and the clever twin-wishbone front Chapman had devised for his racers, in which a high-mounted anti-roll bar doubled as the

upper arms. In place of the Ford torque tube, the back axle was located by twin radius arms and a Panhard rod; the first few cars had a steering box, but thereafter the cars used either a Minor or Herald rack. As for the engine, that was initially the trusty Ford sidevalve, mated to the Ford three-speed gearbox, but soon a Climax became available, while the US market was offered the Sprite A-series unit, both these options being in combination with a BMC four-speed gearbox.

But the Seven wasn't making much money, and it was decided to redesign the car to shave costs. The resultant Series 2 had fibreglass wings and nose-cone and a simplified spaceframe (of reduced strength, alas), along with a re-jigged back axle. Intially the engines were A-series or Ford sidevalve, but soon the revvy new Anglia

RIGHT The Series 4 shown here never had the chance to prove itself: after the Caterham takeover only a further 38 cars were made before boss Graham Nearn decided to revive the S3.

THE CATERHAM SEVEN

Caterham's initial offering was the twin-cam S3. This was joined in 1975 by models powered by 1300 and 1600 pushrod Ford 'Kent' engines. A tuned Sprint version of the 1600 arrived in 1980, being joined in 1984 by the 135bhp 1700cc Supersprint. Other Ford-derived engines fitted over the years include the Vegantune twin-cam, the Cosworth BDR, and – for export only – the CVH unit. The first Vauxhall-powered cars arrived in 1990, a year ahead of the adoption of the Rover Group K-series engine. The K-series, in various tunes, went on to become Caterham's mainstay, but alongside it have latterly been offered small numbers of trackday specials with Honda motorcycle engines. Up until the arrival in 2005 of the CSR, with its new chassis and suspension, mechanical changes have been incremental: two key improvements were the arrival of a de Dion rear in 1985 and a six-speed gearbox in 1995.

105E pushrod unit took over, accompanied by bigger versions of the Ford 'Kent' engine, often Cosworth-tuned. This was pretty much the definitive Seven, the subsequent Series 3 differing – other than in detail – only in that it had a Ford Escort axle.

By the end of the 1960s Chapman had evidently tired of the Seven. The Europa had started out as a would-be replacement, and the Clan Crusader was born of a coterie of Lotus engineers pondering on a 'New Seven'. But in the end it was decided – legend has it without Chapman's knowledge – to stick with a modernised and cheaper interpretation of the original. This was the Series 4 of 1970, which had glassfibre panels bonded onto a simplified spaceframe. Despite being more practical and better-riding than the S3, the S4 was not universally loved, and Lotus pulled the plug in 1972. When Caterham Cars restarted production, it soon switched to making the S3, and this has formed the basis of all subsequent Sevens.

Whichever Seven you choose, you are buying a four-wheeled motorbike, and sports-car motoring at its purest and most intoxicating, with razor-sharp responses, superb roadholding and handling, and heady acceleration from even a mildly-tuned example. No other two-seater offers such a buzz – the author happily admits that a Caterham with supple de Dion rear and tweaked 1700cc 'Kent' engine heads his sports car 'Top Ten'.

I DIDN'T KNOW THAT...

■ A handful of Sevens had de Dion back axles, including the 1957 prototype – which also had a Climax engine and four-wheel discs.

■ The axle on the S2 was a cheaper Standard unit, located by two top-mounted radius arms and a lower A-frame that was at first secured to the axle by its drain-plug. In vigorous use the plug undid itself, thereby both destabilising the handling and emptying the differential of its oil...

■ Thirteen S3s – called Twin Cam SS – were fitted with the Lotus twin-cam. Subsequently a twin-cam S4 was offered, and when Caterham took over manufacture it reintroduced a twin-cam S3, offering this until 1983. Later Caterham twin-cams had their engines built from parts, ultimately with a 1599cc block, Lotus no longer supplying complete power units after 1977.

■ The S4 was more than just a new body and chassis: the suspension was also new, with a twin-wishbone front and a rear axle located by Watt's linkages (ie a lower trailing arm and an upper leading arm each side), with lateral location by a single diagonal brace from one of the lower arms. Lotus made an estimated 664 of the S4, with a further 38 built by Caterham.

■ In 1994 Caterham announced a rebodied Seven, the Caterham 21. Faced with strong competition from the Elise, the 21 was withdrawn in 1999 with only 49 cars made. After this chastening episode Caterham has stuck to the traditional Seven shape, albeit with the option of a longer and wider body from 2000.

SPECIFICATION (SERIES 3)

Engine:	1297cc/1598cc water-cooled in-line 4-cyl; ohv
Power:	72bhp at 6000rpm/84bhp at 6500rpm
Transmission:	four-speed gearbox
Construction:	spaceframe combined chassis and body structure with aluminium panels
Front suspension:	independent by coil-and-wishbone, anti-roll bar forming upper arm; coil springs concentric with telescopic dampers
Rear suspension:	live axle; location by A-frame and twin radius arms; coil springs concentric with telescopic dampers
Steering:	rack-and-pinion
Brakes:	front discs and rear drums
Kerb weight:	9.5cwt (S2 Super Seven)

EVOLUTION

October 1957	Series 1 introduced
February 1958	Climax-engined Super Seven (7C) announced
October 1959	Sprite-powered Seven America (7A) introduced
	Herald steering rack standardised
June 1960	Series 2 announced
January 1961	Anglia 105E engine available: twin SUs or Cosworth-tuned
Mid 1961	Cosworth-engined Super Seven announced
September 1962	1498cc Cortina engine available (standard or Cosworth-tuned)
Early 1968	Crossflow 1600 engine replaces 1500 unit
August 1968	Series 3 introduced
January 1969	Twin-Cam SS introduced
March 1970	Series 4 launched
October 1972	Series 4 discontinued
May 1973	Rights sold to Caterham
June 1974	Caterham halts production of S4 and restarts manufacture of S3
October 1984	De Dion rear axle introduced
February 1999	Last Caterham Seven with 'Kent' engine

1962–74

LOTUS ELAN

Max Speed	121mph*
0–60mph	6.7sec*
	* Sprint

ABOVE The S1 Elan – as the S2 – has unframed windows; the pressed-steel wheels are specific to Lotus. The numberplate letters attached to the air-intake mesh are a clever answer to legal requirements.

BELOW The 'Elanbulance' was so well executed that one regrets that this high-performance micro-estate never made it to production. Only two were built, by dealer Hexagon of Highgate.

It was elegantly put: 'If the E-type is king, we continue to regard the Elan as prince', wrote *Motor* magazine in 1970. That this sums up the Lotus so perfectly – and that it was still a valid comment six years after the Elan's launch – speaks volumes for the abilities of the pint-sized glassfibre sportster. It wasn't journalistic hyperbole. Just as the Jaguar bettered its rivals, so the Lotus was streets ahead of the crude ironmongery offered by mainstream manufacturers.

The Elan was lightweight – as surely a good sports car should be. It was elegantly clean-lined, again as surely a good sports car should be. With a twin-cam adaptation of the Ford 'Kent' engine it was also appropriately rapid. But to these virtues the Elan added not only Spridget levels of crisp agility but a finesse in chassis behaviour that was probably never equalled in a sports car until the MX-5 came along.

Not only did the Elan hold the road as a race-bred Lotus was expected to do, but it did so with an extraordinary level of comfort: Colin Chapman understood that the secret both of good roadholding and good ride was long-travel suspension with strong damping. With a Triumph-derived coil-and-wishbone front end and a coil-sprung strut rear, this goal was achieved with delicious simplicity.

The Elan saved Lotus. The Elite had been a money-sapping catastrophe, expensive to make and impossible to sell. Chapman knew he had to start again, and set out to make a cheap Sprite-eater with the revvy Ford Anglia engine. To keep weight down, he wanted it to be a glassfibre monocoque, despite it being intended as an open car. In the end the Elan moved up-market of the low-cost Sprite, gained the twin-cam engine, and – most significantly

SPECIAL-BODIED ELANS

Various Elans received special bodies, beginning with two aluminium-shelled fastbacks built by Williams & Pritchard for Ian Walker Racing: one was intended for Le Mans and the other was a road car with a luxurious interior and unusual slanting twin headlamps. Then there was a series of 20 Shapecraft Elans with an aluminium fastback bonded to the Elan's glassfibre body, while in Italy a single car was given smart coupé coachwork by Frua; there was talk of series production. Most practical of the lot, though, were the two 'Elanbulance' miniature estates built by dealer Hexagon of Highgate. But the most significant rebodying of the Elan was of course that by Lotus itself, in the shape of the longer and wider +2 model. A total of 3300 was made between 1967 and 1974 – of which a hundred or so were converted into dropheads later in life, by Lotus specialist Christopher Neil.

of all – abandoned the grp monocoque in favour of a plastic shell over a simple folded-steel backbone chassis. Chapman's engineers had to convince him of this stroke of genius, which provided a lightweight cheap-to-make foundation for the car, but so logical was it that all Lotuses thereafter, until the Elise came along, have been based on the same concept.

The first Elans had a bitty interior and counterbalanced sliding windows. The S2 of 1964 offered optional electric windows and a full-length wood dashboard. The subsequent S3 and S4 models added detail changes, nothing more – although the arrival of a fixed-head coupé in 1965 constituted a sensible addition to the range. More significant was the Elan Sprint of 1971, which had a big-valve twin-cam that punched out 126bhp – serious horsepower for such a featherweight. The last cars were also available with a five-speed gearbox.

US regulations, the imposition of VAT on kit cars and Chapman's wish to move up-market all conspired to kill the Elan in 1973. That the name was revived in the 1980s and that the Elise was seen as a return to its values speaks volumes for the rightness of the Elan – as does its status as partial inspiration for Mazda's MX-5. The Elan is still a reference.

I DIDN'T KNOW THAT...

- The design of the Elan was directed by Ron Hickman, who later found fame as the inventor of the Black & Decker Workmate.
- The alloy-head twin-cam engine was created by former Coventry Climax designer Harry Mundy, then working as Technical Editor of *The Autocar* magazine – or *Autocar*, as it became in 1962.
- The Elan was launched with a 1498cc engine but the 22 cars fitted with this unit were recalled and given the 1558cc engine standardised in early 1963.
- The wooden dashboard used from the S2 onwards acts as a body brace, preventing scuttle shake. Other ingenious Elan details include the vacuum-operated retractable headlamps that use a chassis member as a vacuum reservoir, and the integral moulded glassfibre bumpers. The latter in particular was a notable innovation at the time and avoided having to adapt existing production-car bumpers: it was calculated that the entire Elan development budget was less than it would have cost to have tooled up a pair of tailor-made steel bumpers.
- In the 1964–66 period Lotus offered a race-spec Elan, the 26R. This had an engine tuned by Cosworth or BRM, extensively revised suspension and chassis, and a lightwight bodyshell with fixed headlamps; just under a hundred 26Rs were built.
- The five-speed gearbox available on the last Elan Sprints used an Austin Maxi gear cluster.
- The Elan was revived, in re-thought and modernised form, as the 1990s Evante, using a tubular chassis, metal driveshaft joints, and a belt-driven twin-cam engine by Vegantune, the company behind the car.

SPECIFICATION

Engine:	1558cc water-cooled in-line 4-cyl; alloy head and dohc
Power:	105bhp at 5500rpm (S1)/115bhp at 6000rpm (S3 SE)/126bhp at 6500rpm (Sprint)
Transmission:	four-speed or five-speed gearbox
Construction:	folded-steel backbone chassis with glassfibre body
Front suspension:	independent coil-and-wishbone; anti-roll bar; telescopic dampers
Rear suspension:	independent by coil-sprung struts and tubular lower wishbones; telescopic dampers
Steering:	rack-and-pinion
Brakes:	discs front and rear; servo on SE and Sprint
Kerb weight:	11.5cwt (S1); 14.2cwt (Sprint)

EVOLUTION

October 1962	Elan launched
May 1963	Production begins
November 1964	Series 2 announced
October 1965	Fixed-head Series 3 coupé introduced
January 1966	Special Equipment (SE) available: 115bhp engine, c/r gearbox, centre-lock wheels
June 1966	Series 3 convertible announced: framed windows
September 1967	Plus 2 announced
March 1968	Series 4 introduced
November 1968	Stromberg carbs replace Webers
March 1969	Plus 2S announced
August 1969	Weber carbs replace Strombergs
October 1970	Elan Sprint and +2S 130 introduced: Big Valve engine
October 1972	Five-speed gearbox available
February 1973	Last Elan convertible and coupé
December 1974	Last +2S 130/5

BELOW By the time of this S3 the Elan dashboard was a smart veneered-wood item that gave the interior a real lift. The steering wheel, with its delicate spokes, is the correct Lotus type.

MARAUDER

Max Speed	89mph
0–60mph	18.4sec

ABOVE This Marauder is one of those built by Abbey Panels, and has a more domed and higher nose section; the construction of the body also differs and is supposedly heavier.

BELOW The unique Marauder coupé: the interior is also bespoke, and has a slight cabin-cruiser air. The body uses many cut-down Rover P4 panels, and indeed could almost be a Rover.

The idea of a Rover sports car seems more than slightly ridiculous. But that's what the Marauder was, and that's doubtless one of the reasons why production ceased after only 15 cars had been made.

The concept was cooked up by Rover engineer Spen King, his cousin Peter Wilks, and Rover continental sales representative George Mackie. The original scheme was for a skimpy cycle-winged car along the lines of the Healey Silverstone, but Mackie fell for the lines of a Farina-styled Ferrari 166. Inspired by this, he cut about a side-elevation view of a Rover P4, stuck it on a postcard…and so the Marauder was born.

The basis of the car was a modified 'Auntie Rover' P4 chassis, with 9in cut out of the wheelbase, the crossmembers re-positioned, and the 2103cc inlet-over-exhaust Rover engine located 19in further back and 2in lower. A floor gearchange replaced the Rover's column shift, the steering was made quicker, and power boosted from 75bhp to 80bhp. The Rover freewheel remained, allowing clutchless geachanging.

While King stayed at Rover, his two collaborators left, to establish Wilks, Mackie and Company – with the target of manufacturing one car per week. The roadster would be followed by a drophead coupé, it was planned, and a competition model with a tuned engine was envisaged.

With the first car finished in July 1950, and sales in Switzerland, France and the US in prospect, the fledgling company was dealt a serious blow by the British government, which in April 1951 imposed a double purchase tax of 66.6 per cent on cars with a pre-tax cost

THE MARAUDER COUPÉ

The last Marauder made was a closed coupé. Bizarrely, it was built for a gentleman whose wife reared prize goats, and who used the car to tow a trailer containing the pampered beasts, ivy to feed them stowed in the boot. With its turret-like small-windowed top, pinched-in tail and long bonnet, the coupé looks as if Auntie Rover has had an illicit fling with a small Italian, in the form of a 'Topolino' Fiat. The unique front grille has shades of Alfa and Bristol about it, but the rest is pure remodelled P4 – including P4 rear wings, rear skirts and bootlid, a re-raked P4 windscreen, and P4 bumpers, as well as a roof formed from a cut-down P4 panel. Other elements of Rover presswork were used by coachbuilder Richard Mead – who also bodied five of the roadsters – and the result is a car which could easily have passed as a regular Rover model.

of over £1000. At first the company held the basic price down to £999, but by October it was obliged to raise it to £1250, meaning a hefty tax-inclusive price of £2001. The Marauder, already a pricey item, now more than ever failed to offer the performance commensurate with its price-tag: 0–60mph in 18.4 seconds and a maximum speed of 89mph wasn't going to give Jaguar any sleepless nights.

Fitting a bored-out 2393cc engine from the previous P3 Rover, in conjunction with triple carbs and a modified cylinder head, pushed the power up to 100bhp. This wasn't enough to save the project: not only was the car still far too expensive for what it offered, but Wilks and Mackie simply didn't have the capital to keep going. With precious few orders pending, the last Marauder left the Kenilworth works in April 1952.

Should a tear be shed? The Marauder has all the engineering quality and refinement of the P4, with smooth but unsporting responses from the torquey straight-six. This is scarcely a sports car, though: roll is quite pronounced on corners, as is understeer, while straight-line stability is less good than it could be, if the example the author sampled is any guide. But the Marauder was a brave effort. Before criticising it too vigorously, bear in mind that it was made on a shoestring by a company with a staff of only four people.

I DIDN'T KNOW THAT...

- Rover did much to help the Marauder project along – after all, Rover bosses Maurice and Spencer Wilks were uncles to Peter Wilks. One instance was that Rover arranged for P4 chassis frames to be delivered with all the crossmembers just tack-welded in place, making modification much easier.
- This indulgence extended to the use of Rover facilities. 'We cut and shut the chassis, and then on a Saturday we'd take it in and on the production line they'd jig-drill all the holes for the front suspension,' George Mackie told the author. 'I don't think they were bothered in those days by whether it was "on the side" or not. It was neither official nor unofficial…'
- The sole Marauder coupé wasn't the final word on a closed variant: an altogether more elegant fastback was sketched out, and could have given the marque just the boost it needed.
- The part-alloy Marauder bodies at first contained a fair amount of timber, but after body construction moved to Abbey Panels the timber content was eliminated.
- The Marauder team hoped that the 3-litre V6 engine Rover was developing would enter production and be made available. But the engine was never produced.
- The whereabouts of all but three of the 15 Marauders is known.
- One of the survivors is active in historic rallying, fitted with an uprated 134bhp 2.6-litre engine. The performance is excellent, as might be expected, and the owner says it despatches XKs with no problem, and out-handles Austin-Healeys.

SPECIFICATION

Engine:	2103cc six-cyl in-line, water-cooled (IoE) 80bhp at 4200rpm. Optional 2393cc unit develops 100bhp
Transmission:	four-speed gearbox (synchro on third and top only), freewheel or optional overdrive
Construction:	boxed ladder-frame chassis; part-timber body frame (latterly steel); steel/aluminium panels
Front suspension:	independent by double wishbones and coil springs; telescopic dampers
Rear suspension:	live axle with leaf springs; telescopic dampers
Steering:	cam-and-peg
Brakes:	all-drum, hydro-mechanical
Kerb weight:	25.75cwt

EVOLUTION

July 1950	Prototype completed
March 1951	Marauder '100' introduced
April 1952	Last Marauder leaves works

ABOVE Several owners have uprated their cars, and this example has a 3-litre Rover engine. With tweaks to the chassis and a more powerful engine, the Marauder becomes a real sports car.

BELOW The Marauder combines a bench seat with a clunky after-market floor gearchange; the round knurled knob on the dashboard controls the typical Rover freewheel.

MARENDAZ SPECIAL

Max Speed	82mph*
0–60mph	15.8sec*

* 15/90 tourer

ABOVE This catalogue image depicts a 13/70 tourer; the white steering wheel was seemingly always a feature of Marendaz Specials. Apparently WO Bentley considered suing over the shape of the radiator. (*Graham Skillen*)

BELOW In all probability photographed in the 'Jam Factory', this is one of the cars campaigned by Aileen Moss, mother of Sir Stirling; the Moss family were a great support to Marendaz.

The Marendaz Special has attracted far more attention than is merited by its modest production run: almost certainly fewer than 100 cars were made, between 1926 and 1936. Part of the reason for the car's high profile will be familiar to anyone who grew up as a reader of *Motor Sport* during any time from the 1950s to the 1970s.

Quite simply, whenever the Marendaz came up in the magazine, the next issue invariably – to the point of tedium – contained a letter from Captain DMK Marendaz RFC, correcting what he saw as inaccuracies and singing the praises of his creation. Unfortunately the good captain's version of the truth didn't always accord with reality – starting with his claims of an 800-car production run. As a result, establishing what really happened is a genuine challenge.

The Marendaz was an assembled car, built in the main from readily-available proprietary components; but it was none the worse for this, being constructed to a moderately high standard and incorporating clever details such as reduction gearing on the pedals, on later models, to reduce brake and clutch effort. Developed out of the Marseel – soon re-named Marseal – light cars made by Marendaz, the first examples used the 1496cc Anzani ohv 'four', sometimes supercharged. There was also a 9/20hp model listed, with a linered-down 1100cc Anzani engine.

In 1931 a new Marendaz Special was announced, with a six-cylinder sidevalve engine of 1869cc; this power unit was subsequently also offered in 2½-litre form. Disguised with an alloy cover, the origins of this engine have been muddied by Marendaz's continued insistence that it was of his own design. It wasn't – at least not at first. It was an American-sourced

MARENDAZ AND THE JAM FACTORY

The Marendaz Special was initially made in Kennington, London, where Donald Marendaz had a garage specialising in sports cars and tuning. But from 1932, after an estimated 35 cars or so had been completed, the Marendaz was built in the Cordwallis Works in Maidenhead, immortalised as 'The Jam Factory' as a result of subsequently being the home of St Martin's Chunky Marmalade. As is related in Lord Montagu's *Lost Causes of Motoring*, the Berkshire factory was also the last resting place for the friction-drive GWK, the home of the importers of the Belgian-built Imperia, and the site of the workshops where the ill-fated Burney Streamline was developed by Sir Dennistoun Burney, designer of the R100 airship. Given the sticky end of all these ventures, and of Marendaz, Lord Montagu and his co-writer Michael Sedgwick mischievously ponder on whether there was a jinx on the automotive occupants of the Cordwallis Works...

Continental unit as used by Studebaker's budget Erskine brand, but fitted with a Marendaz-originated 'special high-efficiency anti-pinking' cylinder head and latterly offered with a supercharger. Some cars even used refurbished secondhand Erskine engines. Subsequently, apparently as a result of supply problems, Marendaz used blocks and crankcases of his own design, but the basic starting point was the Continental engine.

For 1935 the new 15/90 arrived, and gradually supplanted the sidevalve models. Again this adapted an off-the-shelf engine, the 1991cc inlet-over-exhaust Coventry Climax engine also used by Triumph, and again it was in theory also available in supercharged form – although sources suggest that in the 1932–36 period only two blown cars were produced.

With their elegant Bentley-apeing radiator the later Marendaz Specials were smart and competent cars, blessed with good suspension, in general a pleasant gearbox, and effective hydraulic brakes. They were also successful in competition, not least in the hands of Aileen Moss, mother of Stirling, who owned four examples during the 1930s.

Production ended in 1936, and Donald Marendaz turned to aircraft design. After the war he developed a three-cylinder ohc car engine and spent a spell in South Africa making a small stationary diesel power unit. Back in England, in 1964 he said a new Marendaz Special would be going into production. It never did.

I DIDN'T KNOW THAT...

- Captain Donald Marcus Kelway Marendaz flew in WWI in the Royal Flying Corps and in later years took pleasure in regaling guests with tales of his exploits. He was especially proud of his part in the battle of Cambrai, when he flew a spotter-plane for the British cavalry.
- Marendaz was instrumental in persuading TG John, a fellow Welshman, to begin manufacture of the Alvis car. It is not true, though, that he co-designed the first Alvis.
- The four-seater tourer body style introduced for 1932 was at least in part the work of *The Autocar* cutaway artist Max Millar. Drophead and saloon bodies were also listed, as well as a 'sportsman's coupé', but it seems almost all Marendaz Specials were open four-seaters.
- Marendaz broke various speed records at Brooklands and at Montlhéry, generally in a Marendaz Special but sometimes in a straight-eight Graham-Paige.
- Possibly as a result of a bit of canny product placement by Captain Marendaz, during 1935 a supercharged 17-100 Marendaz Special appeared on stage at the Cambridge Theatre, London, in a scene of George Bernard Shaw's *Man and Superman*.
- A somewhat sceptical *The Autocar* reported in 1932 that a scientific-research mission was leaving for Central Africa with a Marendaz Special as the team's transport.
- During the late 1920s Marendaz experimented with a 1½-litre straight-eight.
- Despite his unquestioned patriotism, Marendaz was interned during the war because of his political views – he was a sympathiser of Sir Oswald Mosley and his British Union of Fascists.

ABOVE The 15/90 road-tested in 1935 by *The Autocar;* the engine is an IoE Coventry Climax 'six', as used by Triumph, but with a Marendaz head and triple carbs.

SPECIFICATION (15/90)

Engine:	1991cc water-cooled in-line 6-cyl; inlet-over-exhaust
Power:	not disclosed
Transmission:	four-speed unsynchronised
Construction:	separate chassis; wood-framed body
Front suspension:	beam axle with semi-elliptic leaf springs; friction dampers
Rear suspension:	live axle with cantilever leaf springs; friction dampers
Steering:	cam-and-peg
Brakes:	drum, hydraulic
Kerb weight:	22.1cwt (tourer)

EVOLUTION

October 1926	Anzani-engined Marendaz Special announced
June 1930	Four-speed gearbox standard (previously optional)
October 1931	13/70 announced – sidevalve 1869cc 'six'
August 1932	First car made at Maidenhead
October 1933	2½-litre 17hp models introduced
April 1934	Possibly unique Continental saloon supplied to Liverpool customer
October 1934	Climax-powered 15/90 joins range
Spring 1936	Production ends

BELOW The christening of the first Marendaz to be made at the Maidenhead works, in August 1932; doing the honours is the Mayoress of the Berkshire town, with DMK Marendaz behind, by her left shoulder.

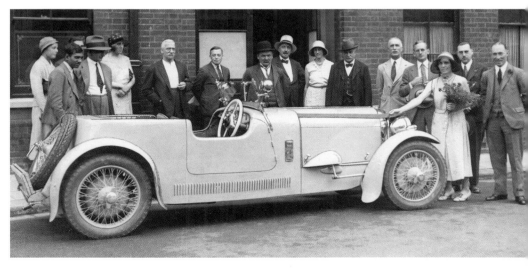

MG 18/80

Max Speed	74–80mph
0–60mph	n/a

ABOVE As a MkII Speed Model, this car has the wider and heavier chassis: better braking and roadholding come at the cost of diminished performance. The coachwork is by Carbodies of Coventry. *(Magna Press Photo Library)*

BELOW The MkIII was never a success. This car is finished in cream, with brown mudguards, a colour scheme much favoured by MG. *(Magna Press Photo Library)*

The 18/80 can claim the distinction of being the first 'true' MG – as opposed to being a modified Morris with a special body, as was the case with the earlier Bullnose-derived and Flatnose-derived models and the M-type Midget. That said, the 18/80, introduced alongside the Midget at the 1928 Motor Show, was very much of Morris parentage.

The starting point for the car was the ill-fated Morris Light Six, as unveiled in 1927. This was by all accounts a pretty wretched device, with a long and narrow chassis of such flexibility that the car was all but undrivable; it did, however, have a brand-new and very promising 2468cc overhead-camshaft engine, supposedly designed at the instigation of MG chief Cecil Kimber.

When the Light Six's shortcomings became apparent, all thoughts of production were abandoned while the car was redesigned into the wider-chassis Morris Six of the following year. Meanwhile, though, Kimber had acquired one of the prototypes, and he used this as the basis for the 18/80, retaining the engine, the cork-in-oil clutch and the three-speed gearbox, but creating a new and suitably rigid chassis and modifying the front and rear axles.

With the crossflow Morris engine given a new block and twin carbs, and the chassis sitting on Rudge-Whitworth centre-lock wire wheels, the new MG looked an attractive proposition, even if the retention of the Light Six's 4ft track made it seem a little narrow. Details included a fly-off handbrake, a full set of up-market Jaeger dials, and an elegant new radiator design with a central rib that was destined to be used on all MGs through to the TD.

Kimber didn't stop there, however, and a year later MG

THE 18/80 MKIII

It is conceivable that the 18/80 would have sold better had it benefited from a halo effect created by competition successes. This wasn't to be, as the racing version created by MG proved something of a dud. Called the MkIII, this ultra-special 18/80 had a dry-sump version of the ex-Morris engine with all new internals and twin-spark ignition, and was intended to deploy a healthy 100bhp. As announced, in May 1930, the output was 83bhp, however, with 96bhp only being achieved after a period of further development. More seriously, on its Brooklands debut the MkIII ran its crankshaft bearings in the early stages of the Double Twelve race, and reliability remained a problem. With its deep-valanced tourer bodywork, built in conformity with international racing regulations, the MkIII looked the business, but manufacture was stopped after only five of the intended first batch of 25 had been made.

announced a MkII version of the 18/80 with a revised and still stiffer wider-track chassis and a four-speed gearbox, along with uprated running gear. Better-braked and with better roadholding, the MkII was a further step forward, but the MkI – which continued in production – was a more sporting machine, three-speed gearbox notwithstanding, as it weighed roughly 3cwt less than the substantially-constructed MkII. In open tourer Speed form, a MkI was capable of just shy of 80mph, a more than respectable performance given the relatively modest 60bhp or so delivered by the overhead-cam 'six'.

In all, 500 of the MkIs were assembled, the last in summer 1931, while the heavier and more expensive MkII continued to be sold until 1934, presumably until stocks of parts had been exhausted; with 236 cars made, it was hardly a success for MG.

With good looks, sound engineering and a delightfully smooth engine, the 18/80 apologised to nobody, and was fast enough to kick sand in the face of such thoroughbred machinery as the 3-litre Lagonda. But it was the cheeky and affordable little Midget that caught the public's imagination, and defined the way forward for the marque; possibly not helped by the débâcle of the MkIII (see box), MG's first 'six' was – alas – destined to remain a minority interest.

ABOVE Carrying drophead bodywork by Carbodies, this is a MkII 18/80; the track is 4in wider than on the MkI. Also featured on the MkII is a four-speed gearbox, still with a cork clutch. (Magna Press Photo Library)

I DIDN'T KNOW THAT...

- The 18/80 was available as an open tourer, a two-seater with dickey, a two-door closed salonette and a four-door saloon; the last two were at first offered either fabric-covered or metal-panelled. Later a drophead arrived, with coachwork by Carbodies, the source for all MG's catalogued 18/80 body styles. Sales of closed models constituted a clear majority.
- Famous aviator Amy Johnson was presented with an 18/80 by Sir William Morris; the car carried a special radiator mascot in the form of a Gipsy Moth aeroplane.
- The 18/80 was nicknamed 'Quick Six' at the MG works, and as a result some parts numbers for the car had a 'QS' prefix.
- The bulkhead featured the letters 'MG' cast into the aluminium uprights; this charming detail was however not visible once the chassis was bodied.
- The full catalogued name for the MkIII was the 'M.G. Six Sports Mark III Road Racing Model'; sometimes referred to as the 18/100, the car was also known as the Tiger or Tigress, and sometimes as the Tigresse. Ready to go racing off the showroom floor, the MkIII was priced at £895, when a MkI Speed Model cost £525, so its lack of commercial success is perhaps understandable.
- The outstanding 20 MkIII bodies were fitted to MkI (and possibly a few MkII) chassis, and sold as Speed Models.
- The first 18/80s were built at MG's factory at Edmund Road, Cowley, near the Morris works; the company only moved to Abingdon in September 1929.

SPECIFICATION

Engine:	2468cc water-cooled in-line 6-cyl; chain-driven ohc
Power:	58–60bhp at 3500–3800rpm (no definite figures available)
Transmission:	three-speed (MkI) or four-speed (MkII and MkIII) gearbox; no synchromesh; cork-in-oil clutch
Construction:	separate chassis
Front suspension:	beam axle with semi-elliptic leaf springs; friction dampers
Rear suspension:	live axle with leaf springs; torque tube; friction dampers
Steering:	worm-and-roller
Brakes:	drum, mechanically operated; Perrot shaft and cable on early MkI and thereafter by cable
Kerb weight:	22.75cwt (MkI Speed Model) 29cwt (MkII metal-panelled saloon)

EVOLUTION

August 1928	'MG Sports Six' announced
September 1929	MkII introduced
April 1930	Production of MkII starts
May 1930	MkIII announced
September 1930	MkI Speed Model introduced: fabric body
July 1931	Last MkI built
October 1932	Final MkII chassis number issued; last car sold 1934

BELOW The MkI tourer, viewed from the rear. As befits an expensive car, the dashboard is suitably well-stocked. 'Octagon-itis' had yet to break out, but the accelerator pedal has a cast octagonal 'MG' pad. (Magna Press Photo Library)

MG MIDGET M-TYPE

Max Speed	63mph
0–60mph	n/a

ABOVE The car that defined the marque: this M-type is a later model, with metal panelling. The fabric body continued to be offered, for £20 less. All factory M-types have this speedboat-style split screen.

BELOW The C-type is an 'M' completely rethought for racing. Only the first cars had the cowled radiator, in a form rather more elegant than that on this example.

The modest little M-type is one of the most important cars in this book. It brought into being the small British sports car. It set MG on its way as a manufacturer in its own right. It spawned a whole generation of four-cylinder and six-cylinder models that made MG the world's premier maker of sports cars. Its engine provided the building block for specialised power units that ended up developing more bhp per litre than a V16 Auto Union racer. That's a lot of weight to be carried on the shoulders of a cheap 20bhp two-seater.

The M-type Midget was nothing more involved than a Morris Minor rolling chassis, complete with its Wolseley-designed 847cc overhead-cam engine and three-speed gearbox, with the springs reset and a jaunty fabric-covered plywood body popped on top. Styled under the direction of

MG boss Cecil Kimber, who had a good eye for the line of a motor car, the M-type looked both cute and sporting, with its elegant boat tail, stylish vee-screen and helmet wings. Nor was the recipe over-egged: the louvred sideskirts were the only frippery.

Such was the car unveiled at the 1928 Motor Show. Production began in 1929, at a price of £175, rising to the same £185 as the unblown Austin Ulster by the time of the 1930 show. In the autumn of 1929, meanwhile, a chic Sportsman's Coupé joined the range. For 1932 the body became steel-panelled, but this was only a prelude to the M-type being replaced in August that year by the bigger J-type.

The M-type was as good-natured as its looks suggested, with safe handling, quick steering and acceptable (and

THE C-TYPE: MG's FIRST RACING MIDGET

The C-type or Montlhéry Midget was a specialist racing model available in both supercharged and unsupercharged form. Announced in March 1931, it had a shorter-throw crankshaft, to reduce capacity to under 750cc, and an all-new chassis. Underslung at the rear and with tubular crossmembers, the simple ladder frame became the basis of all MG sports car chassis up to and including the TC; ingenious details included sliding-trunnion rear shackles for the springs. The engine, thoroughly revised and mated to a remote-change four-speed gearbox, ultimately delivered 41.1bhp unblown and 52.5bhp blown. The first 14 cars, with an elegantly cowled radiator, were hurriedly built for the 1931 Double-Twelve race, where they occupied the first five places and scooped the Team Prize; this success was followed by victories in the Irish Grand Prix and the Ulster TT, thereby firmly establishing MG's sporting credentials. In all 44 C-types were built, the last in mid-1932.

latterly improved) cable-operated braking; with a weight of 10cwt, it could turn in over 60mph while returning close to 40mpg. No wonder, then, that it was soon a popular choice amongst sportsmen, with no fewer than 30 entered in the 1930 Lands End Trial, for example. The M-type was also the perfect springboard for MG, who soon gave the Midget more 'go', not least with a 'Double Twelve' racer and the celebrated EX120 single-seater, with its shorter-stroke supercharged engine, which was the first 750cc car to achieve 100mph.

MG's first Midget gained a four-seat sister in September 1931, the new D-type using a longer-wheelbase adaptation of the C-type racer's underslung chassis. There was also a snappy remote-control gearchange, whereas the M-type always made do with a willowy direct change; the possibility of making faster gearchanges was doubtless appreciated, as the D-type carried a fair bit more weight than the two-seater, and disposed of the same 27bhp as later M-types.

Anyone used to modern sports cars will find an 'M' quite coffee-grinder noisy, with a pitchy ride and a hop-skip-and-jump approach to directional stability. But the clutch and gearchange are sweet, the engine is happy to rev, and the brakes are better than an Austin Seven's. It doesn't take long to appreciate that the little MG was surely the start of something big, back in the late 1920s.

I DIDN'T KNOW THAT...

- In its initial report *The Autocar* described the MG as the 'Morris Midget'; this becomes more understandable when one considers that the MG 14/28, which was based on the Flatnose Morris, was still being described in 1927 as the 'M.G. Super Sports Morris-Oxford' and still carried Morris badging. The 'Morris Garages' marque was still young...

- Although the Sportsman's Coupé was formally announced with the 1930 range in October 1929, *The Autocar* published a 'scoop' photograph in August, depicting five Coupés in a line, each with slightly different styling – proof, said the magazine, of the lengths MG would go to in order to evolve the most attractive body style.

- Special-bodied M-types included an open-backed two-seater by Jarvis (looking like a four-seater, it in fact had an open luggage area behind the seats, enclosed by the hood) and a drophead 'University Foursome' offered by University Motors.

- The distinctive feature of shaft-and-bevel drive for the M-type's overhead camshaft led to a notorious failing common to all the overhead-cam MGs: the lower part of the shaft formed the armature of the vertically-mounted dynamo and as wear began to take place, so oil leaked into the dynamo. Re-machining the dynamo shaft to enable installation of a modern oil seal solves the problem.

- That the M-type was a huge success for MG is proved by the production figures: 3235 were made, more than any other 'cammy' MG. Next most numerous were the PA/PB, with 2500 made, and the J1/J2, of which 2463 left Abingdon.

ABOVE The standard 'M' has a whippy 'magic wand' non-remote gearchange for the three-speed gearbox; some cars were however given remote-change four-speeders.

SPECIFICATION

Engine:	847cc water-cooled in-line 4-cyl; shaft-driven ohc
Power:	20bhp at 4000rpm; 27bhp at 4500rpm (later cars)
Transmission:	three-speed gearbox; no synchromesh
Construction:	separate chassis; wood frame with fabric or steel panelling
Front suspension:	beam axle with semi-elliptic leaf springs; friction dampers
Rear suspension:	live axle with leaf springs; friction dampers
Steering:	worm-and-wheel
Brakes:	drum, cable operated
Kerb weight:	10cwt (fabric-bodied)

EVOLUTION

September 1928	M-type announced
March 1929	Production begins
October 1929	Sportsman's Coupé introduced
October 1930	Jarvis two-seater introduced
March 1931	C-type announced
October 1931	Steel body available
	D-type introduced
August 1932	M-type and D-type replaced by J-type

MG MIDGET J-TYPE & P-TYPE

Max Speed	74mph*
0–60mph	32.2sec*
	* PA

ABOVE As a PA, this Midget lacks the slatted grille of the later PB. The body had become relatively heavy for the 847cc engine, so the boost to 939cc for the PB was most welcome.

BELOW Only 42 P-types received this Deco-looking Airline body; this example, however, in typical MG coffee-and-cream, is one of six or seven fitted to the N-type Magnette chassis.

If the M-type launched the breed, the two generations of Midget that followed were to define the style and character of the MG sports car over the next 20-odd years.

The J-type was introduced in August 1932 as a two-seater J2 and a four-seater J1, and thus replaced both the M-type and the D-type. In simple terms it was a better M-type, using the improved chassis of the D-type and a detuned 847cc version of the C-type engine mated to a four-speed gearbox with a remote change. For those wanting closed transport, there was also a J1 coupé – effectively a four-cylinder sister to the F-type Magna coupé. For competition motoring, finally, the J3 was a supercharged J2, and the J4 a no-holds-barred blown racer with a high-set Brooklands exhaust and no doors; both had 746cc engines.

What gave the J-type its edge was the sparse elegance of its lines – at least in classic two-seat form. To perfect proportions were added a dual-cowl scuttle and an abbreviated tail with a slab tank and exposed spare wheel. When a set of swept wings replaced the original cycle wings in late 1933 the result was an aesthetic rightness that has probably never been bettered in a traditionally-styled sports car and which could still be seen in the last MG TF of 1955.

The J3 and J4 were short-lived: after 22 J3s and a mere nine J4s had been built the two models were deleted at the end of the 1933 model year – as was the slow-selling J1 four-seat tourer. This was a prelude to the J2's replacement with an improved model, the P-type launched in March 1934.

THE AIRLINE COUPÉ

The closed Salonette version of the J-type was a clear stylistic follow-on from the M-type Sportsman's Coupé and shared its coachwork with the Salonette-bodied F-type Magna. For the P-type, however, MG created an altogether more striking body. Designed by Henry Allingham and built by Carbodies of Coventry, this was a delicious two-seat fastback known as the Airline, and featured a sliding roof with three celluloid panels. Introduced at the 1934 Motor Show, only 42 were made, in both PA and PB form. The body – a surprisingly complex wooden structure with square-tube steel windscreen pillars – was also fitted to an estimated six or seven N-type six-cylinder MGs and to a couple of TAs. As mounted on the P-type chassis, the extra weight of the Airline body inevitably blunted performance, especially in the case of the 847cc PA; the launch price of £290, against £222 for an open two-seater, also counted against it.

With 36bhp, courtesy of a crossflow cylinder head and twin SU carburettors, the J-type had been adequately swift, and its son-of-C-type chassis gave it good handling. But the two-main-bearing engine was prone to crankshaft breakages and the brakes – by cable, as on all ohc MGs – weren't the best. The PA, as it was retrospectively called, addressed these problems – and moved the game on in other areas.

The key change was to go over to a crankshaft with three main bearings. This was accompanied by an increase in brake diameter from 8in to 12in and by an uprated gearbox and back axle, the whole housed in a strengthened longer-wheelbase chassis. The Midget now had road manners that were largely irreproachable, and reserves of reliability, but it could hardly be said it was a firebreather, so for the 1936 model year the engine was up-gunned to 939cc – giving an output of 43.3bhp. This was sufficient to give the new PB a top speed of roughly 75mph and measurably improved acceleration, aided by a closer-ratio gearbox.

With its crisp little engine, responsive steering and nicely easy gearchange, the PB was hard to fault. But getting this far, alas, had meant deviating too much from the regular Morris and Wolseley products of the parent Nuffield Organisation, which is why in 1936 it gave way to the first of the T-types.

I DIDN'T KNOW THAT...

- The J-type caused MG serious problems when a tuned-up version was sent out as a road-test car to the press. The car duly achieved 80mph in the hands of *The Autocar* – way beyond the normal top speed. Abingdon was deluged with complaints from owners who couldn't get more than 70mph out of their J-type, and was obliged to fit higher-compression cylinder heads to the cars of dissatisfied customers.
- The J-type and P-type were the bedrock of MG sales: 4962 were built (excluding J3s and J4s), against a little over 2900 six-cylinder road cars. Of the total, 2463 were J1/J2 models and 2499 were P-types.
- Special-bodied J-types included a coupé by Uhlik of Czechoslovakia and another by Vanden Plas.
- After it became clear that the J4 had too much power for its chassis, MG came up with a new Midget-based racer, the Q-type. This had a longer wheelbase and track, N-type Magnette brakes and steering, and a supercharged 746cc PA engine driving through a pre-selector gearbox. Power rose from 100bhp to 146bhp over the years – an output per litre substantially better than that achieved by the V16 Auto Union racers.
- The last racer based on the ohc Midgets was the R-type announced in April 1935. This featured a backbone-type chassis with independent suspension to all four wheels, using longitudinal torsion bars. Powered by a beefed-up Q-type engine, it was the only single-seater MG ever offered to the public: its price was £750, when a P-type cost £222. Only ten were made before MG announced its withdrawal from racing in July 1935.

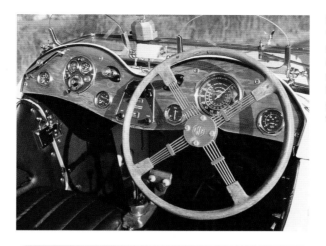

LEFT This is what is meant by 'octagon-itis' – the P-type dashboard features octagonal instrument surrounds, while the controls by the (octagonal-knobbed) gearlever are equally in the traditional MG shape.

SPECIFICATION

Engine:	847cc/939cc water-cooled in-line 4-cyl; shaft-driven ohc
	36bhp at 5500rpm (J-type); 35bhp at 5600rpm (PA); 43.3bhp at 5500rpm (PB)
Transmission:	four-speed gearbox; no synchromesh
Construction:	separate chassis; steel over ash frame
Front suspension:	beam axle with semi-elliptic leaf springs; friction dampers
Rear suspension:	live axle with leaf springs; friction (J-type) or Luvax hydraulic dampers (P-type)
Steering:	cam-and-peg (Marles/Bishop)
Brakes:	drum, cable operated
Kerb weight:	11.25cwt (J2); 13.5cwt (PA)

EVOLUTION

August 1932	J-type introduced
March 1933	J4 announced
September 1933	J1 four-seater and saloon deleted
	J3 and J4 deleted
	Swept front wings
January 1934	J2 discontinued
February 1934	P-type (PA) introduced
August 1935	PB announced
June 1936	PB discontinued

BELOW The infamous road-test J2, which was tuned to achieve a rousing 80mph no regular J-type could match – a ploy which backfired on MG in no uncertain terms.

MG MAGNA & MAGNETTE

Max Speed	80mph*
0–60mph	22.8sec*

* N-Type Magnette 2-seater

ABOVE The two-seater L2 version of the L-type Magna, with its flowing wings; salonette and four-seat tourers were also offered, as well as the unloved Continental Coupé. *(Magna Press Photo Library)*

BELOW The K3 in its more normal pointed-tail form; the bulge in the fairing between the dumb irons houses the supercharger. It is not unusual for K3s to have been created from the remains of K1 saloons.

The family of six-cylinder overhead-cam MGs is gruesomely complicated – quite surprisingly so, given that the models were only in production for five years.

The F-type arrived in September 1931, and used the D-type Midget chassis with an extra 10in added to the wheelbase to accommodate an MG-developed version of the 1271cc Wolseley Hornet engine – itself a six-cylinder adaptation of the Minor/Midget 'four'. Available as a two-seater, a four-seat tourer or a closed coupé, it was not a hugely good car: 'it was a car of length but no breadth, I used to say – and it had directional qualities roughly what you'd expect from that,' former MG boss John Thornley once told the author, before regaling him with an imitation of the noise made by its whippy crankshaft.

September 1932 saw the announcement of the 1086cc Magnette, conceived as a more specialised sporting model to get MG into the under-1100cc racing class. Available as a pillarless four-door K1 saloon with a pre-selector gearbox, as an open two-seater K2 or a four-seater K1 long-wheelbase tourer both generally with a normal 'crash' gearbox – and as the supercharged racing K3 – the Magnette had a comprehensively revised engine ('KA' or 'KB') and a wider-track chassis with improved brakes and steering. Power output of the new engine was however disappointing, at 39/41bhp, and in July 1933 a new 48bhp 1271cc version – known as the KD-series – was introduced: excluding cars supplied as chassis, most of these bigger-engined K-types were pillarless saloons with pre-selector gearboxes.

The L-type Magna that replaced the F-type in March 1933 used a detuned twin-carb version of the more robust 1086cc engine of the Magnette, and continued with the same basic body styles, but with cutaway doors, a dual-cowl

MG K3: ABINGDON'S MINIATURE BENTLEY?

The 1933–34 K3 was the off-the-shelf racing six-cylinder MG. Based on the K2 Magnette chassis (with an additional crossmember), it was a very special beast indeed. At its heart was a supercharged 1087cc Magnette engine developing up to 120bhp and mated to a pre-selector gearbox; each engine was stripped and rebuilt by the race shop. The body was initially a 'door-less' slab-tank affair, but this soon gave way to one with a pointed tail. The K3 was blooded in the 1933 Mille Miglia, where first and second positions in the 1100cc class gained MG the Team Prize, and went on to win the Ulster TT in the hands of Nuvolari; in the course of the race he broke nine class records and established a winning speed not bettered until 1951. Only 33 K3s were built, one receiving a Jensen body and one forming the basis of the EX135 recordbreaker.

scuttle, and flowing front wings incorporating running boards; the coupé, meanwhile, gained rear side windows and was renamed the Salonette.

The L-type never received the 1271cc power unit and lasted barely 18 months before the N-type Magnette, with a 56.6bhp version of the 'KD' engine, replaced both it and the K-type. Available in sweeping two-tone paintwork, the N-type was offered as two-seater and four-seater open cars and as an Airline coupé, the two-seater marking a departure from practice in that it had a sloping rear rather than one with an exposed slab tank.

Meanwhile, there were still stocks of L-type Continental bodies, so this model continued to be listed, while in September 1934 the pillarless-saloon K-type reappeared as the KN saloon, with the N-type engine; another stock-clearing exercise saw the last slab-tank K2 two-seater bodies being mounted on N-type chassis and sold as the ND. The last of the 'cammy' MGs to survive, the N-type was given forward-hinged doors and a lower scuttle for 1936, and was deleted in September of that year.

Although the six-cylinder ohc MGs evolved into fine sports – or sporting – motor cars, the constant chopping-and-changing meant they made little money for Abingdon; while purists might appreciate their beautiful presentation and zingy engines, commercial realities ultimately sealed their fate.

I DIDN'T KNOW THAT...

- The F-type was the most successful of the ohc 'sixes', with 1250 cars sold in little over a year.
- The L-type Continental Coupé with its French-style coachwork has sometimes been referred to as 'Kimber's Folly': 100 bodies were optimistically sanctioned when production began in March 1933, and cars were still being sold as late as 1936.
- Of the 486 L-types built, 35 were supplied in chassis form to outside coachbuilders.
- Cecil Kimber used a supercharged K1 with Corsica drophead coachwork as his personal car – it was good for an indicated 100mph.
- The pillarless Magnette saloon might have been pretty, but its rigidity was awful, while standards of construction and finish were often sub-standard. Many customer complaints are to be found in surviving MG service files.
- The improved KD-series engine used in the later K-type and the N-type was frequently described as being of 1287cc. In fact it retained the 1271cc capacity of the original Hornet-derived unit. Cecil Kimber however didn't want the new MG engine to be confused with the Wolseley 'six', and so arbitrarily added a fictitious extra millimetre to the stroke of the engine.
- The K-type was a waste of time in commercial terms: only 20 two-seaters were made, and 200 or so K1 saloons and tourers.
- Special bodies on the 'sixes' included dropheads by Abbey and University Motors (the latter by Carlton), coupés by Abbey and Windover, and the catalogue-model N-type Allingham Coupé, which was a dickey-seat open car by Whittingham & Mitchel.

SPECIFICATION

Engine:	1086cc/1271cc water-cooled in-line 6-cyl; shaft-driven ohc
Power:	37.2bhp at 4100rpm (F-type) to 56.6bhp at 5700rpm (N-type)
Transmission:	four-speed gearbox; no synchromesh; pre-selector standard on KA and KD series of Magnette and K3 and optional on 41bhp KB-series open cars
Construction:	separate chassis; body aluminium over ash frame
Front suspension:	beam axle with semi-elliptic leaf springs; friction dampers
Rear suspension:	underslung live axle with leaf springs; friction dampers (hydraulic Luvax on N-type)
Steering:	worm-and-wheel (F-type), then cam-and-peg (Marles/Bishop)
Brakes:	drum, cable operated
Kerb weight:	18.5cwt (N-type Magnette two-seater)

EVOLUTION

September 1931	F-type Magna introduced
September 1932	Improved brakes
	Two-seater F2 Magna introduced
	K1 and K2 Magnettes announced
March 1933	L-type Magna (1086cc) replaces F-type
	K3 Magnette introduced
July 1933	1271cc KD engine fitted to Magnette
	Pre-selector gearbox standard on Magnette
September 1933	L-type Continental Coupé announced
January 1934	L-type Magna discontinued (except Continental Coupé)
March 1934	N-type Magnette introduced – including ND two-seater
	K1 and K2 Magnette production stops
August 1934	Last K3 laid down
September 1934	KN Magnette saloon introduced
May/June 1935	Final K3 sold
August 1935	Forward-hinged doors on N-type ('NB')
	KN saloon deleted
January 1937	Final NB delivered

BELOW The first-of-line F-type, here again in two-seat (F2) form, as introduced a year after the four-seat tourer and salonette models; cycle wings are still found on all body styles. *(Magna Press Photo Library)*

MG T-TYPE

Max Speed	73.5mph*
0–60mph	23.9sec*
	* TD

ABOVE Today much coveted, in its time the TF was not well received. The dashboard with its octagonal dials is specific to the TF, the wire wheels a popular option.

RIGHT The Arnolt TDs were sponsored by American sports-car dealer 'Wacky' Arnolt, and were built by Bertone; Arnolt also had Bertone body a series of Bristols with lightweight open coachwork.

When the first T-type arrived, in June 1936, for some loyalists this marked the end of MG. In place of the revvy little PB here was a car that wasn't just bigger but one that was based on run-of-the-mill Morris and Wolseley components, from the pushrod engine to the cork-in-oil clutch. The TA's announcement followed the shifting of MG from the personal ownership of Lord Nuffield: henceforth it would be part of his Nuffield Organisation, with design executed at Cowley. Not only that, but the racing programme was cancelled.

If these were bitter pills to swallow, the truth is that commercial realities had to prevail. More to the point, the TA was every inch a real sports car, with deft handling, more than adequate performance, excellent hydraulic brakes, and well-proportioned lines that defined the British sports-car

breed. The new Midget – it still carried that name – sold better than any preceding model, was nicely profitable, and MG never looked back.

In 1939 the TA gave way to the TB, identical but for a new pushrod engine – derived from that of the Morris Ten Series M – and the disappearance of the archaic cork clutch. Post-war the TB was revived as the TC, the principal difference being a wider body tub.

It was with the TC that MG broke into the American market, but despite its commercial success on the other side of the Atlantic it was pretty out-dated mechanically. With no obvious replacement under way at Cowley, MG took matters into its own hands, and evolved the TD by the simple expedient of cut-and-shutting a Y-type saloon chassis and slotting it underneath a modified T-type wood-framed

SPECIAL-BODIED T-TYPES

Other than the Tickford drophead TA/TB, a catalogued model, one-offs based on the TA-TC include a TA drophead by Park Ward, and the TC racer built for George Phillips and entered at Le Mans in 1949 and 1950. On the TD chassis the most numerous – 67 coupés and 36 cabriolets – were the Bertone-built Arnolt TDs. A handful of TDs were given smart convertible and coupé coachwork by Swiss firm Ghia Aigle, while in Italy Motto made a single barchetta and two similar cars using a tubular chassis, and a sole barchetta was built by Schiaretti. In Holland, Veth made a razor-edged coupé. Then there were various German or Austrian TDs, some by small local bodyshops, some by better-known firms such as Wendler. Finally, a single TD coupé was built in 1953 by Nottingham dealer Shipsides, and a grp-bodied TD drophead was constructed by Dick Jacobs's Mill Garage.

body. The resultant TD thus had coil-spring independent front suspension and precise rack-and-pinion steering: it was a modern car in 1930s clothing.

The driving experience was transformed. Sample a TC, as the TA and TB before it, and you'll find it stiffly sprung, with instant responses but limited adhesion, and requiring a certain style of driving: on poor roads you aim for the horizon, and let the car find its natural path, without fighting the machinery. The TD, on the other hand, rides more comfortably, holds the road better, and has slightly slower but less heavy steering. It's still a zippy, endearing fat-free blast of true sports-car motoring, but you have to work less hard to cover the ground.

By the early 1950s it was clear, however, that a more modern style of MG was needed. Abingdon had the MGA ready, as recounted overleaf, but initially had to make do with facelifting the TD into the TF. Nobody was much fooled. The arrival of the 1500 engine gave more power, at the expense of some loss in sweetness, but the TF couldn't compete with the new breed of sports cars. Only 9600 were made, of which 3400 were TF-1500s, whereas 29,664 TDs left Abingdon – a figure well up on the 10,000 TCs produced, and the 3003 TAs and 379 TBs that found buyers before the war.

I DIDN'T KNOW THAT...

■ An estimated 260 TAs and 60 TBs received Tickford drophead coachwork. The cars weighed an extra 2cwt, which probably explains why some Tickfords – as well as one or two ordinary TAs – were latterly given the 1548cc engine of the bigger MG VA.

■ This same engine, soon enlarged to 1708cc, was used in the works-supported Cream Cracker team of trials TAs.

■ The XPAG engine introduced in the TB was a robust unit responsive to tuning, and was used in many sports-racers, from Tojeiros and Coopers to Lesters and Lotuses. One of the author's abiding memories is driving a Y-type MG saloon with a 134bhp supercharged XPAG...

■ In milder tune the engine was used in the pre-war Wolseley Ten and the post-war Wolseley 4/44, as well as in the Y-type.

■ The T-type's moment of international racing glory came when photographer George Phillips took his TC special to second in his class in the 1950 Le Mans 24-hours.

■ Many Australian TDs and TFs received Buchanan glassfibre bodies, the Buchanan shell, moulded off an Aston Martin DB3S, being primarily intended for the MG chassis.

■ It was not uncommon for down-under T-types to be fitted with the Holden 2.2-litre straight-six engine – complete with a Holden back axle to give higher gearing. Conversely, some racing Holdens used the rugged TC gearbox in place of the Holden column-shift three-speeder.

■ A run of 25 TD chassis were given near-identical copies of the Abingdon body by a German bodyshop; most probably went to GIs posted to Germany.

SPECIFICATION

Engine:	1292cc (TA)/1250cc (TB-TF)/1466cc (TF-1500) water-cooled in-line 4-cyl, ohv
Power:	52.4bhp at 5000rpm (TA); 54.4bhp at 5200rpm (TB-TD); 57bhp at 5500rpm (TD MkII and TF); 63bhp at 5000rpm (TF-1500)
Transmission:	four-speed gearbox, with no synchromesh on first TAs and then only on third/fourth; 2-3-4 synchronised from TB onwards; cork-in-oil clutch on TA
Construction:	separate chassis, underslung at rear on TA/TB/TC; wood-framed body with steel panels
Front suspension:	beam axle with semi-elliptic leaf springs (TA/TB/TC); independent by coil and wishbone thereafter; lever-arm hydraulic dampers
Rear suspension:	live axle with leaf springs; lever-arm hydraulic dampers
Steering:	cam-and-peg (TA/TB/TC); thereafter rack-and-pinion
Brakes:	drum, hydraulic
Kerb weight:	17.3cwt (TA); 17.75cwt (TD)

EVOLUTION

June 1936	MG TA announced
August 1938	Tickford drophead introduced
May 1939	First TB laid down
August 1939	Last Tickford laid down
September 1939	Announcement of TB 2-seater and drophead
October 1939	TB production ends
October 1945	TC announced
January 1950	TD announced
May 1950	TD MkII available – tuned engine, high-ratio axle
November 1953	TF announced – 'export only'
July 1954	First TF-1500
September 1954	1250cc model deleted
April 1955	Last TF

BELOW The TA has a narrower body than the TC – as does the shortlived 1939-only TB: you can tell a TA/TB from a TC by its broader running boards, with two rather than three protective strakes.

MGA

Max Speed 96.3mph*
0–60mph 13.3sec*
* 1600 MkI

ABOVE The MGA Twin-Cam is distinguished by knock-on steel wheels – also found on some pushrod cars, notably the De Luxe.

BELOW The coupé, available in both pushrod and Twin-Cam form, features a three-piece rear window; it gets quite hot and noisy in the tight cockpit. A nice detail is the small vertical door handle.

The MGA was the first modern MG, and relaunched the company after a rocky period when the traditional 'square-rigger' models had fallen from favour and competitors had started eating into Abingdon's lucrative US market. The 'A' changed all that, and went on to sell over 100,000 examples, a feat never before achieved by a sports car. It achieved this success as much as anything because it was a genuinely delightful motor car with no significant weaknesses.

The starting-point for the 'A' was a special-bodied TD racer built for photographer George Phillips to campaign in the 1951 Le Mans race. This had the basic shape of what was to become the MGA, but looked somewhat odd on the road, as the TD chassis made the driver sit up very high in the car. A new perimeter-style chassis was designed, and the car was put forward in 1952 as the intended replacement for the TD. But by this time Nuffield and Austin had merged to form BMC, and it had just been agreed that Healey's Austin-based prototype would be put into production as the Austin-Healey 100. Accordingly the new model was not authorised, and MG had to fall back on facelifting the TD into the TF. After the lukewarm reception this received, BMC recanted, and the MGA entered production in 1955, equipped with the combine's B-series engine and gearbox but otherwise as the 1952 prototype.

Clean, elegant styling was matched to straightforward mechanicals, there being the TD/TF coil-and-wishbone front,

THE MGA IN COMPETITION

The MGA's competition career began when three aluminium-bodied cars competed in 1955's Le Mans, resulting in a 12th place overall. In rallying the 'A' achieved some honourable results, including a second and third in class in the 1956 Mille Miglia, a Coupe des Dames and Coupe des Alpes in the 1956 Alpine, and a class win with a lightweight Twin-Cam in the 1962 Monte. The MGA also secured class wins at Sebring. The year 1959, meanwhile, saw completion of EX186, a Twin-Cam streamliner, with a de Dion rear, intended for Le Mans. Built without BMC authorisation, it never raced, and ended up being shipped to California. Privateer Ted Lund did however contest 1959's Le Mans, in a works-supported Twin-Cam. He retired when he hit a dog, but returned the following year with the car bored to 1762cc and given a fastback, finishing 13th overall and winning the 2-litre class. Re-entering the same car in 1961, he retired after three hours.

with its rack-and-pinion steering, and a leaf-sprung live back axle. With the 1489cc engine delivering 68bhp, the more aerodynamically-efficient MGA had lively performance and crisp, forgiving handling in the true 'Safety Fast' tradition.

Over the years the 'A' changed little, other than receiving two increases in engine capacity and gaining disc front brakes; in 1956, however, the roadster was joined by a fixed-head coupé while in 1958 the high-performance Twin-Cam variant was announced. This proved a catastrophe, as its engine demanded high-octane petrol and judicious tuning if it were not to hole its pistons. It soon developed a bad reputation, and was withdrawn in 1960. The Twin-Cam used a special chassis with all-round disc brakes and knock-on steel disc wheels, and rather than scrap the large stock of components lingering at Abingdon these were used in a run of pushrod-engined cars known as the MGA De Luxe.

These days, people know how to make a Twin-Cam reliable, and the alloy-head engine gives a gutsy carved-from-the-solid performance that is intoxicatingly Alfa-ish, so the car makes an intriguing choice for the bravely non-conformist MG enthusiast – although high prices mean a deep pocket will be needed.

Smaller and narrower than the MGB, the 'A' is far less spacious, with a tighter cockpit and a minimal boot; it also has to make do with slot-in sidescreens rather than winding windows. Counterbalancing this, it has a delicacy and an instantaneousness to its responses that make it more 'alive' than its more refined successor: driving a well-sorted MGA is truly a pleasure.

I DIDN'T KNOW THAT...

- A prototype MGA chassis was the basis for the EX179 record-breaker, a streamlined special using the TF-1500 'XPEG' engine. Over 120mph was averaged for 12 hours at Utah in 1954, at speeds of up to 153.69mph. With a prototype Twin-Cam engine fitted, in 1956, the car exceeded 170mph and captured 16 class records; later records were broken with a 948cc A-series engine installed.
- There is some controversy over the MGA De Luxe. It seems likely that only 50 or so genuine De Luxes – with the Twin-Cam chassis – were made, and that subsequently the Twin-Cam wheels and four-wheel disc brakes were offered as an option on the regular chassis, cars so-equipped being mistaken in later life for genuine De Luxes.
- At one stage Abingdon considered a drophead coupé MGA, to be built by Vanden Plas; additionally it looked at building a longer-wheelbase 2+2 MGA roadster, possibly selling this as a Riley.
- In the quest for a replacement for the MGA, Italian stylist Frua was commissioned to build a car on the 'A' chassis. The result was an imposing Maserati-like vehicle.
- In a bid to create a cheap sports car, a stripped-out MGA was fitted with a 948cc A-series engine. The car had no performance and would not have been financially viable.
- Independent rear suspension was considered for the MGB, and a semi-trailing set-up was tried on an MGA 'mule'; an MG engineer wrote the car off, and the project was rapidly canned.

ABOVE The dashboard remained essentially unchanged throughout the MGA's life, but only coupés, Twin-Cams and Mk II 1600s have a Rexine covering rather than being painted body colour.

SPECIFICATION

Engine:	1489cc/1558cc/1622cc four-cyl water-cooled in-line four; ohv/dohc
Power:	68bhp at 5500rpm/72bhp at 5500rpm/79.5bhp at 5600rpm (1600)/86bhp at 5500rpm (1600 MkII)/108bhp at 6700rpm (Twin-Cam)
Transmission:	four-speed gearbox
Construction:	separate chassis, steel panels
Front suspension:	independent coil-and-wishbone, with lever-arm damper as upper arm
Rear suspension:	live axle with leaf springs; lever-arm dampers
Steering:	rack-and-pinion
Brakes:	all-drum until July 1959; thereafter front disc; Twin-Cam has four-wheel Dunlop discs
Kerb weight:	17.75cwt (1500 roadster)

EVOLUTION

September 1955	MGA announced
October 1956	Coupé introduced
May 1958	Twin-Cam introduced
July 1959	1588cc engine and front disc brakes; renamed MGA 1600
June 1960	Twin-Cam discontinued
June 1961	MkII, with 1622cc engine; inset grille slats; larger horizontal-set rear lights
September 1962	Replaced by MGB

MGB & MGC

Max Speed 102mph*
0–60mph 11.0sec*
* MGB

ABOVE An early MGB, with pull-type rather than press-button door handles, sitting on the pierced steel wheels that were standard equipment until Rostyles arrived for 1970.

If there's one sports car that is a British institution, it's the MGB. Over half a million were made; not only that, but it is one of the few cars in the world to have been brought back into production after having been discontinued. Unfortunately, familiarity sometimes breeds contempt, so let's begin by putting the record straight: the 'B' is a thoroughly able sports car that does everything that could reasonably be expected of it, while at the same time being the most practical of two-seaters available. It deserves those half-million sales – even if it didn't deserve its messy and undignified end.

The 'B' is mechanically an evolution of the MGA, the only significant change being an engine enlarged to 1798cc: thoughts of independent rear suspension or of a coil-sprung live axle were ultimately abandoned, as was the use of V4 and V6 engines when these failed to materialise. Where the car differed was in its use of an immensely strong monocoque. MG knew that discarding the MGA's heavy chassis was the way forward, but the consequence of this decision was that the massive investment in the new shell could only be amortised over a long period during which no significant changes could be made to the car. That said, it was never intended to keep the 'B' in production right through the 1970s.

In a bid to replace the 'Big Healey', the MGC arrived in 1967, two years after the MGB GT had been launched as realisation of boss John Thornley's dream of a 'poor man's Aston Martin'. The MGC used the lacklustre Austin 3-litre engine in a 'B' shell modified to take torsion-bar front suspension: leaden handling and performance and a poor press meant it died, unloved, after two years, and it was only in 1973 – shamefully late – that BL revived the big-engined 'B' in the shape of the Rover-powered MGB GT V8.

Up until 1974 the MGB received only the most piffling

RIGHT The RV8 has modernised suspension with a twin-wishbone front and telescopic dampers all-round, but the leaf-sprung rear axle remains; the interior is in stone-colour ruched leather.

THE MG RV8 (1992–95)

Nobody quite knew what to make of the RV8. If it was a new sports car, it was no rival for the TVR. If it was a new MG, it wasn't that new at all. And if it was a revived MGB, how come it cost a huge £25,000? Rover had its answer: the RV8 was a 30th birthday celebration of the MGB, and not to be compared with more modern machinery. What wasn't said was that the car was as much as anything a marketing exercise to build up marque consciousness ahead of the MGF. The RV8 was in fact a prisoner of its circumstances. Once it became clear that the Heritage MGB shell made a new 'B' possible, the only way the economics of hand-building could add up was to make the car a high-value model: hence the 3.9-litre V8, the posh trim, and the restyled body. Most went to Japan.

changes but for 1975 it was given ungainly impact bumpers to meet US legislation; worse, to meet bumper-height requirements the car was raised up on its suspension. The result was an uglified car with its handling ruined – not to mention its power increasingly sapped by engine de-toxing in its US-market 'Federal' specification. Despite this wretched bastardisation, and the US deletion of the GT, the 'B' carried on selling strongly in the States, and indeed outsold the TR7. The MG factory never knew from year to year whether it would survive, but plans were well advanced for the MGB at last to receive the updated O-series engine when a crisis-wracked BL decided to close the Abingdon plant. Miraculously the MGB body tooling was preserved, and in 1988 production of the monocoque re-started – an unprecedented event which ultimately led to the creation of the RV8.

Spacious (just compare it with a Midget), safe-handling, peppy if not outright fast, the 'B' – ideally with overdrive – is a relaxed long-distance touring sports car with a broad-shouldered friendly nature. With endless aftermarket possibilities to update it, from leather seats to independent rear suspension, what more could you want?

I DIDN'T KNOW THAT...

- The front of the 'B', with its headlamp 'scoops', was inspired by the Frua-designed Renault Floride.
- The MGB's rigidity was partly due to a square-tube brace under the dashboard. At one stage lengths of the tube were forever going missing at the Pressed Steel works, where it was being purloined for making golf trolleys on the side...
- The engine of the MGC is not the C-series unit used in the 'Big Healey'. Although of the same 2912cc capacity it is an all-new seven-main-bearing unit. An Austin-Healey version of the MGC was vetoed by Donald Healey.
- In all, only 8999 MGCs were made; many of the final cars were sold to dealer University Motors, who upgraded the cars and in some instances fitted Downton tuning kits.
- Belgian garage-owner Jacques Coune built a run of an estimated 56 fastback MGB coupés; additionally a single WSM special-bodied 'B' was built in England by Doug Wilson-Spratt.
- The MGB competed at Le Mans in 1963 and 1964, finishing 12th the first year and 19th and highest-placed British entry the following year: thoroughly honourable results for a largely standard mass-production sports car.
- MG never offered a V8 roadster. Abingdon chief engineer Roy Brocklehurst told the author this was not only because engine availability was limited but also because of worries about scuttle shake. Today, however, you can buy new Heritage roadster bodyshells adapted to take the V8 engine – just as you can buy RV8-type twin-wishbone front suspension assemblies, complete with modern telescopic dampers.

SPECIFICATION

Engine:	1798cc/2912cc water-cooled in-line 4-cyl or 6-cyl; ohv (MGB/MGC). 3528cc water-cooled alloy V8; ohv (MGB GT V8)
Power:	95bhp at 5400rpm (MGB)/145bhp at 5250rpm (MGC)/137bhp at 5000rpm (MGB GT V8)
Transmission:	four-speed gearbox; overdrive optional/standard
Construction:	steel monocoque
Front suspension:	independent coil-and-wishbone; anti-roll bar optional/standard; lever-arm dampers (MGB and MGB GT V8). Independent by longitudinal torsion bars; telescopic dampers; anti-roll bar (MGC)
Rear suspension:	live axle with semi-elliptic springs; lever-arm dampers; anti-roll bar from 1976
Steering:	rack-and-pinion
Brakes:	front discs, rear drum; servo standard from 1973 (standard on MGC and MGB GT V8)
Kerb weight:	19.0cwt (MGB roadster); 20.75cwt (MGB GT); 23.3cwt (MGC GT automatic); 21.3cwt (MGB GT V8)

EVOLUTION

October 1962	MGB announced
October 1964	Five-bearing crankshaft
October 1965	MGB GT introduced
October 1967	MGC introduced
	All-synchro gearbox for MGB
September 1969	MGC discontinued
October 1969	BL facelift: recessed grille
October 1972	Chrome grille with plastic mesh inserts
August 1973	MGB GT V8 introduced
September 1974	Rubber-bumper MGB launched
May 1975	Anniversary Edition MGB GT
July 1976	New dashboard; front and rear anti-roll bars standard
September 1976	MGB GT V8 deleted
October 1980	Last MGB

BELOW A 'rubber-bumper' MGB with the factory hard-top; the Rostyle wheels would normally be painted rather than chromed, while the spoilers front and rear are not original.

MORGAN THREE-WHEELER

Max Speed	73mph*
0–60mph	n/a*

* Matchless w/cooled ohv Super Sports

ABOVE The archetypal Morgan trike, this beetle-back 1930 Super Sports Aero, owned by marque expert Chris Booth, is powered by a water-cooled 1100cc overhead-valve JAP vee-twin.

Morgan's trike counts as an institution. First seen before WW1, as a minimalist runaround, it evolved into pretty much the only three-wheeler with sports-car status, and remained in production into the 1950s; not only that, but a development of its suspension is still used by current Morgans.

HFS Morgan built his first tiller-steered car in 1909 and by 1911 was offering a two-seater with steering-wheel. Active in motorsport from the outset, two years later he offered a Grand Prix model, and thereafter there was always a sports model in the range.

The Morgan was built around a simple but rigid brazed-tube frame incorporating a large central tube to enclose the propshaft that took drive to the rear-mounted gearbox – from which final drive was via chains to the quarter-elliptic-sprung rear wheel. At the front was independent suspension – a

highly advanced feature for the time – using sliding pillars and coil springs. Power units varied over the years, with sundry permutations of side and overhead valves and air and water cooling, but before Ford power units were adopted the engines were principally JAP or Matchless vee-twins.

Bodies evolved over the trike's currency, but were always open two-seater or open four-seater. The best-loved were the beetle-back two-seaters, current in one form or another from 1927 to 1934, and the barrel-back type that replaced it and featured a round-section tail. Four-seaters, unsurprisingly, are less elegant and less sought-after.

In 1933 Morgan began to move away from motorcycle engines, launching a new model, the F4, that used a four-cylinder 933cc Ford Eight engine equipped with a Derrington 'Silver Top' alloy cylinder head. Retaining the rear-mounted

RIGHT The Sandford was built by the one-time Paris importer for Morgan; the engine was usually a 950cc Ruby unit, as found in many French light cars of the 1920s and 1930s.

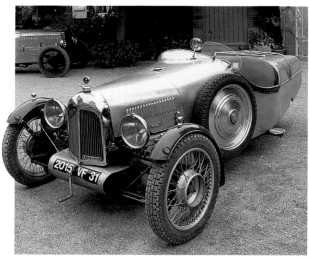

MORGAN'S FRENCH CONNECTION

The Morgan three-wheeler spawned three French spin-offs. The first was the 1919–39 Darmont, which started off as a licence-built Morgan. But Darmont wriggled out of paying his licence fees and the Darmont-Morgan became the Darmont pure and simple, ending up with French-built copies of the British vee-twin engines. Top of the range was a supercharged model supposedly good for a terrifying 100mph. The 1923–36 Sandford, meanwhile, featured either an in-line four-cylinder engine or, latterly, an air-cooled flat-twin. A trike for the connoisseur, the high-priced Sandford was called 'The Aeroplane of the Road'. The final French interpretation of the Morgan was the 1923–30 D'Yrsan, built by a French aristocrat who decided to market his own trike when Sandford turned down a joint venture; the D'Yrsan used the same Ruby four-cylinder engine as the Sandford, and had transverse-leaf independent front suspension.

gearbox, the F-type had a new chassis with Z-section sidemembers – as subsequently adapted (and still used today) on the four-wheelers.

Priced mid-way between the cheapest and the most expensive of the vee-twins, the new car had a barrel-back four-seater body and an orthodox bonnet and radiator. A two-seater followed, as did a Super Sports using the 1172cc Ford Ten sidevalve: good for over 70mph, this was the most expensive Morgan trike. In all, 1216 Ford-powered cars were produced, the last in 1952; meanwhile, the vee-twins continued until the outbreak of war.

The Morgan trike was always a low-priced vehicle, and it was also pretty crude. It was only for 1932 that the two-speed gearbox was replaced by a three-speed unit, and until the 1929 model year the steering was direct-acting rather than geared-down; a reverse gear, meanwhile, only arrived with the three-speed gearbox, a year before detachable wheels were standardised. Such rudimentary engineering helped keep weight down, and when a potent engine was fitted the result was a car with an impressive turn of speed but with roadholding, braking and steering that could be somewhat challenging. The author still breaks into as cold sweat when recalling a terrifying drive of an early '20s Morgan: the guys who fearlessly piloted the cars in inter-war competition, not to mention those still racing the cars today, have to rate as true heroes.

I DIDN'T KNOW THAT...

- In 1913/14 Morgan produced approximately 1000 trikes pa and was Britain's third-largest motor manufacturer, behind market-leader Wolseley (3000 cars) and Austin (2000 cars).
- The first Morgan agent was famous London store Harrods.
- In early trials, HFS Morgan carried a small suitcase on the back of his Runabout. This contained not a change of clothing, as some thought, but a handful of bricks to ballast the rear wheel.
- Sales were given a fillip by changes to the Road Fund Tax in 1920, these establishing a rate of £1 per RAC horsepower for cars but a flat rate of £4 for 'motor tricycles'.
- From 1913 to 1923 Morgan offered the installation of a second gearbox as an option, for competition use, thereby providing four gears.
- Peak output of Morgan three-wheelers was in 1923, with 2300 cars produced. By 1935 the figure had fallen to 286 cars, and by 1939 to an insignificant 29. The Morgan's principal three-wheel rival, the front-wheel-drive BSA of 1929–35, outsold it by roughly four-to-one.
- In the period 1928–35 roughly 40 Morgan 3cwt delivery vans were made.
- The following vee-twin engines were used on the trikes: Anzani, Blackburne, Blumfield (pre-WW1), JAP, Matchless, MAG (Swiss-built, by Motosacoche), Green-Precision (pre-WW1). Most, however, were JAP or Matchless, the most powerful used being the 1096cc water-cooled ohv JAP and the 990cc water-cooled ohv MX4 Matchless. Both these developed 42bhp, when a Morris Eight then mustered a puny 23.5bhp – hence the sports-car performance of the sub-8cwt Morgans so equipped.

SPECIFICATION

Engine:	various vee-twins, air-cooled or water-cooled; sidevalve or ohv 933cc/1172cc water-cooled in-line four-cylinder; sidevalve
Power:	25bhp at 2600rpm (981cc SV air-cooled JAP) to 42bhp at 4800rpm (990cc ohv water-cooled Matchless); 22bhp at 3500rpm (993cc Ford); 32.5bhp at 3500rpm (1172cc Ford)
Transmission:	two-speed unsynchronised (no reverse), by bevel-box and dog-clutched shafts, final drive by chain; three-speed unsynchronised (with reverse), final drive by chain
Construction:	separate tubular chassis (vee-twin models) or separate Z-section chassis (F-type); wood body frame with steel panels
Front suspension:	independent by sliding pillar and coil springs; telescopic dampers from 1928
Rear suspension:	swinging arm and quarter-elliptic leaf springs; friction dampers from 1927
Steering:	direct-acting until 1929 models; thereafter Morgan reduction box
Brakes:	mechanically-operated drum, external-contracting until 1929 (rear); drum, cable-operated (front, phased in from 1923)
Kerb weight:	5–9cwt (approx), depending on model

EVOLUTION

November 1910	Public debut of Runabout
August 1911	Two-seater with steering wheel launched
November 1919	Aero sports model introduced
November 1927	Super Sports Aero introduced (low chassis)
October 1929	Strengthened (M-type) chassis
October 1931	Three-speed gearbox introduced
Early 1932	Sports replaces Aero
October 1932	Magna detachable wheels; standard chassis lowered
October 1933	Barrel-back body introduced
November 1933	Ford-powered F4 four-seater announced
September 1935	Two-seater Ford-powered F2 introduced
End 1936	Vee-twin Family models deleted
September 1937	F Super Sports introduced (1172cc engine)
July 1952	Last Morgan three-wheeler

BELOW At speed in a later barrel-back car, equipped with the more robust Dunlop Magna wire wheels introduced for 1933; trikes never had pressed-steel wheels.

MORGAN FOUR-WHEELER

Max Speed	80mph*
0–60mph	18.6sec*

* 1340cc 4/4 SIV

ABOVE Built in 1969, this Plus 8 shows how early cars are much narrower than later models: it is just 4ft 9in wide. At this stage the Plus 8 still had an archaic separate gearbox.

To call the four-wheel Morgan unique is to sell it short. No other car still in production can boast a basic design unchanged since 1936. In its 70-year history the Morgan has used countless different engines, and has had two restyles, while the brakes, steering and rear axle have been uprated as necessary. But underneath there is still an underslung Z-section chassis dating back to 1933, sliding-pillar front suspension as used on the first Morgan trikes, and a body built of panels nailed to an ash frame.

The first 4-4 was essentially an adaptation of the F-type three-wheeler, but with first an 1122cc Coventry Climax IoE engine and latterly an ohv version of the Standard Ten unit. When this became obsolete, Morgan changed to the bigger Vanguard engine, re-naming the car Plus 4; with the 1955 revival of the 4/4, as a bargain-basement model powered by the 1172cc Ford sidevalve, Morgan established a two-tier

range that has underpinned the company ever since. The 4/4 switched to pushrod Ford power in 1960, and has retained Ford engines ever since – with a brief spell when a Fiat twin-cam was also offered. The Plus 4, meanwhile, kept to Vanguard or TR-tune versions of the Standard 2-litre engine until replaced in 1968 by the Rover-powered V8 Plus 8 – but was then revived between 1985 and 2000, with first a Fiat and then a Rover Group twin-cam 'four'.

Other than changes of engine, modifications to the running gear have been few. Disc front brakes arrived in 1959, the separate gearbox finally disappeared in 1972, rack-and-pinion steering began to be used in 1984, and telescopic rear dampers were phased in on the Plus 8 in 1991. As for the body, this received a cowled radiator for 1954, and low-set faired-in headlamps. This was satisfactory neither aesthetically nor in terms of legality – the headlamps

RIGHT The Plus 4 Plus has unusual looks, with a tall and somewhat domed glasshouse. Only in 1964, the first full year of production, did sales attain double figures.

THE PLUS 4 PLUS

The Plus 4 Plus is the most unlikely of Morgans – a car with a modern all-enveloping body. Not only that, but the two-seater coupé is constructed in glass-fibre. If this seems an aberration, it should be remembered that in the early 1960s Morgans were not the cult cars they are in today's retro-obsessed society: back then they just looked like creaky old relics from another era. Company chief Peter Morgan, fearing dwindling sales, accordingly commissioned grp body specialist EB (Staffs) Ltd to come up with a new body for the Plus 4 chassis. The resultant Plus 4 Plus was unveiled at the 1963 Motor Show, but a mere 26 were made – with the last only being sold in January 1967. Odd looks and a price substantially above that of a regular Plus 4 counted against it – but maybe in the end people preferred a Morgan to be traditionally-styled after all...

were positioned too low – and a more curved grille and higher-set headlamps were introduced in the course of 1954. Since then the tail has become more raked, the body has become lower, and the wings have been progressively widened – but the style has never changed in its essentials.

Nor has the Morgan's deportment. Good roadholding on smooth roads, aided by quick if heavy steering, has always been accompanied by unsettled behaviour on poor surfaces and a board-stiff ride – although cars with rear telescopic dampers are slightly less unyielding, and the rack has improved steering precision. Other constants are a firm pedal action and – on Moss-gearbox cars – a deliberate gearchange that is not to be rushed. Where the cars differ is in their performance, which ranges from the borderline-anaemic of a sidevalve 4/4 to the broad-shouldered torque-rich power of the Plus 8 – via the acceptable liveliness of a pushrod 4/4 and the surprising refinement of an M16-powered Plus 4.

Whichever Morgan one chooses, the experience is an intriguing blend of vintage and modern sufficiently seductive to make one accept the car's shortcomings as part of its dyed-in-the-wool character.

I DIDN'T KNOW THAT...

- In the 1950s and 1960s the ash for Morgan bodies came from Belgium, some from trees on WWI battlefields. It was not unknown for the wood to contain shrapnel or .303 bullets...
- Drophead two-seat coachwork was available on the first series of 4-4 (latterly 4/4) and on all Plus 4s until the model was discontinued for 1969; additionally 51 four-seater dropheads were made in the 1954–56 period.
- One-off Morgans have included a flat-rad 4/4 'woodie' estate and a Plus Four coupé inspired by a Touring-bodied Ferrari.
- A Super Sports Plus 4 was catalogued from 1961 until 1968. It had a twin-Weber Lawrence Tune engine and a lightweight aluminium body – of 'lowline' type from 1963. In all, 101 Super Sports were made, including a single four-seater. Additionally 42 examples of a Plus 4 Competition model were made between 1965 and 1967, with a 'lowline' body in steel and a more mildly tuned engine.
- Morgan quality took a major leap forward 1986, when the chassis became powder-coated or (optionally) galvanised and the wood frames were for the first time given a preservative treatment.
- Morgan built a V8-powered prototype as early as 1937, using the small 2.2-litre version of the flathead Ford engine. The car was subsequently fitted with a supercharged sidevalve Standard Eight power unit.
- Today's Aero 8, the first all-new Morgan in the firm's history, still uses a wooden body frame – but the car's strength comes from a bonded and riveted aluminium tub.
- The post-1955 4/4 was only offered with non-Ford power from 1981 until 1984, when a 1600cc Fiat twin-cam was available – with the alternative of the Ford CVH from April 1982.

SPECIFICATION (SELECTED MODELS)

Engine:	1172cc water-cooled in-line 4-cyl, sidevalve (4/4 SII); 2088cc water-cooled in-line 4-cyl, ohv (Vanguard-engined Plus 4); 3528cc water-cooled in-line V8, ohv (1968–72 Plus 8)
Power:	36bhp at 4400rpm (4/4 SII)/68bhp at 4200rpm (Vanguard-engined Plus 4)/160bhp at 5200rpm (1968–72 Plus 8)
Transmission:	three-speed gearbox in unit with engine (4/4 SII); separate four-speed gearbox linked to engine by torque tube (Plus 4 and 1968–72 Plus 8)
Construction:	separate chassis, underslung at rear, with Z-section main rails; ash-framed body panelled in steel or aluminium
Front suspension:	independent by sliding pillars and coil springs; telescopic dampers
Rear suspension:	live axle with leaf springs; lever-arm dampers
Steering:	cam-and-peg
Brakes:	all-drum (4/4 SII and Vanguard-engined Plus 4); front discs and rear drum, servo-assisted (1968–72 Plus 8)
Kerb weight:	14cwt/16.1cwt/17.7cwt

EVOLUTION

January 1936	4-4 announced
September 1950	Plus 4 announced
February 1951	4/4 deleted
October 1953	'Interim cowl'; TR engine introduced
June 1954	Last flat-rad and interim-cowl cars
October 1955	Single spare wheel; 4/4 reintroduced
October 1958	More sloping rear deck on Plus 4 two-seater and drophead
October 1960	4/4 Series III (105E engine)
October 1961	4/4 Series IV (1340cc Classic engine)
February 1963	4/4 Series V (1498cc Cortina engine)
November 1964	Plus 4 Plus introduced
December 1966	Lowline body standardised on Plus 4
February 1968	1600 engines for 4/4
October 1968	Plus 8 and 4/4 four-seater announced
January 1969	Last Triumph-engined Plus 4

BELOW Drophead coachwork was available up until the 1969 demise of the Triumph-powered Plus 4; this 1951 car carries the 'flat-rad' front that was phased out in 1954.

RILEY IMP/MPH/SPRITE

Max Speed	83mph*
0–60mph	18.8sec*
	* Sprite

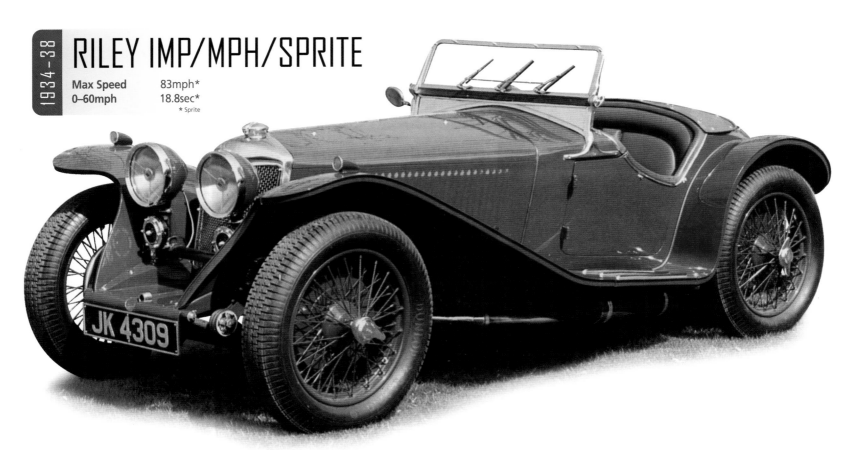

ABOVE The Imp and the MPH share their basic body, and have delicate Alfa-like looks, thanks to their more spare wings; this is a four-cylinder Imp. Alas, few were sold. *(Arnold Wilson)*

BELOW The supercharged White Riley, in company with an ERA: the two cars are more related than you might think, the ERA six-cylinder engine being based on a Riley block.

Elegant, well-engineered and powered by efficient twin-cam engines, the Riley Imp, MPH and Sprite were competition-honed aristocrats in comparison to the cheaper and more commonplace MGs of the time.

It was with the arrival of Percy Riley's famous twin-high-camshaft Nine engine in 1926 that a truly sporting model became possible, this advanced hemi-head power unit being the basis of all Riley engines until the 1957 demise of the ill-fated Pathfinder saloon. It wasn't long before a low-slung sports Nine, the Brooklands Speed Model, was available. This broke class records at Brooklands, won its class in the 1928 and 1929 Ulster TTs, and won the TT outright in 1932, before going on to a third place in 1933's Le Mans and a class win and fifth place in the 1934 event.

To fill the gap after the Brooklands Nine had been discontinued in 1932, for 1933 Riley listed a slab-tank 2/4-seater sports model under the March Special name; most had a 9hp four-cylinder engine but a handful had a 12hp six-cylinder unit. The March was an exercise in marking time, as at the 1933 Motor Show the 9hp Imp was unveiled – as a 2/4-seater with a squared-off tail. By the time it entered production in 1934, however, the Imp was offered only as two-seater, with a body clearly related to a new six-cylinder sister car, the MPH.

Both models used a diagonal-braced underslung chassis and their bodies differed only in their tail treatment: the MPH had an Alfa-like finned spare-wheel cover while the shorter-wheelbase Imp had a simple detachable surround for the spare. Powering the MPH was either an uprated version of the 1458cc 12hp engine or a similarly breathed-upon 14hp

RILEY, ERA AND THE WHITE RILEY

Riley was intimately involved with the ERA: the engine of the famed racers was based around a modified six-cylinder Riley block and part-assembled at the Coventry works. But the links with Raymond Mays go back before then, to a racing Riley that was effectively the prototype ERA. Known as the White Riley, this was a 1933 TT-spec rolling chassis loaned to Mays, with further financial backing from Riley. It was duly given a 1486cc Riley 'six' modified by future ERA designer Peter Berthon, with a supercharger installation by Murray Jamieson – the brains behind the twin-cam Austin Seven racers. With a heady 12psi boost, this ultimately pushed out 160bhp. Mays duly broke the existing record for the Shelsley Walsh hillclimb and claimed the Mountain Circuit record at Brooklands, and the White Riley had further successes in the hands of Kay Petre before being converted to road use after the war.

unit of 1633cc; for 1935 this latter engine gave way to a 1726cc 15hp variant. The Imp, meanwhile, retained the classic 1087cc 'four' of the Nine, further up-gunned when used in a racing version known as the Ulster Imp. With the MPH coming second and third overall in 1934's Le Mans – beaten only by a 2.9-litre Alfa Romeo – you would have thought that Riley would have been content to sit pretty.

But for the 1935 Motor Show the family-run Coventry firm discontinued both the MPH and the Imp and introduced a restyled sports model using the company's new 1½-litre four-cylinder engine. Known as the Sprite, this was built on a more rigid boxed version of the MPH chassis and featured a raked 'fencer's mask' grille and fuller valanced wings front and rear.

What was the logic behind this model? Quite likely it was decided to leave the bottom end of the sports car market to MG, and at the top of the range offer a more affordable model than the MPH, which at the Aston Martin money demanded had attracted fewer than 20 buyers. But even if the £425 Sprite was more attainable than the £550 MPH, it was still a car for the moneyed few; although production figures are not available, the last of the sports Rileys, desirable though it was, constituted little more than a blip on the screen.

I DIDN'T KNOW THAT...

■ The Riley Nine Speed Model – as it was originally called – was conceived not by Riley but by record-breaker and former Leyland engineer JG Parry Thomas, the man behind the huge Leyland Eight. After Thomas's death on Pendine Sands, at the wheel of his aero-engined Land Speed Record car 'Babs', development was continued by Reid Railton of Brooklands specialists Thomson and Taylor.

■ The height of the Brooklands Speed Model was only 36in at scuttle level, making the car sufficiently low for a driver to be able to rest the palm of his hand on the ground.

■ A single Brooklands Nine was bodied as an unusual and very low-slung closed coupé.

■ It was with Riley specials that famed motorcycle racer and tuner Freddie Dixon made his name in motor racing. His particular skills were in weight-saving and in extracting maximum power through the use of carefully conceived carburettor installations using multiple motorcycle Amals.

■ It seems that in all no more than 80 or so of the Imp were made.

■ MPH engines featured duralumin con rods and a more efficient oil pump. The pre-selector gearbox seems to have been used on all production MPHs and most Imps.

■ At least one MPH was given two-seater bodywork by Bertelli, the former in-house coachbuilder for Aston Martin.

■ In France, three racing Sprites were given streamlined Pourtout roadster bodies designed by Georges Paulin – better known for his Darl'mat Peugeots. Two of the cars were entered in 1937's Le Mans, without any success, but all three came home 2-3-4 in the same year's French GP – behind a conventionally-bodied racing Sprite.

SPECIFICATION

Engine:	1087cc four-cyl water-cooled twin-cam (Imp); 1458cc/1633cc/1726cc six-cyl water-cooled twin-cam (MPH); 1496cc four-cyl water-cooled twin-cam (Sprite)
Power:	50–70bhp depending on model
Transmission:	four-speed 'silent third' gearbox or ENV pre-selector
Construction:	underslung chassis, wood body frame, aluminium panels and steel wings
Front suspension:	beam axle and leaf springs; torque reaction rods (MPH); friction dampers
Rear suspension:	underslung live axle with leaf springs; friction dampers
Steering:	worm-and-wheel
Brakes:	cable-operated drum (Imp/MPH); rod-operated drum (Sprite)
Kerb weight:	19.7cwt (Sprite)

EVOLUTION

August 1927	'Racing Riley Nine' (Speed Model) announced
May 1932	1½-litre 6-cylinder racing model
October 1933	9hp Imp 2/4-seater shown – never produced
May 1934	MPH six-cylinder (1458cc/1633cc) introduced, alongside production Imp
September 1934	New 12hp/15hp engines for MPH
October 1935	Sprite replaces MPH; Imp deleted
February 1938	Riley in receivership

BELOW The Sprite is heavier-looking than the Imp and MPH, thanks to its valanced wings and 'fencer's mask' grille. It was described by *The Autocar* as 'A Proper Little Sports Car of High Efficiency'.

SINGER LE MANS

Max Speed	70mph*
0–60mph	34.2sec*

* Nine Le Mans

ABOVE This Nine Le Mans Special Speed dates from 1936. The cars are every bit as elegant as the MGs of the day, and performance compares well with that of the P-type Midgets.

BELOW Two Roadsters: the red car is a 1939 example, one of 862 made, while the white car is one of the 700 or so twin-carb 1500s made between 1952 and 1956.

To those of you who think a Singer is nothing more than a Hillman Minx in a party frock, the idea of the Coventry marque making a sports car – and one that was successful in competition, furthermore – doubtless seems on the bizarre side of improbable. But the Singer Le Mans was every inch a sports car, and indeed there are those who regard it as a better machine than the equivalent MGs of the time.

At the heart of the better-known 9hp Le Mans was an advanced – for the era – overhead-cam 972cc engine, a derivative of the chain-driven ohc power unit first seen in the otherwise banal Junior of 1926. The Nine was introduced in 1932 as a replacement for the Junior, and for 1933 became available as an open four-seater Sports and an elegant Sports Coupé.

When one of the former managed to finish the 1933 Le Mans 24-hours, in 13th and last position, but as the first unsupercharged sub-1000cc British car to qualify for the Rudge Whitworth Cup, this prompted the announcement for 1934 of the two-seater Le Mans with its slab rear tank and twin spares. The engine was tuned and would happily rev to 6000rpm, a close-ratio gearbox was fitted, and there was a new double-dropped chassis, as well as details such as a fly-off handbrake. At the same time a six-cylinder 1½-litre Le Mans was introduced, using a 1493cc ohc engine. This model was also available as a more highly-tuned Le Mans Special, boasting a big-valve engine with a higher compression ratio and triple SU carbs.

Another foray to Le Mans in 1934 saw five Singers

THE SINGER ROADSTER

Introduced in 1939, the Roadster was a clever bit of marketing: it had something of the Le Mans about it, yet was a practical four-seat tourer at an affordable price, slotting above the Morris Eight tourer yet below a run-of-the-mill 10hp saloon. Based on Singer's Bantam saloon, it had a similar underslung chassis and used the 1074cc engine of later Bantams. Reintroduced post-war, it gained a four-speed gearbox for 1950, independent front suspension and hydro-mechanical brakes for 1951, and a 1500 engine from March 1951. Production continued into 1956, but long before then the wood-framed Roadster had become an unsaleable anachronism. Not that the car was bad, in itself: a late 1500 with twin carbs gives a strong if unrefined performance, has sportingly firm suspension, and taut, quick-acting steering. Put a Singer man on the spot, though, and he'll most likely say an '1100', preferably beam-axled, is the sweetest of the line.

finishing, with 1½-litres coming home seventh and eighth overall and Nines taking first, third and sixth in class. Building on this honorable performance, a Special Speed version of the Le Mans was introduced for 1935. Only ever made as a 9hp (although a 1½-litre was announced), this had an enlarged body, running boards, and twin SUs in place of Solexes; for 1936, when an underslung chassis was introduced, this was the only Le Mans to be offered.

Spurred by the continuing success of the Le Mans in motor sport – 64 out of the 300 entries in the 1935 Lands End Trial were Singers, and 31 won premier awards – Singer built four special racers for 1935, and the marque returned to Le Mans, coming in first, third, fourth, sixth and seventh in class. But this was where things came unravelled. Four of these new cars were entered for the 1935 Ards TT, and three crashed more or less at the same corner, victims of an identical steering failure; indeed one of the cars landed on top of another. This widely-reported incident did Singer's reputation no good at all, and early on in 1937 the Le Mans models were deleted.

With their demise, financially constrained Singer never made another series-production sports car, contenting itself instead with the more staid Roadster. That's a shame, as the pert little Le Mans Nines were sparkling performers, handled well, and had effective hydraulic brakes – something no 'cammy' MG ever boasted. Today their virtues are a well-kept secret...

I DIDN'T KNOW THAT...

- At a 1934 price of £595, against £215 for a 9hp Le Mans, the 1½-litre Le Mans was very much a connoisseur's motor car, and few were sold. Indeed, during its 1933–35 life only 71 were made. Most had a more efficient crossflow engine, the triple SUs of the Special, and the revised chassis introduced after the first 12 cars had been made – but never the underslung frame.
- For 1935 Singer renamed the four-seater open Nine the Le Mans, but this slight of the marketing hand only lasted a year before the car lost the slightly spurious Le Mans tag – as did the Coupé. Even more short-lived was a drophead coupé Nine Le Mans with a body by specialist coachbuilder REAL: one was exhibited at the 1934 Motor Show but it is not certain if any further examples were ever built.
- A keen competitor in Le Mans Singers was the flamboyant Merlin Minshall. By all accounts quite a character, he went on to work in British Naval Intelligence during the war, being issued with the code 007... and serving under author Ian Fleming. It is generally understood that a certain fictional Mr Bond was modelled on Minshall.
- A 1½-litre Singer Le Mans is the only car ever to have won an Olympic gold medal. A special rally was held as part of the 1936 Berlin Olympics, this being the only time that motor-sport has been included in the Olympics, and the event was duly won by Betty Haig in her Singer.

LEFT The nicely appointed and businesslike cockpit of the Nine, complete in this instance with a 'Brooklands' steering wheel. Folding flat the screen gives roughly another 5mph.

SPECIFICATION (NINE LE MANS)

Engine:	972cc four-cyl water-cooled; ohc
Power:	38bhp at 5000rpm
Transmission:	four-speed gearbox, unsynchronised
Construction:	separate chassis, wood body frame, aluminium panels and steel wings
Front suspension:	beam axle and leaf springs; friction dampers
Rear suspension:	live axle with leaf springs; friction dampers
Steering:	worm-and-nut
Brakes:	hydraulic
Kerb weight:	15.8cwt (Nine Le Mans Special Speed)

EVOLUTION

October 1933	Nine and 1½-litre Le Mans introduced
April 1934	New chassis; revised triple-carb crossflow engine for 1½-litre
October 1934	Special Speed models announced Four-seater and Coupé renamed Le Mans
July 1935	TT-bodied (round-tail) Le Mans Replica announced – but none ever sold
August 1935	1½-litre Le Mans deleted
Spring 1937	Last Le Mans believed built

BELOW This works TT 1½-litre went on to be campaigned in trials and rallies. The body – with cutaway rear wings – has been moved back on the chassis, as have the twin spares, to move weight rearwards for trials.

SS 90 AND SS-JAGUAR 100

Max Speed	101mph*
0–60mph	10.9sec*

* 3½-litre SS 100

ABOVE The graceful lines of the SS 100. The shape was copied for the Panther J72 replicar of the 1970s, while today you can buy an extremely authentic reproduction based on XJ6 parts.

BELOW The SS-Jaguar 100 coupé attracted much attention at the 1938 Motor Show, but remained a one-off. In style it clearly anticipates the post-war XK120 coupé and the MkV and MkVII saloons.

Like father, like son. Just as with the E-type, the SS 100 was considered in its day to be too fast, too cheap and too flashy for its own good. It wasn't a suitable car for a gentleman – for whom only a BMW 328 was good enough – and was always going to be out of its depth in motorsport. It was a cad's car.

As with the E-type, such jibes were unfair – even if there were, all the same, an element of truth hidden behind the snideness. The good looks of the SS were part of the problem: the first Jaguar sports car was almost implausibly attractive, being a perfect interpretation of the tense long-bonnet feline sleekness that marque founder William Lyons sought to impart to all his cars.

Yet underneath its sensuous lines lay an adaptation of a chassis used on one of Britain's most banal mass-produced saloons, the 16hp Standard. Not only that, but the power

unit of the SS 90 was an unexciting Standard sidevalve 'six'. Looked at coldly, the car makes one recall engine specialist Harry Weslake's supposed remark to Lyons, when he said 'Your car reminds me of an overdressed lady with no brains – there's nothing under the bonnet'.

But things weren't so black-and-white. The underslung cruciform chassis was indeed Standard-derived, and an adaptation of the frame used on the preceding SS 1; for the SS 90, however, it was shortened by approximately 15in, and emerged from this cut-and-shutting effectively a new component. The 2663cc engine, too, was somewhat removed from the regular Standard seven-main-bearing unit, having an alloy head and twin RAG carburettors; output, never quoted by SS, was in the region of 70bhp.

In any case, the SS 90, introduced in March 1935, was short-lived, being replaced in September by the SS 100,

THE SS-JAGUAR 100 COUPÉ

With only 308 built, over four years, the SS 100 was such a sideline for SS Cars that you can understand why just the one body style was offered. But that didn't stop William Lyons exhibiting a stunning one-off 3½-litre coupé at the 1938 Motor Show – and even affixing to it a £595 price-tag, some £150 more than the regular 3½-litre SS 100. With a wooden dashboard, its interior evoked that of the saloon Jaguars, while in its lines it anticipated the XK120 coupé. The car was bought by an SS-Jaguar enthusiast as a 17th birthday present for his lucky son. Sold after the war, it passed through various hands, including a film producer and one owner who had it clocked by the police doing 105mph downhill. Eventually, in the 1970s, it was rescued from the States, in a derelict state, and duly restored.

after only 22 production cars had been made. The SS 100 shared with the 2½-litre SS-Jaguar saloon a revised engine with a Weslake-designed overhead-valve head. Delivering 102bhp, this gave the SS 100 entirely honourable performance: a maximum of 96mph with a 0–60mph time of 12.8 seconds was moving it some for the mid-1930s. When a 3½-litre option became available for 1938 the SS 100 became a genuine 100mph car – and there were few of those around at the time.

With its new engine – and with revised steering, brakes and suspension – the SS 100 went as well as it looked. Yet even as a 3½-litre, it cost no more than a 1½-litre Riley Sprite – and was more than £300 cheaper than a 2-litre Aston Martin; as for the BMW 328, that cost £695 against the £445 of the SS 100.

The SS 100 was soon making a name for itself in competition, a Glacier Cup in the 1936 Alpine Trial being followed by victories in the 1937 RAC and Welsh rallies.

When the VSCC eventually accepted it as a Post-Vintage Thoroughbred, the SS 100 at last achieved social respectability, and today it is a highly-coveted classic with a price-tag to match. It was never, though, a car to be seen on every street corner: only 308 were built, 191 of the 2½-litre and 117 of the 3½-litre. At last count, there were over 260 known survivors.

I DIDN'T KNOW THAT...

- The SS 100 was cheaper to make than the SS saloons yet could be sold at a premium. SS-Jaguar specialist Barrie Price estimates that the profit-per-unit on the SS 100 was £25 for the 2½-litre and £30 for the 3½-litre – against £5 for the 1½-litre saloon and £6.50 to £15 for the bigger-engined saloons.
- The 1933-on AC was related to the SS 90 and SS 100, both cars using an adapted SS 1 frame, as built by John Thompson Motor Pressings for Standard. Not only that, but as a parts-bin assembled car the 2-litre AC also used the same Alford & Alder front axle, ENV rear axle, Bendix brakes and Moss gearbox as the SS.
- The same Standard/SS chassis was modified for use on the post-war AC 2-litre, the last example of which was built in 1958 – making this antique pre-war left-over a strange blood-brother indeed to the sassy SS 100.
- Prince Michael of Romania was the owner of an SS 100; bucking the received wisdom, he apparently preferred it to his BMW 328.
- Avon built two drophead coupé SS 100s. Other special-bodied SS 100s included a sleek Cooper-like racer by Paul Pycroft, an overbodied horror of a roadster shown by Vanden Plas of Belgium in 1947, a flamboyant drophead with enclosed wheels by Bernath of Switzerland, and a very XK120-ish drophead (a post-war rebodying) by Czechoslovak coachbuilder Uhlik.
- Post-war, Ian Appleyard won the 1948 Alpine Rally in an SS 100, and came second in the following year's Tulip Rally.

SPECIFICATION

Engine:	2663cc water-cooled in-line 6-cyl; sidevalve/2663cc or 3485cc water-cooled in-line 6-cylinder; ohv
Power:	70bhp estimated (SS 90)/102bhp at 4600rpm (SS 100 2½-litre)/125bhp at 4250rpm (SS 100 3½-litre)
Transmission:	four-speed, synchromesh
Construction:	separate chassis; aluminium body over ash frame
Front suspension:	beam axle with semi-elliptic leaf springs; friction dampers (SS 90); friction and hydraulic dampers (SS 100)
Rear suspension:	underslung live axle with leaf springs; friction dampers
Steering:	cam-and-lever (SS 90); worm-and-nut (SS 100)
Brakes:	drum, cable-operated (SS 90); drum, Girling rod-operated (SS 100)
Kerb weight:	23.7cwt (2½-litre SS 100)

EVOLUTION

March 1935	SS 90 introduced
September 1935	SS 100 announced
September 1937	3½-litre engine available
December 1941	Last SS 100 leaves factory

LEFT The plain painted dash of the SS 100 is austere – if well stocked with smart white dials. For its era, its performance-per-pound made the SS extraordinary value.

BELOW The tightly-drawn rear gives the SS 100 a cat-ready-to-pounce tension: William Lyons at his best. The first SS 90, in contrast, had a bobbed tail, and looked slightly Riley-ish.

SUNBEAM 3-LITRE

Max Speed	90mph
0–60mph	n/a

ABOVE This late car carries striking Barker open tourer coachwork, and was built for famous racing motorist Earl Howe, later Lord Curzon. *(Bruce Dowell collection)*

BELOW The '1000hp Sunbeam' on display in the National Motor Museum at Beaulieu, which also houses the Golden Arrow. The Sunbeam was the first car to crack the 200mph barrier. *(National Motor Museum)*

Sunbeam is a marque that dips on and off the sports-car radar, rather than having a continuous history of manufacturing such vehicles. If one looks at the vintage years – before it was bought in 1935 by Rootes – the company was known primarily as a producer of beautifully engineered but essentially conservative luxury cars at the top end of the British market. This might seem strange, given that the Wolverhampton firm's pre-WW1 incursions into motor racing culminated in the creation of an advanced double-overhead-cam racer that won the 1914 TT, and given that in the 1920s it was active in motor-racing and record-breaking. Yet the only sports car to be offered during this period was the Three-Litre Super Sports – to give the model its correct name.

Available from 1925, the Three-litre was a spin-off from the Sunbeam twin-cam racers designed by former Fiat engineer Vincent Bertarione; caustically referred to as 'Fiats in Green Paint', one of these won the 1923 French Grand Prix and another, supercharged, triumphed in the 1924 Spanish event at San Sebastian.

The new model used a freshly-designed dohc six-cylinder engine of 2916cc, developing a healthy 90bhp at 3800rpm. The work of Bertarione, assisted by former Fiat colleague Walter Becchia, the engine had seven main bearings, hemispherical combustion chambers, and camshafts driven by a train of helical gears rather than by chain. Other details included dry-sump lubrication and fuelling by twin Claudel Hobson carburettors; the dynamo was crank-driven, with all other auxiliaries taking drive from the camshaft geartrain. If one excludes 50 cars made by Ballot in 1923, the Sunbeam is the first twin-cam power unit to be series-made in Europe.

THE '1000HP SUNBEAM'

One of the more unusual cars to carry the marque name was the so-called '1000hp Sunbeam' of 1927. Nicknamed 'The Slug', this extraordinary vehicle was built for regular Sunbeam racer Henry Segrave, to contest the Land Speed Record. Powered by two Sunbeam Matabele aero-engines removed from a racing motor boat – one engine at the front and one at the rear – the somewhat portly streamliner in fact mustered closer to 900bhp. All the same, this was sufficient for Segrave to push the record up to 203.7mph at Daytona Beach, in Florida – making him the first man to crack the 200mph barrier. The combined capacity of the two quad-cam V12 engines was a massive 44,888cc; drive was by chain, a somewhat horrifying thought. The car can be seen in the National Motor Museum, at Beaulieu, as can the Golden Arrow in which Segrave achieved a new record of 231.44mph in 1929.

When first seen, in Spring 1924, the new engine – with in-unit gearbox – was mounted in a modified version of the chassis used for the 2½-litre pushrod-engined 16/50 Sunbeam, but production models had their own design of chassis. This had cantilever semi-elliptic springs at the rear and an axle located by torque tube; the fully-equipped chassis, fitted with cycle wings, was available to outside coachbuilders for £950, or was bodied in open tourer form by Sunbeam for an all-in price of £1125. To put this in perspective, a Morris Oxford tourer cost £260 in 1925, or less than a quarter of the Sunbeam's price; in modern-day terms this equates roughly to the Sunbeam being in the class of today's Jaguar XK.

For his money the purchaser of a Three-Litre had a very special motor car, more revvy and responsive than the four-cylinder Bentleys, with a faster and easier gearchange, better refinement, lighter steering, and a 90mph top speed comparable to that of the rival make's 4½-litre – whose engine was half as big again.

Less of a blunderbuss than the Cricklewood cars – but regarded as less secure in its roadholding – the Sunbeam was a true thoroughbred, with its English solidity tempered by a quantifiable dose of Italian brio. Owners of the 42 known survivors are guardians of one of vintage motoring's better-kept secrets.

I DIDN'T KNOW THAT...

- Although having the same bore and stroke as the ohv 20.9hp Sunbeam introduced for 1927, the Bertarione twin-cam is not related to this power unit.
- Walter Becchia, the ex-Fiat colleague of Vincent Bertarione, went on to work for Talbot in France, before ending up at Citroën – where he was responsible for the 2CV flat-twin, with its many ingenious features.
- Owners of the Three-Litre included Bentley financier and racer Woolf Barnato, Lady Rocksavage of the Rothschild banking family, racing driver Earl Howe, and comedian Harry Lauder. Barnato owned at least two Three-Litres, including one with a tautly-drawn two-door 'Surbico' saloon body by Surbiton Coach and Motor Works.
- The Three-Litre wasn't just a sports car for wealthy customers: it was also Sunbeam's contender for glory at Le Mans, and construction of the first cars was hurried through so that the model would be eligible for the 1925 event: in due course a Three-Litre came home second to a Lorraine-Dietrich.
- The Three-Litre was catalogued until 1930, and 315 examples were built, with many different types of bodywork: over 20 coachbuilders tried their hand on the chassis.
- A supercharged Three-litre was catalogued from early 1929, but no more than six such cars were made, and only two were sold – the other examples having their supercharger removed before leaving the factory as normal Three-Litres.
- A few Three-Litres may have been made to special order after the car was withdrawn from the price lists in 1930; additionally, final cars had hydraulic brakes.

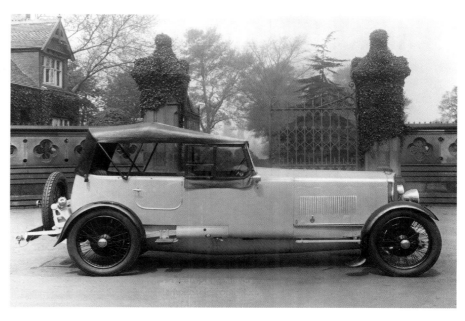

SPECIFICATION

Engine:	2916cc water-cooled in-line 6-cyl; dohc
Power:	90bhp at 3800rpm
Transmission:	four-speed unsynchronised gearbox; right-hand change
Construction:	separate chassis; body construction varies
Front suspension:	beam axle and semi-elliptic leaf springs; friction dampers
Rear suspension:	live axle with cantilever semi-elliptic leaf springs; torque tube; friction dampers
Steering:	worm-and-nut
Brakes:	all-drum, mechanical
Kerb weight:	30.3cwt (steel-bodied tourer)

EVOLUTION

May 1924	'Three-Litre Sunbeam' announced
Spring 1925	First six cars built
February 1929	Supercharged model catalogued
March 1930	Three-litre last catalogued

ABOVE One of the earliest 3-litres – indeed, quite possibly the first; the bodywork is standard-issue Sunbeam. These Sunbeams were good for 90mph or so. *(Bruce Dowell collection)*

BELOW Racer and recordbreaker Sir Malcolm Campbell in a late 3-litre with the standard Sunbeam-built tourer coachwork. In all likelihood it was not his personal car. *(Bruce Dowell collection)*

SUNBEAM (-TALBOT) ALPINE

Max Speed	95mph
0–60mph	18.9sec

ABOVE Based on the Sunbeam-Talbot, the 1953–55 Alpine has certain specific sporting details, such as a louvred bonnet and vents in the front wings.

BELOW Two pre-war Sunbeam-Talbot Ten tourers: the red car is from the 1938 model year, and the white car is a 1936–37 example with a different tail treatment. Both are based on Hillman components.

The Sunbeam-Talbot was the parts-bin sports saloon that had the purists snorting into their scotch. So can a cut-down roadster version really claim to be a sports car? Having driven a nicely set-up ex-works example that doesn't give anything much away to a Healey 100 or a TR2 in its responses or performance, the author is happy to stick his head over the parapet and take a few pot-shots from the Outraged of Tunbridge Wells contingent.

In any case, the Alpine's mechanicals are no better or no worse than those of its ostensible rivals: a torquey 2.2-litre pushrod 'four', a close-ratio gearbox (initially, at least) with optional (latterly standard) overdrive, and orthodox but well-executed coil-and-wishbone suspension. Admittedly the Alpine was no lightweight, so its 80bhp

made it less sprightly than the opposition, but it was still a 90mph car. Look beyond the dodgy pedigree, look beyond the steering-column gearchange (which is actually no hardship to operate), and there's a car of real worth – and relative rarity, as only 3000 or so were made.

Sold simply as a Sunbeam, rather than as a Sunbeam-Talbot, the Alpine was inspired by a one-off roadster which rally driver and major Rootes dealer George Hartwell had built by cutting down a Sunbeam-Talbot drophead. Styling was by the famed Loewy Studios in the United States, consultants to the Rootes Group and previously responsible for styling the Sunbeam-Talbot's interior. This the Alpine inherited: indeed, from the Americanised dashboard forward the Alpine is pure

THE SUNBEAM-TALBOT

The Sunbeam-Talbot was a confected make that emerged in 1938, three years after Rootes had finished absorbing the British arm of Sunbeam-Talbot-Darracq. The first models were the Ten, which was a renamed Talbot Ten and thus a derivative of the pseudo-sporting Hillman Aero Minx, the 3-litre, which was a renamed Talbot 3-litre and therefore a dolled-up Humber Snipe, and the 4-litre, which was a 3-litre fitted with the 4086cc Humber Super Snipe engine. In September 1939 the range was completed by a 2-litre model, this essentially being a Ten fitted with a 1944cc Hillman sidevalve engine. Reintroduced after the war, the Ten and 2-litre gave way in 1948 to restyled '80' and '90' models, both built on the old 2-litre chassis. For 1951 a new chassis with independent front suspension was introduced, and the underpowered 1185cc '80' deleted. Latterly called the Sunbeam MkIII, the '90' continued in production until late 1956.

Sunbeam-Talbot MkIIA, the only departure being the louvred bonnet.

Aft of the windscreen all is different, there being removable sliding sidescreens and a long rear deck; the body was built and trimmed at Mulliners of Birmingham, as opposed to the Sunbeam-Talbot drophead, which had a Pressed Steel body trimmed at in-house Rootes coachbuilder Thrupp and Maberley.

In keeping with its sports-car pretensions, the Alpine was given a modified cylinder head, a revised carburettor and manifolding, and a more efficient exhaust, all this giving an extra 10bhp over the regular Sunbeam-Talbot models. The chassis was also improved, with a beefed-up front section and uprated front springs, while a quicker-ratio steering box was fitted.

The Alpine didn't catch on in its intended main market, the United States, but a string of competition successes made it a fine publicity tool for the Rootes Group. These in addition prompted a series of around 120 Alpine Specials, replicas of the works rally cars fitted with uprated engines and with overdrive as standard.

Although the Alpine continued to be listed until October 1955, it was never sold with the 1955 model year's porthole side vents and more prominent side grilles. This may have been a question of aesthetics, but more likely it was simply a matter of disposing of stocks of unsold obsolete-specification Alpines before calling it a day. Whatever its virtues, the car was somehow neither fish nor fowl, and that's rarely a recipe for success.

I DIDN'T KNOW THAT...

- The Alpine has a celluloid claim to fame as the automotive star of the 1955 Hitchcock film *To Catch a Thief*, starring Grace Kelly and Cary Grant. Featured is a chase sequence in which Kelly, at the wheel of the Sunbeam, is pursued by the police in a Traction Avant Citroën.
- The Alpine appropriately enough had its competition debut in the 1953 Alpine Rally. Stirling Moss took a car home to sixth position, and the team of six cars won four Coupe des Alpes awards. The same year also saw second place for an Alpine in the RAC Rally.
- In 1953 regular winner of ladies awards and Sunbeam-Talbot stalwart Sheila van Damm clocked in excess of 120mph over the flying kilometre at Jabbeke in Belgium with an Alpine. The author has fond memories of driving the same car more than 30 years later…
- If you don't like the idea of a column shift, a floor-change Hillman Hunter or Sunbeam Rapier gearbox (or similar Rootes unit) can be easily fitted. At the time, Rootes dealer Castles of Leicester offered a floor-change conversion.
- The coil-and-wishbone Sunbeam-Talbot suspension ended its days on the Commer forward-control van last made – as a Dodge – in 1983. The same somewhat unlamented light commercial also used the S-T engine, which can be traced back to a sidevalve unit first seen in a Humber in 1932.

SPECIFICATION

Engine:	2267cc water-cooled in-line 4-cyl; ohv
Power:	80bhp at 4200rpm (at 4400rpm from October 1954)
Transmission:	four-speed gearbox, optional/std overdrive on top only
Construction:	cruciform chassis, steel body
Front suspension:	independent by coil and wishbone, with anti-roll bar; telescopic dampers
Rear suspension:	live axle on semi-elliptic leaf springs; location by Panhard rod; lever-arm dampers
Steering:	worm-and-nut
Brakes:	all-drum
Kerb weight:	26.5cwt

EVOLUTION

July 1948	Sunbeam-Talbot 80 and 90 introduced
September 1950	Sunbeam-Talbot 90 MkII
September 1952	MkIIA introduced
March 1953	Sunbeam Alpine announced
October 1954	Sunbeam MkIII replaces S-T MkIIA; Alpine receives same revised 80bhp engine as MkIII, and standard overdrive
October 1955	Alpine and MkIII drophead deleted
July 1957	Last Sunbeam MkIII despatched

ABOVE The long rear deck results from the Alpine being a converted four-door saloon. The doors are equipped with removable sidescreens rather than winding windows.

BELOW The Alpine was last listed in 1955, by which time Sunbeam sales were dwindling: saloons made at the end of that year or in January 1956 were still being despatched in June and July 1957!

SUNBEAM ALPINE/TIGER

Max Speed	98mph*
0–60mph	14.9sec*

* Series III Alpine

ABOVE The Alpine retained its fins until 1964. This is a Series III car, recognisable by its doors having quarterlights; the 1592cc engine is uprated from the Series II specification.

BELOW Nowadays regarded with admiration, in their time the Le Mans Tigers were a failure: the Rootes competition manager would have rather spent the money making the Imp competitive in rallying.

The Sunbeam Alpine was the Johnny-come-lately of the British sports-car scene, arriving well after the MGA, the Triumph TR and the Austin-Healey. Rootes had no experience of sports-car manufacture, so was bound to take its time before venturing into this field. Also it was a slenderly-resourced company whose activities largely centred around two model ranges. Until it had a suitable set of components in mass-production, it could not contemplate a niche sports two-seater.

The starting-point was simple: as such a car obviously couldn't be based on the hefty Humber, it would perforce have to wait until it could be spun off from the new unitary-construction Hillmans and related Singers and Sunbeams that started to emerge in 1955. The Alpine was as a consequence designed around the short-wheelbase

floorpan of the Husky, a two-door utility estate variant of the Hillman Minx. The new car would thus be a monocoque, and to be sufficiently rigid it was necessary to add a beefy cruciform to the Husky underpan – as well as bolt-in scuttle braces under the bonnet.

Coil-and-wishbone front suspension was shared with the Minx family of cars, as was the recirculating-ball steering, the leaf-sprung rear axle, and the 1494cc engine and its matching four-speed gearbox. These components were clothed in an elegant shell styled by former Loewy Associates and Ford-US designer Kenneth Howes. Ignoring the supposed tradition that British sports cars had sidescreens and an impossible-to-erect hood, the Alpine's sleek body, with those please-the-Americans fins, incorporated wind-up windows and a neat integral hood that hid behind hinged panels. The Sunbeam might have

THE LE MANS TIGERS

The idea of Rootes taking two grunty Lister-built Tiger fastbacks to Le Mans might seem like the stuff of romance, but misty-eyed nostalgics might care to reflect that the man who campaigned the works Tigers at 1964's Le Mans, Rootes competition manager Marcus Chambers, sums the cars up quite simply as 'deplorable', and as a waste of half a year's rallying budget. The Tigers were hurriedly built and overweight, had poor roadholding and brakes, and unsatisfactory engines. One retired after three hours with piston failure and the other broke its crankshaft after nine hours, blowing up its engine in such spectacular style that the debris blocked the steering mechanism. The two cars were sold off promptly after the event, but the original development vehicle was passed to Rootes racer Bernard Unett, who was successful with it, but still described it as 'a pretty horrible car, with horrible handling'.

lacked pedigree, but it was Britain's first civilised modern sports car – and that shouldn't be forgotten.

Over its eight-year life the Alpine's mechanicals evolved little, other than progressively better engines being fitted, culminating in the last cars having 92.5bhp five-main-bearing alloy-head 1725cc power units. Aesthetically, the only change of import was the elimination of the tail fins on the Series IV model.

The Alpine was a pleasing and well-finished car with less of a sporting edge than its rivals – but with an extra dose of comfort. What it lacked was performance, but this was more than made up for by its 1964–67 stablemate the Tiger. Cooked up by the Rootes team in the States, in cahoots with racing driver Carroll Shelby, the Tiger was nothing more – or less – than an Alpine with a 4.2-litre Ford V8 and matching gearbox shoehorned under the bonnet. The only running-gear changes were a move to rack steering and the fitment of a beefier rear axle with additional location by a Panhard rod.

Pussy-cat docile if driven with decorum, the Tiger was a different matter entirely when its performance was exploited, especially in the wet: the primitive suspension simply couldn't put the power down. The last examples of this exhilarating Q-car had a 4.7-litre engine but were never officially sold in Britain.

In all, 69,251 Alpines were made, and 7067 Tigers; it seems Rootes never made a profit out of the exercise.

I DIDN'T KNOW THAT...

- Until 1962 the Alpine was built by Armstrong-Siddeley, as part of a deal that saw Armstrong design the engine – effectively a revised version of its own 'six' – for the 1958-on Humber Super Snipe.
- Rootes campaigned Alpines at Le Mans in 1961, 1962 and 1963. In the first year a Harrington-bodied car won the Index of Thermal Efficiency, in 1962 one car finished 15th overall, and in 1963 both cars retired.
- Sussex coachbuilder and Rootes dealer Harrington built three different variants of a coupé conversion of the Alpine. The most elegant was called the Le Mans, and had a full fastback and de-finned rear wings. In all roughly 450 Harringtons were built, of which approximately 250 were of the Le Mans model; all but a handful were based on the SII or SIII Alpines.
- The Tiger was assembled by Jensen, using Alpine bodies supplied painted and trimmed by Pressed Steel. Part of the procedure was dressing back the bulkhead – in other words bashing it with a large hammer so that it would clear the engine.
- The Tiger had a brief rallying career. High points were a fourth place in the 1965 Monte and victory in the same year's International Police Rally.
- Only 533 of the 4.7-litre (289cu in) Tiger IIs were built, between December 1966 and June 1967; they are identifiable by their egg-crate grille and by go-faster stripes in place of the Tiger I's chrome waist strip. It is understood that about 27 stayed in the UK.

SPECIFICATION

Engine:	1494cc/1592cc/1725cc water-cooled in-line 4-cyl, ohv (Alpine); 4261cc/4727cc water-cooled V8, ohv (Tiger)
Power:	78bhp at 4600rpm (SI)/80bhp at 5000rpm (SII)/82bhp at 5200rpm (SIII)/80.5bhp at 5000rpm (SIV)/92.5bhp at 5500rpm (SV); 136bhp at 4200rpm/174bhp at 4400rpm (Tiger)
Transmission:	four-speed gearbox; optional overdrive on Alpine
Construction:	steel monocoque
Front suspension:	independent coil-and-wishbone; anti-roll bar; telescopic dampers
Rear suspension:	underslung live axle with leaf springs; Panhard rod (Tiger); lever-arm (SI/SII) or telescopic dampers (SIII-V and Tiger)
Steering:	recirculating ball (Alpine); rack-and-pinion (Tiger)
Brakes:	front discs and rear drum; servo on SIII-V Alpines and Tiger
Kerb weight:	20cwt (SIII)

EVOLUTION

August 1959	Series I Alpine introduced
October 1960	Series II Alpine – 1592cc
March 1963	Series III Alpine – uprated engine
January 1964	Series IV Alpine – fins cropped
March 1964	Tiger introduced
September 1965	Series V Alpine – 1725cc engine
End 1966	Tiger MkII (289ci) production begins
June 1967	Tiger production ends
January 1968	Last Alpine

BELOW The egg-crate grille identifies this Tiger as a MkII; most subsequent owners have removed the cheapskate 'ape tape' MkII stripes from the lower body of their car.

SWALLOW DORETTI

Max Speed	97mph
0–60mph	13.4sec

ABOVE With its longer wheelbase and 3in wider front track, the Doretti is less stubby than the TR2 whose mechanicals it borrows. The doors have sidescreens rather than winding windows.

BELOW This MkII Doretti originally had a restyled front to match its more voluminous rear, but received a regular front end after an accident; only three of these revised cars were built.

The Swallow Doretti was in production for barely a year, and only 274 cars were made. It's tempting to assume, therefore, that it was just another half-baked parts-bin special, almost certainly made by an some tinpot company that duly collapsed when the money ran out. In fact the Doretti was an intelligently designed vehicle made by an offshoot of one of Britain's more important manufacturing businesses, and it was selling well when it was discontinued.

The Doretti was the fruit of a collaboration between three men. Arthur Andersen ran a Californian company making thin-wall tubing, and with his daughter Dorothy Deen sold sports-car accessories through their firm Cal Specialties; to add European glamour the brand Doretti was created by italianising Dorothy's name. Andersen and Deen were keen to start selling British sports cars.

Eric Sanders, meanwhile, was boss of Helliwell, a subsidiary of British tubing specialist Tube Investments that also had under its wing the Swallow Coachbuilding Company; this was the sidecar-making enterprise out of which Jaguar had grown, and had been sold on by William Lyons in 1944. Sanders and Andersen clearly had interests in common and soon established friendly relations.

Completing the trio of collaborators was Standard-Triumph chief Sir John Black, a close friend of Eric Sanders. He was just putting the Triumph TR2 into production, and had always followed a policy of making Standard-Triumph parts available to other manufacturers. The three men agreed in late 1952 that Black would supply TR components for a car to be made by Swallow, and marketed alongside the TR in the western states of the US by two new subsidiaries of Cal Specialties.

DOROTHY DEEN

Dorothy Deen – she kept the name of her first husband, whom she divorced in 1950 – inherited father Arthur Andersen's love of machinery. The enthusiastic owner of an MG TD, when she couldn't find the bolt-on goodies she wanted she set up Cal Specialties with her father. With the expansion into distributing Triumphs and the Doretti in all states west of the Mississippi, Deen became the only woman running a US car-distribution business. Advertising talked this up, to the point where she was quite incorrectly described as the designer of the Doretti. In essence it was Deen who made Triumph a success in the west, and her influence extended to getting Triumph to change its TR3A colour schemes to more sporting shades. When Triumph took over its own distribution in 1960, Deen moved into the aviation business and latterly into the legal profession. In 1991 she married motoring historian Jim Sitz.

The resultant Swallow Doretti used TR2 running gear in its entirety, with the addition of radius arms bars to the back axle. The chassis, however, was particular to the Doretti, and used a mix of square and round tube; a wheelbase 7in longer meant that in effect the engine was positioned 7in further back, which improved handling. Clothing these mechanicals was a simple but inoffensive aluminium body, built – by Panelcraft of Birmingham – on a substantial steel under-structure. The prototype was finished by the end of summer 1953, and US sales started at the beginning of 1954 – fast going by any standard.

The Doretti was heavier than the TR, more expensive, less spacious, and had a useless boot. But that didn't deter moneyed West-Coasters, and sales were soon running at almost a car a day. In any case, a MkII Doretti was being developed, with a bigger cockpit and a more acceptable boot; a related coupé was also in prospect.

But in February 1955, production stopped. What had happened? Quite simply, TI was leant upon by some of those in the motor industry whom it supplied with steel – including Jaguar. It seems it was suggested that if it carried on making a car in competition with their products, then they might well be inclined to look to other suppliers for their steel. And so ended a brave little venture.

I DIDN'T KNOW THAT...

- The Doretti was the work of Swallow engineer Frank Rainbow, who had previously created the Swallow Gadabout scooter for the company.
- A key component of the Doretti chassis was Reynolds 531 chrome-moly tubing – beloved of generations of cyclists whose racing bikes had '531' frames.
- It was in his personal Doretti, driven by Triumph development engineer Ken Richardson, that Sir John Black was involved in an accident outside the Standard-Triumph works, breaking an arm. Although his injuries were not serious, they were given as the reason for Black's departure after he was ousted in a boardroom coup in January 1954.
- Black closely followed the Doretti project, regularly asking Richardson for his opinion on the car; Richardson also carried out some development testing.
- Because boot space in the Doretti was minimal, Cal Sales Inc offered a fitted suitcase for stowage behind the seats.
- Three MkII (or 'Sabre') Dorettis were built – two convertibles and a single coupé. One of the convertibles was at one stage fitted with a de Dion back axle and was owned by Standard-Triumph.
- Peter Kirwan-Taylor, the amateur stylist who came up with the basic shape of the Lotus Elite, designed a fastback coupé rear for his Doretti.
- Legendary Californian racer Max Balchowsky, famous for his Ol' Yaller special, re-engined six Dorettis with American V8s. Four had Buick engines, one a Cadillac unit, and one a small-block Chevy. This last disposed of approaching 300bhp, and weight was up by only 40lb.

LEFT The simple front uses Austin-Healey bumpers. Road behaviour of the Doretti is good – and probably better than that of the TR2 – while performance is only marginally inferior.

SPECIFICATION

Engine:	1991cc four-cyl water-cooled; ohv
Power:	90bhp at 4800rpm
Transmission:	four-speed gearbox; optional overdrive
Construction:	separate chassis, steel body understructure, aluminium panels
Front suspension:	independent by coil-and-wishbone; telescopic dampers
Rear suspension:	underslung live axle with leaf springs; radius arms; lever-arm dampers
Steering:	cam-and-peg
Brakes:	all-drum
Kerb weight:	19.25cwt

EVOLUTION

January 1953	Design work begins
October 1953	First production Doretti completed
January 1954	Launch of Doretti in Los Angeles
February 1955	Production stops

BELOW Again, the rear bumpers are Austin-Healey items; the boot is not generous, but then few sports cars of the era had much luggage space. The dashboard uses TR dials.

TRIUMPH GLORIA SOUTHERN CROSS

Max Speed	81.8mph*
0–60mph	19sec*
	* 6-cyl

ABOVE This Southern Cross is a four-cylinder car, as opposed to the shortlived six-cylinder 2-litre variant, and the author still has fond memories of a day behind its wheel.

BELOW The straight-eight Dolomite was inspired by the 8C-2300 Alfa Romeo. Triumph and Alfa discussed a possible joint venture, and there was even talk of the Italians building Triumph motorcycles.

For a company latterly best known for its sports cars, it's perhaps a surprise to realise that Triumph had no great tradition of such vehicles before the TR came along. In fact the only serious contender for the label, the Gloria Southern Cross, had a life of a mere two years.

Before the Gloria range came along in 1933 the company was making pretty undistinguished stodge. But for the 1934 model year the inlet-over-exhaust Coventry Climax engines that Triumph used were transplanted into a new cruciform chassis, together with a basket of mechanical and body components bought in from well-known proprietary suppliers in the Midlands.

The new Gloria was an assembly job – but it was a good one: the chassis was underslung, the 'crash' gearbox had a freewheel to aid gearchanging, there were meaty 12in hydraulic brakes, and – perhaps most importantly of all –

the cars had a well-contrived elegance of line. Not for nothing did Triumph's advertising people come up with the slogan 'The Smartest Cars in the Land'.

It was for the 1935 model year that the Southern Cross arrived, as a short-wheelbase two-seater sister car to the sporting four-seat Monte Carlo tourer. Sharing the Monte Carlo's exposed slab tank and twin rear spare wheels, it was offered in 1087cc 9.5hp form to suit under-1100cc competition classes as well as in 1232cc 10.8hp and six-cylinder 1991cc Vitesse formats – the Vitesse tag indicating a hotter camshaft, bigger valves, a modified high-compression cylinder head, and a more efficient twin-carb installation. These mods translated into an output of 50bhp for the 10.8hp Southern Cross and 65bhp for the 'six'.

The result of these endeavours was a delicious-looking flowingly-winged sports car that must have been every

THE DOLOMITE STRAIGHT-EIGHT

The first Dolomite was nothing less than a chinese copy of the 2.3-litre straight-eight Alfa Romeo. The idea of an ultra-fast super-sports model was cooked up by Donald Healey. Finding the Alfa the best of the breed, he had Triumph buy an 8C-2300, take it to bits, and copy it. Latterly he approached Alfa, who gave authorisation and even discussed calling the car the Triumph-Alfa. Although the initial engine was pure 8C, albeit reduced to 1990cc, the chassis was a Triumph design, as was the Alfa-like body. Completed in 1934, the prototype was entered by Healey in the 1935 Monte, but hit a train; rebuilt with a 2.5-litre engine and the supercharger removed, Healey drove it to eighth place in the 1936 event. Only two other chassis were laid down, of which only one may have been built into a complete vehicle, and in 1936 cars and parts were sold as a job-lot.

1930s boy-racer's dream. From the slight rake of the stoneguard-adorned radiator to the twin spares, there wasn't a detail that didn't make the Triumph a little bit special: big Lucas headlamps, twin aeroscreens, paired rear numberplates, quick-release filler cap, fuel-tank stoneguards, a stylish tripod-type chrome retaining strap for the spare wheels…

The six-cylinder Southern Cross only lasted a year, being deleted from the 1936 range along with the Monte Carlo, and so is a real rarity today; the two 'fours' continued for a further season, however, before Triumph switched its attention to the bigger, flashier and less sporting Dolomite range, with its stunning waterfall grille.

The four-cylinder Southern Cross was a sports car of real distinction, a clear cut above such cheaper competition as the last of the ohc MGs, and driving one today is a real pleasure. The gearchange is snappy, and easy to operate even for amateur double-declutchers (and even easier if you wind the freewheel in), the performance is adequately brisk in a surprisingly robust way, and secure and accurate cornering is matched by effective brakes. The steering could be sharper (maybe a flaw of the particular car the author sampled), and the ride is lively, but the overall feel is of a friendly high-quality motor car, less instant than one of the MGs, but more carved-from-the-solid.

I DIDN'T KNOW THAT...

- Although a Coventry Climax design, the inlet-over-exhaust power units of the Southern Cross were built by Triumph from castings supplied by Coventry Climax. They had cooling deficiencies and tended to burn out their exhaust valves, and were consequently revised into ohv format by Triumph for the new 1937 model-year cars.
- Doing much to boost Triumph's credentials was a much-publicised third place in the 1934 Monte Carlo by Donald Healey, who was recruited to Triumph in 1933 as experimental manager but soon became the company's technical director. Although his performance was billed as being achieved by a Gloria, the car used was in fact a hybrid. It combined a tuned IoE 'four' with the chassis of a pre-Gloria Southern Cross, the whole perched on huge tyres and topped with a modified Monte Carlo tourer body.
- In the following year's event a Gloria Monte Carlo much closer to the real thing came in second overall and first in the Light Car class.
- MG historian Wilson McComb briefly owned one of the 1934 Monte Carlo Rally hybrids in the 1950s – only he thought it was a Rover, as it had been given a Rover engine and radiator.
- The evolution of the Triumph range in the 1930s is massively complicated, with a huge variety of different models. This is one of the reasons why the firm went into receivership in 1939. The company was bought as a going concern by steelmaker Thomas Ward, who sold it on to Standard in 1944.

LEFT The cockpit of the Southern Cross; beside the snappy remote-change gearlever is the knob for the freewheel, which ensures crunch-free gearchanging when engaged.

SPECIFICATION

Engine:	1087cc/1232cc/1991cc water-cooled in-line 4-cyl/6-cyl; IoE
Power:	46bhp at 4600rpm/50bhp at 5000rpm/65bhp at 4750rpm
Transmission:	four-speed gearbox, unsynchronised ('silent third'), with freewheel; option of Warren Synchroniser for 1936
Construction:	cruciform underslung chassis, wood body frame, aluminium panels except bonnet and wings
Front suspension:	beam axle and semi-elliptic leaf springs; lever-arm dampers
Rear suspension:	live axle on leaf springs; lever-arm dampers
Steering:	worm-and-nut
Brakes:	all-drum, hydraulic
Kerb weight:	21.75cwt (6-cyl)

EVOLUTION

October 1933	Gloria range announced
January 1934	Monte Carlo sports tourers introduced
October 1934	Southern Cross joins range. Special/Speed appellations replaced by Vitesse. Chassis and engine improvements
October 1935	Monte Carlo and 6-cyl Southern Cross models deleted
October 1936	New ohv range; Southern Cross remains listed until stocks exhausted

BELOW The paired rear numberplates were dubbed 'Continental' and are accompanied by a flamboyant three-armed clamp for the spare wheel; the indicators are a modern addition.

TRIUMPH TR2-TR3A

Max Speed 102mph*
0–60mph 12.5sec*
* TR3

ABOVE The 'dollar grin' grille identifies a TR3A; mechanically the cars changed little over the years. The cutaway-door TRs received a lot of hand-finishing to make panels fit, and body restoration is not easy.

RIGHT Deliciously elegant, the Italia was intended to be sold only in Europe but some cars made it to the United States. Its styling is clearly related to that of the TR4, also by Michelotti.

The original TR is testimony to the value of a good development engineer – because the starting point was a design calamity of the highest order. Standard-Triumph boss Sir John Black was determined to have a slice of the US sports-car market so lucratively being milked by MG and Jaguar. Having been politely rebuffed in an attempt to buy Morgan, in early 1952 he ordered his engineers to come up with a suitable Triumph sports car in time for the 1952 Motor Show – which by this time was only a matter of months away.

The result was an ugly little pug of a car cobbled together in eight weeks from whatever parts were available: a Standard Vanguard engine and gearbox, Triumph Mayflower front suspension and rear axle, and a chassis based on that of the 1936 Standard Nine...as a stock of these had been unearthed in the bowels of the

Standard factory. This unholy mish-mash was never going to be a competitor to the elegant Healey 100 unveiled at the same show; more to the point the car drove like a pig. Having given his forthright opinion, former BRM test-driver Ken Richardson was drafted in as development engineer to supervise a complete redesign. All the mechanicals were revised, a new chassis was drawn up, and the body was restyled to eliminate the prototype's stubby tail with its exposed rear wheel. Unveiled at the 1953 Geneva show, this was the definitive TR2, and to efface all memory of the original, Richardson took a prototype to Jabbeke, achieving a much-publicised 124.9mph maximum down this celebrated stretch of Belgian motorway.

Triumph had a winner. The TR2 was more modern than the T-type MG, but with its cutaway doors still had something of the MG's traditional appeal; it lacked the

THE TRIUMPH ITALIA 2000

The Michelotti-styled 1959–62 Italia was first seen on the Vignale stand at the 1958 Turin show, sporting an unusual 'droop-snoot' front. A more orthodox nose was evolved, and the 1960 Turin show saw the definitive version, with a squared-off boot. The Italian Standard-Triumph distributor contracted Vignale to produce the car, and there was talk of 500 being produced in the following year, for sale purely in the European Free Trade Area: Europe-based Americans had to sign a form saying they understood that no body parts would be stocked outside Italy. Despite this, attempts were made to sell the Italia in the States, but buyers were hard to find. They were hard to find in Europe, too, and in 1961 a batch of 30-odd unsold Italias was shipped to the US by Standard-Triumph; the last US cars were registered as late as 1965. It is thought 329 Italias were made.

elegance of the Healey but was cheaper and barely any less fast. Ruggedly indestructible, deep-chestedly torquey in performance and surprisingly economical, the nicely-trimmed TR was both a seductive boulevardier for fashionable Americans and a successful race and rally car. That fast driving, especially on the tyres of the time, demanded a degree of commitment was neither here nor there: the TR was just the right recipe for the era, and re-established the Triumph name.

Unsurprisingly, the changes over the years were few. The TR3 of 1955 was essentially a cosmetic facelift, bringing in an uprated engine and an eggbox grille, and the TR3A of 1959 was again basically a new grille and little else. The only improvement of significance was the arrival of disc front brakes for 1957, the TR being one of the world's first cars to be so equipped.

Despite sales having fallen off, and despite the new TR4 being a much more civilised vehicle, the original TR was regarded by the US Triumph importers as still having a market, and a final run of cars was made during 1962, after the launch of the TR4. Unofficially known as the TR3B, all but 530 of the 3331 made used the 2138cc engine and all-synchro gearbox of the TR4. This took total output of the TR2/3 family to 83,656 units.

I DIDN'T KNOW THAT...

■ Early TR2s had deeper doors, but from October 1954 they were shortened and external sills fitted – the original 'long' doors fouled high kerbs.

■ The TR was one of the most popular cars in national and international rallying, and had many successes to its name. Famous drivers included Paddy Hopkirk and the inventor of the 'Gatso' speed camera, Maurice Gatsonides.

■ Triumph entered three special TRs in 1959's Le Mans. Carrying glassfibre bodywork and built on a longer wheelbase, the cars looked superficially like TR3As but ran a new part-aluminium twin-cam engine. Developing 150bhp or so, this exciting power unit had oddly bulbous front cam-covers and was soon nicknamed 'Sabrina', after a certain well-endowed TV starlet. Overweight and under-developed, the three cars – known as the TR3S – all failed to finish the event.

■ The TR engine was used in the Morgan Plus 4 (which had begun life with the Vanguard engine) and in the Peerless – latterly the Warwick – glassfibre-bodied GT of the 1957–62 period.

■ With work on a new TR caught up in Standard-Triumph's growing cash crisis of 1960–61, thought was given to canning (or at least postponing) the putative TR4 and instead bringing out a revised TR3A with the TR4's wider-track chassis and rack-and-pinion steering. Two such cars, known as the TR3 Beta, were produced, their body having the wings pulled out to clear the wider track.

■ Several hundred TR2s and TR3s were assembled by Imperia in Belgium, and these included 22 fixed-head coupé TR2s called the Francorchamps.

LEFT The TR interior (here a TR2) is nicely presented, and has the virtue of a decent luggage platform behind the seats; the handbrake is of the fly-off type, whereby you lift the lever to release the brake.

SPECIFICATION

Engine:	1991cc/2138cc four-cyl water-cooled; ohv
Power:	90bhp/95bhp at 4800rpm/100bhp at 5000rpm/100bhp at 4600rpm
Transmission:	four-speed gearbox; optional overdrive
Construction:	separate chassis, steel body
Front suspension:	independent coil-and-wishbone; telescopic dampers
Rear suspension:	underslung live axle with leaf springs; lever-arm dampers
Steering:	cam-and-peg
Brakes:	all-drum
Kerb weight:	22cwt (TR3)

EVOLUTION

October 1952	Triumph 20TS shown at Earls Court
March 1953	TR2 unveiled
July 1953	Production starts
October 1954	Short doors introduced
October 1955	TR3 introduced: new grille, 95bhp engine
October 1956	Front disc brakes standard; 100bhp engine
October 1957	TR3A announced
September 1961	TR4 launched
March 1962	TR3B introduced, for US only
December 1962	Last TR3B

BELOW This TR2 sits on non-standard wide-rim wire wheels. Note how the spare wheel is kept in its own compartment. Separate orange flashing indicators only came in with the TR3A.

TRIUMPH TR4-TR6

Max Speed	109mph*
0–60mph	11.4sec*
	* TR4A

ABOVE The TR6 shell retains the centre section of the TR4-4A-5 Michelotti body, with a new front and rear designed and tooled by Karmann; early 150bhp cars achieved 119mph and a 0–60mph time of 8.2 seconds.

BELOW The Dové cost 30 per cent more than a hardtop TR4; Triumph thought sufficiently of the quality of the conversion to allow full factory warranty. Roughly 25 are believed to survive.

The second-generation TRs are the perfect example of an intelligently modernised product evolving steadily and unspectacularly, without losing its essential character.

The process began with the TR4 of 1961, which retained the sturdy mechanicals of preceding TRs while adding a civilised and more spacious winding-window body, elegantly Michelotti-styled. The engine was a little bigger, at 2138cc, and there was now synchromesh on first gear, but otherwise the only mechanical changes were a wider track and the addition of more precise rack-and-pinion steering. A clever feature was an optional 'Surrey top', a two-piece hardtop with a removable roof section.

Although the TR4 handled well, in a somewhat elemental way, it never rode with any refinement, and in 1965 a revised chassis was introduced, incorporating the semi-trailing-arm independent rear of the Triumph 2000. The resultant TR4A was recognisable by its wooden dashboard (also on the very last TR4s) and by unusual indicator/sidelight units incorporated in the new chrome side-strip. Not for the first time, the Americans then put a spanner in the works, one importer saying it was quite happy with the old rigid axle; accordingly a special US-only TR4A was made, with the chassis adapted to take a live axle on leaf springs...

Even if the new IRS was a bit of a cobble-up, it made the TR a more comfortable car, with marginally better roadholding; but it also added weight, highlighting the performance fall-off since the days of the TR2. The answer was to drop in a fuel-injected 2.5-litre version of the

THE DOVÉ GTR4

Before the MGB GT, the idea of a modestly-priced British 2+2 never quite took off; such cars were either from specialist manufacturers or were pricey conversions of existing sports cars. The Dové GTR4 is an example of the latter, being the work of Hove-based Harrington's – better known for its similar adaptations of the Sunbeam Alpine. Built on behalf of Wimbledon dealer LF Dove, the Dové – the accute accent was a bogus-French affectation – had a glassfibre rear with lift-up tailgate and a miniature rear seat with a fold-down back (complete with centre armrest). Optional was a tuned engine, and this doubtless helped put back the performance eroded by the extra 4cwt kerb weight over a regular TR4. The snag, though, was that a Dové cost a third as much again as a regular TR4; it is thought 50–80 cars were converted, including a few TR4As and a solitary TR5.

Triumph 'six' to create the TR5. The TR now had smooth and muscular performance but was arguably starting to look old-fashioned; consequently the TR5 turned out to be little more than a stop-gap, being replaced barely a year after its autumn 1967 introduction.

The new TR6, announced in January 1969, was developed in haste, on a small budget, and consisted of nothing more than restyled front and rear panelwork married to an unchanged centre section. Carried out by Karmann in Germany, it was an effective facelift, giving the TR a visual strength to go with its robust manners on the road. From this point on the TR6 was only changed in detail. There was however one important and unheralded modification: in early 1973 the engine was slyly de-rated to 125bhp in a bid to make the injected power unit easier to keep in tune.

The Lucas mechanical injection was in fact always something of a liability, and rarely gave owners complete satisfaction. Not only that, but despite its supposed efficiency Triumph found itself incapable of setting it up to meet US emission requirements – or so the story goes. As a result, all US-market TR5s and TR6s ran on twin Stromberg carburettors – more reliable, no doubt, but reducing power, on the last TR6s, to a weedy 106bhp. Even thus emasculated, the TR6 had an endearing Old-English-Sheepdog character: with its beefy power and unsophisticated chassis it was truly the last 'trad' British sports car.

I DIDN'T KNOW THAT...

- The TR4 was preceded by another set of racers powered by the 'Sabrina' twin-cam. Known as the TRS, these cars had TR4-like bodies in glassfibre, and ran at Le Mans in 1960 and 1961. In both events all the cars finished, and in 1961 the Triumphs came home ninth (and highest-placed British car), eleventh and fifteenth – sufficient to win the manufacturers' prize.
- It was intended to use a detuned 'Sabrina' engine in the TR4, but with Triumph in financial difficulty such extravagances inevitably had to be shelved.
- An extraordinary later TR was the TR250K – or the 'K-car'. Styled by Pete Brock, responsible for the lines of the AC Daytona Cobras, it was a slick wedge-shaped roadster created at the behest of 'Kas' Kastner, Standard-Triumph's US competitions manager. Intended as a publicity exercise, the TR250K was completed in 1968 and entered in that year's Sebring 12-hour race – retiring after a wheel failed. BL never capitalised on the car's publicity value, and it ended up in a museum.
- The US-market carburettor-fed TR5 was called the TR250 and was distinguished by a striped band across the nose. Despite being slower than the TR4A, in all 8484 were sold, compared with 2947 injected TR5s. Only 1200 or so TR5s stayed in the UK, making it the rarest of the TR series in its home country.
- The Federal TR6 met US bumper regulations without the need for a restyle, but later cars had huge rubber over-riders to comply with American legislation.

SPECIFICATION

Engine:	2138cc water-cooled in-line 4-cyl; ohv/2498cc water-cooled in-line 6-cyl; ohv (TR5-6)
Power:	100bhp at 4600rpm (TR4/4A)/150bhp at 5500rpm (TR5 and early TR6)/125bhp (DIN) at 5500rpm (later TR6)
Transmission:	four-speed gearbox; optional overdrive
Construction:	separate chassis, steel body
Front suspension:	independent coil-and-wishbone; telescopic dampers
Rear suspension:	underslung live axle with leaf springs; lever-arm dampers (TR4); independent with semi-trailing arms and coil springs; lever-arm dampers (TR4A-5-6)
Steering:	rack-and-pinion
Brakes:	front discs and rear drum; servo on TR5 and TR6
Kerb weight:	21.0cwt (TR4A); 22.1cwt (TR6)

EVOLUTION

September 1961	TR4 introduced
March 1965	TR4A replaces TR4
September 1967	TR5 announced
January 1969	TR6 replaces TR5
Early 1973	TR6 power reduced to 125bhp
February 1975	TR6 no longer UK-available
July 1976	Last TR6 built

BELOW The TR4 has a simple pressed aluminium grille, and lacks the bulky sidelight and indicator repeater units of the TR4A and TR5; inside, on all but the final cars, is a painted-metal dashboard.

TRIUMPH TR7

Max Speed 114mph*
0–60mph 10.7sec*

* TR7 convertible

ABOVE The convertible arrived too late to save the TR7. Canley-built cars have a wreath badge in sticker form, while Solihull cars have a black enamel-style badge: an easy identification point.

BELOW The Lynx wasn't wanted by the Americans; those who tell you it could have made the TR7 project viable are kidding themselves. This surviving car signally failed to impress the author when he drove it.

It's difficult to write about the TR7 without offending enthusiasts of the model. But let's not hide the truth behind weasel words. The TR7 was ugly, it was shoddily assembled and unreliable for much of its life, and it was a commercial catastrophe. Arguably, it should never have been produced. That said, when it came to driving the TR7, it was not a bad car at all. Indeed, it had the best roadholding-handling-ride combination of any Triumph sports car; it also had more than adequate performance, especially in V8 form.

The TR7 was intended to be BL's new corporate sports car, replacing both the TR6 and the MGB – the latter either directly or by means of an MG version. There was a logic behind this, although whether the men at the helm of BL should have looked beyond their Triumph loyalties and instead backed the better-selling and better-regarded

Abingdon marque is another question. The fact remains, though, that this policy was seen as justifying the establishment of a dedicated sports-car assembly plant at Speke, in Liverpool, to produce the new model in unprecedentedly large – and frankly unrealistic – numbers.

The TR7 therefore had to be right. It wasn't. Having pushed aside more staid in-house proposals, management backed a flashy wedge design created by Austin-Morris stylist Harris Mann. By the time this had been adapted for production, and given the bulky impact bumpers required by American legislation, it looked both contrived and ungainly. Not helping matters, fears that convertibles would be outlawed in the US saw it launched only as a fixed-head – without even the removable roof panels of previous prototypes; when the threatened ban on soft-tops never

THE TRIUMPH LYNX

The Lynx was an integral part of plans for the TR7 range, and was at one stage intended to represent 30 per cent of Speke's output. But although prototypes were built and at least some tooling completed, the Lynx never reached production. Built on a wheelbase extended by 11in, the Lynx was a 2+2 with a lift-up tailgate, and was powered by the Rover V8. It is often said that but for the closure of Speke the Lynx would have gone into production, but in fact it was a firm thumbs-down from BL's top marketing man in the States that signed its death warrant. BL looked at using the longer doors of the Lynx – and its scalloped side treatment – in a revised longer-wheelbase TR7, and convertible and 2+2 coupé prototypes were built, under the 'Broadside' codename; before anything could come of these the TR7 was discontinued.

happened, BL was saddled with a closed car in a market where the demand was still for convertibles.

At least the mechanicals chosen by BL were perfectly adequate, with a strut front, a well-controlled live axle on long-travel coil springs, and an eight-valve 1998cc version of the Triumph Dolomite engine. But it took too long to make a five-speed gearbox available, and mechanical reliability was as patchy as build quality. Also delayed was the V8 version that had always been planned, and which eventually only arrived in 1980 – and then only for the US market. Meanwhile, production had plummeted, the strike-torn Speke factory had been closed, and TR7 production had been shunted first to Triumph's Canley factory and then to Rover's Solihull plant – an industrial and logistical nightmare. The arrival of a full convertible TR7 in 1980 was too late to save the TR, even though in V8-powered TR8 form it was deservedly well-received in the States.

The end came the following year, when a desperately retrenching BL simply couldn't sustain the increased losses incurred on the TR as a result of an unfavourable pound-to-dollar exchange rate. The car has never made any money, and one telling figure merits being shared: planned production of the TR7 and its intended derivatives was 84,000 in the first full year, yet over the TR7's troubled six-year life BL made only 115,000 cars.

I DIDN'T KNOW THAT...

- There was intended to be a version of the TR7 powered by the 16-valve Dolomite Sprint engine, but this was another casualty of the Speke closure.
- The five-speed TR7 also used the stronger Rover SD1 back axle.
- The TR7 was campaigned by BL in rallies in both four-cylinder and V8 forms, with an embarrassing lack of success.
- The Californian version of the TR8 had fuel injection from the start, and all US versions were injected for the 1981 model year. Power steering was standard.
- There was never a catalogued TR8 fixed-head, although a substantial number of cars – one source says 145 – were built just before Speke closed, and ended up as development/demonstration cars in the States.
- After the decision had been taken to close the MG factory at Abingdon, there were hasty attempts to confect an MG version of the TR7 – at limited cost. Thankfully nothing came of these proposed cheapskate tart-ups, one of which was by Panther creator Robert Jankel.
- The TR8 convertible was ready to be announced on the UK market when the decision to end TR7/8 production was taken, and the first examples had already left the Solihull lines. It is thought that 36 such cars were made.
- Of the total TR7/8 productions of 115,090 – or 114,512, according to a different statistical breakdown – figures suggest that only 2715 were TR8s. As all but a handful went to the States, many enthusiasts have converted TR7s to V8 power; kits are readily available.

SPECIFICATION

Engine:	1998cc water-cooled in-line ohc 4-cyl; alloy head (TR7); 3528cc all-alloy ohv V8 (TR8)
Power:	105bhp at 5500rpm/137bhp at 5000rpm (1981 injected TR8)
Transmission:	four-speed or five-speed gearbox; automatic optional
Construction:	all-steel monocoque
Front suspension:	independent by strut; anti-roll bar
Rear suspension:	live back axle and coil springs; four-link location; anti-roll-bar; telescopic dampers
Steering:	rack-and-pinion (power-assisted on TR8)
Brakes:	front discs and rear drums; servo
Kerb weight:	21.1cwt (TR7 convertible)

EVOLUTION

January 1975	TR7 announced
May 1976	UK launch
September 1976	Five-speed gearbox standard for US; optional for UK. Automatic option introduced
December 1976	Five-speed gearbox no longer available in UK
March 1977	Silver wheel trims; plaid interior; optional sunroof
October 1977	Five-speed gearbox option reintroduced for UK. Sixteen-week strike begins at Speke
May 1978	Last Speke-built cars
October 1978	Production restarts at Canley; five-speed gearbox standard
July 1979	Convertible announced
March 1980	Convertible available in UK
May 1980	TR8 convertible launched in US
Mid-1980	Production starts at Solihull
October 1981	TR7 and TR8 discontinued

BELOW The TR7/TR8 cockpit – strictly a two-seater – is well designed and comfortable if not particularly sporting; a leather-rim Moto-Lita steering wheel is fitted to the TR8.

TRIUMPH SPITFIRE

Max Speed   95mph*
0–60mph   14.5sec*
* MkIII

ABOVE The MkIII has the same body as the MkI and MkII, but with the bumpers raised. Wire wheels were a popular option, as was overdrive – the latter feature never being available on the Spridget.

BELOW The 'square-tail' restyle works well on the MkIII GT6. From February 1973 the revised rear with its Rotoflex rubber couplings was replaced by the cheaper Spitfire MkIV swing-spring.

The Spitfire was Triumph's riposte to the Sprite, and similarly was based on mass-production components – in this case those of the Herald. Thus underneath the body – styled by Michelotti – is a cut-down Herald backbone chassis, shorn of its outriggers. Having this minimal frame, the strength of the car is in its bulkhead and in the substantial sill structure.

Introduced in 1962, with an 1147cc engine, the Spitfire brought a new level of civilisation to the small sports car, having wind-up windows and a more spacious cockpit: it's no secret that its imminent arrival was a key reason the Sprite was updated in 1961 and given a separate boot. But if the Triumph scored with its better comfort, it lacked the razor-sharp responses of the Sprite-Midget duo; worse, the crude swing-axle rear suspension, if provoked, could lead to

worrying instability if the car were cornered over-exuberantly. Not for nothing did wags coin the rejoinder 'Hark the Herald axles swing'.

Over the years the Spitfire was steadily improved. A wood instrument panel, a better hood and a 1296cc engine arrived with the 1965 MkIII, recognisable by its raised front bumper, while overdrive was available from the 1964 model year. The biggest change came in late 1970, when the car was restyled into a sleek square-tailed form and given improved rear suspension. In this form the car continued until 1980, with a 1500cc engine standardised from late 1974.

Pity, though, the poor Americans, who saw power of the de-toxed 1300 engine plummet to a miserable 48bhp by 1972. This led to the earlier fitment of the 1500 engine

THE TRIUMPH GT6

You could say that the GT6 is nothing more than a Spitfire with a fastback roof and a six-cylinder engine. That's certainly true of the original GT6 of 1966 – give or take a full-width wood-veneer dashboard and some rally-style seats. But that was the car's undoing, as the rear suspension was also nothing more than that of a Spitfire – and the crude swing axles weren't capable of coping with the 95bhp of straight-six in the GT6's elegantly power-bulged nose. Triumph's would-be mini-E-type was consequently slated for its potentially dangerous handling. This prompted a clever redesign for 1969 that gave the GT6 what was in effect a double-wishbone rear. Lightly titivated at the same time, the GT6 MkII was genuinely transformed – a prelude to it adopting the flat-tail restyle of the MkIV Spitfire for 1971. But sales never picked up, and the car was deleted at the end of 1973.

for the US market, from the 1973 model year, but even then only 57bhp was squeezed from the bigger unit – and that figure fell in subsequent years.

For many years it was fashionable to sneer at the Spitfire as not being a 'real' sports car – whatever that means. That's poppycock. Yes, you have to treat early cars with caution when cornering fast – although a few simple modifications will make the car less wayward. In compensation, the Triumph is a more comfortable and better equipped car than the Spridgets, and has more room for people and their goods; add the option of overdrive, unavailable on the BMC cars, and you have a car that is arguably a better proposition for touring, thanks to the relaxed cruising – and better economy – the overdrive offers. A further bonus is the availability of an attractive hardtop.

The foregoing is true to a greater extent with the 'square-tail' cars, which are genuinely civilised sports cars and which are blessed with much improved roadholding. The 1500 is more sought-after, but the 1300 MkIV has a sweeter and more durable engine, making it a cannier purchase at the slightly lower prices it commands. Whereas the final Midgets were manifestly well past their sell-by date, the Spitfire 1500 was still highly rated in its last years, having matured into a thoroughly competent little sports car, well-appointed, agreeably swift, and blessed with fail-safe handling.

I DIDN'T KNOW THAT...

- The Spitfire was campaigned at Le Mans in 1964 and 1965, one car coming home 21st – and third in class – in the '64 event and two cars finishing 13th and 14th – and first and second in class – in 1965. In both years the cars wore GT6-style fastback bodywork. The small Triumph was also briefly rallied, and managed a few class wins.
- A one-off single-seater open racer was built for the Hong Kong importer, who wanted to compete with it in the Macau GP. The so-called 'Macau Spitfire' was later given GT6 mechanicals.
- The MkIV style of full-width dashboard was first seen on the 1969 model-year US-market MkIII. Another mid-run detail change was that for 1970 cars for all markets gained a matt-black windscreen surround; this was dropped with the late-1970 restyle.
- A total of 314,342 Spitfires were made – against 355,888 Sprites and Midgets – the BMC cars, of course, being made over a longer period, the Sprite having been launched in 1958. Only in one year – 1969 – did the Spridget outsell the Spitfire. Over three-quarters of all Spitfires were exported, with a peak figure of 90.9 per cent being sold abroad – principally to the US – in 1979.
- The US Spitfires avoided the indignity of the Midget's rubber bumpers for most of their life, making do with ever-larger rubber over-riders instead, with the front licence-plate holder latterly also serving to give some impact protection. But from 1979 the 'Federal' Spitfire was forced to wear moulded plastic bumpers front and rear.

SPECIFICATION

Engine:	1147cc/1296cc/1493cc water-cooled in-line 4-cyl, ohv
Power:	63bhp at 5750rpm (MkI)/67bhp at 5000rpm) (MkII)/75bhp at 6000rpm (MkIII)/71bhp DIN at 5500rpm (1500)
Transmission:	four-speed gearbox; optional overdrive from 1963
Construction:	separate backbone chassis with steel body
Front suspension:	independent coil-and-wishbone; anti-roll bar; telescopic dampers
Rear suspension:	independent by swing-axle and transverse leaf spring; location by radius arms; lever-arm dampers
Steering:	rack-and-pinion
Brakes:	front discs and rear drum
Kerb weight:	14.25cwt (MkI); 15.9cwt (1500)

EVOLUTION

October 1962	Spitfire 4 introduced
September 1963	Overdrive and hardtop available
March 1965	Spitfire MkII introduced
October 1966	GT6 introduced
March 1967	Spitfire MkIII announced
October 1968	GT6 MkII introduced
October 1970	Spitfire MkIV and GT6 MkIII introduced
October 1972	US Spitfire receives 57bhp de-toxed 1500 engine
February 1973	Swing-spring IRS for GT6
December 1973	GT6 discontinued
November 1974	European-market Spitfire 1500 available
August 1980	Last Spitfire made

ABOVE The MkIV Spitfire lost the bonnet-top seams as well as gaining the new rear-end styling; there were also new door handles. In February 1973 the dashboard was given a wood facing.

VALE SPECIAL

Max Speed	64mph
0–60mph	37.6sec

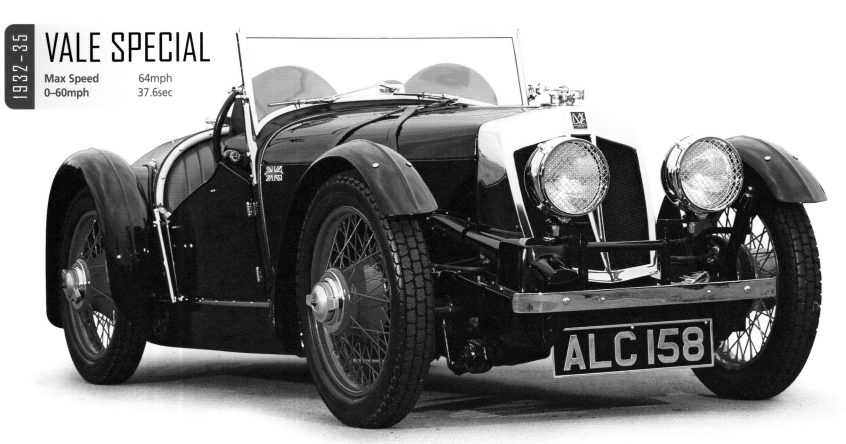

ABOVE The bulge on the front apron hides the steering box. The Vale certainly looks the part, but circumstances alas conspired against it.

BELOW Ian Connell in the one-off supercharged racing Vale; originally intended to be road-usable, it has two staggered seats. The car survived the war but then disappeared from view.

If you want to get a vintage purist in a lather, a good start is to mention the Vale Special. But then the Vale – of which an estimated 55–60 were made between 1932 and 1935 – does rather present an easy target. The trouble is that the little two-seater simply tried too hard, and was over-burdened with the boy-racer accoutrements of the day, from its exaggerated scuttle cowls to its soup-plate instruments, from its bold bonnet straps and quick-release filler caps to – crime of crimes – its dummy knock-on hubcaps. With its ultra-low build and helmet wings (the fronts moving with the steering), the Vale was too camp for its own good. The reality, however, is somewhat removed from the polemics: the Vale was in fact a car not without virtue.

Named after the Maida Vale area of London where it was

built, the Vale was the brainchild of the Hon Pownoll Pellew, latterly the ninth Viscount Exmouth, assisted by Allan Gaspar, a one-time member of the Frazer Nash trials team. Unhappy with the handling of small sports cars of the day – was he perhaps thinking of the sports Austin Sevens? – Pellew built an Austin-powered prototype, with the unusual feature of a chassis that was underslung at both ends. Praised for its roadholding, this ultra-short-wheelbase concoction led to the announcement in September 1932 of the altogether more elegant Vale Special, using the engine, gearbox and low-slung worm-drive rear axle of the 832cc Triumph Super Eight – along with the Triumph's advanced hydraulic braking system.

The sidevalve Triumph engine normally developed a

THE RACING VALE

Whilst there might have been reservations about the performance of the regular Triumph-engined model, no such quibbles could be made of the racing Vale Special built in 1935 for Cambridge undergraduate Ian Connell. Fitted with a 1496cc version of the Coventry Climax inlet-over-exhaust engine, boosted by a Centric supercharger, the boat-tailed Vale was good for over 100mph. The chassis was standard Vale, but with the unusual feature of dual drop arms and two lateral steering links instead of the normal transverse track rod; this supposedly gave steering reactions similar to those of a car with independent front suspension. Intended to showcase Vale's policy of building cars to the customer's specification, the racer remained a one-off, although Vale did offer to build replicas at £625 a time. By this time, in May 1935, the company had wound down, so the idea of using any engine the customer wished never came to fruition.

slender 21.5bhp, but The Vale Motor Co stripped the three-main-bearing unit and balanced it, polished the ports, and raised the compression ratio, before reassembling it with special valves and springs, more efficient manifolding, and a downdraught SU carburettor. Meanwhile, the aluminium-panelled body was built around a rigid cast-aluminium bulkhead and a frame of steel angle-iron, and so was stiffer than the average timber-framed body of the time. Other details included a Vale-made straight-tube axle, a neat remote change for the four-speed gearbox, and a steering box unusually positioned forward of the front axle.

The result was a car that had exceptionally safe and flat roadholding, and more than adequate performance: despite weighing nearly 2cwt more than an MG J2, the Vale was faster from 20mph to 40mph in third and barely slower from 30mph to 50mph, even if its top speed was inferior.

With the Vale priced close to the MG, a full order book soon developed, but then disaster struck. Pellew went down with tuberculosis and retired to a Swiss sanatorium, and then the third partner was sidelined after being injured in a racing accident. Production fell off, orders were cancelled, and car assembly was halted. A new company was set up, and it was hoped to raise capital to re-start manufacture. This never came about, and after a final car, with an 1100cc Coventry Climax engine, had left the works in mid 1935, the brave little Vale Special was no more.

I DIDN'T KNOW THAT...

- 'All customers are measured for their cars, if required, at no extra charge,' proclaimed the sales catalogue, stating that the company was the first 'in the lower-priced car ranges' to offer 'Tailor Made Motoring'.
- A four-seater Vale, the Tourette, was offered, but only 4–6 were made – there were concerns that the car would be unacceptably slow when travelling four-up.
- Plans for a larger-engined model, the Vixen, never came to fruition. But after manufacture had stopped, Vale announced that for £150 it would fit customer vehicles with an 1100cc engine – the inlet-over-exhaust Coventry Climax unit. The price included a re-paint, new tyres, and a year's guarantee. Other engines could also be fitted: at least one car received a 1242cc Meadows unit.
- A Vale completed the 1934 Monte Carlo Rally without losing a single point on a road section. The car averaged 43.5mpg and 41.5mph.
- Allan Gaspar won a gold in the MCC One-Hour High-Speed Trial at Brooklands in 1933, achieving 65.26mph, two-up, in a road-equipped Vale.
- Vale used to demonstrate the car's handling qualities by powering off down the road, swinging the car round a lamp-post without lifting the throttle, and then continuing back to base. 'If the customer did not collapse with a nervous breakdown he usually paid for a Vale on the spot,' recounts Bill Boddy in *The Sports Car Pocketbook*.
- Presumably because someone from the company owned a Vale, one features in the mid-1930s sales catalogue for Raven caravans – making it surely one of the most unusual of tow-cars.

ABOVE Underslung at both ends, the Vale is indeed very low, as this on-the-road photo shows. The rear treatment, with the spare wheel recessed into the barrel-tail, is unusual but effective.

SPECIFICATION

Engine:	832cc water-cooled in-line 4-cyl; sidevalve
Power:	output not quoted
Transmission:	four-speed gearbox; no synchromesh
Construction:	separate chassis, underslung front and rear; aluminium body over steel frame
Front suspension:	beam axle with semi-elliptic leaf springs; friction dampers
Rear suspension:	worm-drive live axle with leaf springs; friction dampers
Steering:	cam-and-peg
Brakes:	drum, hydraulic
Kerb weight:	13cwt

EVOLUTION

September 1932	Vale Special announced
Summer 1934	Last production cars made
	Company reformed as Vale Engineering Co Ltd
September 1934	Larger engines available as retro-fit
Early 1935	Final Vale leaves works

BELOW The omelette over-egged: for a little 832cc sports car the huge soup-plate dials are striking, to say the least – as are the dimensions of the scuttle cowls.

VAUXHALL 30/98

Max Speed	85mph
0–60mph	19sec

ABOVE This OE, with the overhead-valve engine, carries the rare Wensum door-less sports body. The nautical vee-screen is matched to an unusual reverse-raked dashboard.

If you want to attach a label to the 30/98, the most apt is The Last Edwardian. For this is a car that was indeed first seen before the First World War, but which continued until well into the Vintage period, keeping to the end certain features that were indubitably pre-WW1 in flavour.

The most salient of these is an engine which in spite of its capacity of over four litres is only a four-cylinder unit – although the same can be said of the 4½-litre Bentley. Another is a chassis that is somewhat less than adequately rigid. But it is these two elements, in particular, that give the Vauxhall its appeal, as taken together they endow the 30/98 with a power-to-weight ratio that results in truly impressive performance. With 90bhp in a car weighing 24cwt, the original 4½-litre E-type model was good for 85mph and a 0–60mph time of 19 seconds – phenomenal figures for the time, and achieved with a fixed-head

sidevalve engine with exposed valve springs that was pure Edwardian in its conception.

The 30/98 was first seen in 1913, and a short production run was laid down before war stopped play – at an impressive £900 for the chassis alone. In essence the newcomer was a Prince Henry fitted with a new and larger engine. This was in response to a customer's request for a car swift enough to triumph at Shelsley Walsh, and the prototype duly set a record for the hillclimb that was to stand for 15 years.

Reintroduced post-WW1, the sidevalve 30/98 was replaced in 1923 by the OE model, which featured an overhead-valve engine of 4224cc. This was a cut above the average pushrod unit of the time, featuring exceptionally large valves, double valve springs, and roller-rockers to increase valve lift; reciprocating weight was kept down

RIGHT The Prince Henry, with its characteristic pointed prow, was the starting-point for the 30/98. This very early example, with four-seat tourer coachwork, is preserved by Vauxhall.

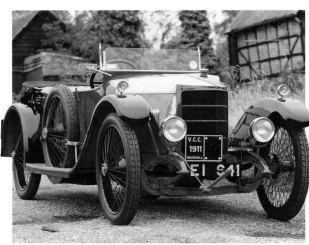

THE VAUXHALL PRINCE HENRY

The 30/98's progenitor was the Prince Henry model of 1911–14, a car that is sometimes put forward as Britain's first sports car: certainly it was both fast on the road and effective in pre-WWI competition. The 'Henry' was derived from three special 20hp models that successfully completed Germany's arduous Prince Henry reliability trial in 1910. Although the cars didn't win, they were timed at over 70mph, which for a sidevalve 3-litre engine of the time wasn't bad going. The production model was unveiled in October 1911, featuring the same elegant pointed nose as found on the trio of works cars and carrying four-seat tourer coachwork. Other body styles were available, and from 1912 the Vauxhall used a 4-litre engine developing a robust 75bhp. It is thought roughly 190 examples of the Prince Henry were built, of which 50 or so had the smaller engine.

by using aluminium con-rods and pushrods. Less massively torquey and more refined than the old 4½-litre unit, this sturdy engine revved easily and pushed out a strong 112bhp – which put a certain demand on the brakes, which were only on the rear wheels, with a foot-operated transmission brake.

Vauxhall soon saw the error of its ways, and from the end of 1923 the foot brake also operated cable-actuated front drums via a convoluted mechanism housed in a so-called 'kidney-box' between the dumb-irons. In late 1926, by which time Vauxhall had been taken over by General Motors, a crude hydraulic system was in use – but by this stage the 30/98 was only being made in occasional batches, and the last cars were completed in early 1927. Latterly they had a more robust balanced crankshaft, resulting in a genuinely smooth engine for a 'big four' – along with a healthy 120bhp power output.

Mostly sold with Vauxhall's own Velox tourer coachwork, the 30/98 combines effortless performance with precise steering and a four-speed gearbox that is easier to manipulate than that of a contemporary Bentley. Such are its virtues that it has been dubbed 'one of the greatest cars of all time'; no wonder it is a cornerstone of the Vintage Sports-Car Club.

I DIDN'T KNOW THAT...

■ The 30/98 was massively expensive. In 1921 a Velox cost £1675, when a Morris Oxford tourer cost £590; the first Bentley 3-litres, available from late 1921, were priced at £1350 in open tourer form.

■ Vauxhall guaranteed 100mph from a 30/98 stripped for racing. Additional to this, some special racers were built, and campaigned at Brooklands and elsewhere.

■ WO Bentley confessed his admiration for the 30/98, which he recognised as the closest rival to his cars and as having superior acceleration and top speed to a 3-litre Bentley. But his cars had better braking and roadholding, and were thus faster across country, he said – while admitting that the idea of the Vauxhall engine in a Bentley chassis had a certain appeal...

■ As well as the Velox tourer, from 1924 Vauxhall also offered a raffish boat-tailed open four-seater with a vee screen and door-less coachwork, called the Wensum. Only a dozen were built, to special order. Various other styles were offered by house coachbuilder Grosvenor, including some closed bodies; most 30/98s, however, wore open coachwork.

■ Post-WWI production of the 30/98 amounted to 586 cars: 274 E-types and 312 OE-types. Peak annual production was 112 cars, in 1924, and thereafter 30/98s were only made in small batches, with only 23 leaving Luton in 1926 and 27 the following year.

■ More than half of all 30/98s made were sold in Australia. The global figure for survivors is in the order of 170 cars.

■ The designer of the 30/98, Lawrence Pomeroy, latterly experimented with an overhead-cam engine for the car; he also initiated a 3½-litre sidevalve V12.

SPECIFICATION

Engine:	4525cc (E-type)/4224cc (OE) water-cooled in-line 4-cyl; sidevalve (E-type) or ohv (OE)
Power:	90 bhp at 3000rpm (E-type)/112bhp at 3300rpm/120bhp at 3500rpm (OE)
Transmission:	four-speed unsynchronised; separate from engine
Construction:	separate chassis; wooden-framed body
Front suspension:	beam axle with semi-elliptic leaf springs; latterly friction dampers
Rear suspension:	live axle with leaf springs; location by torque arm; latterly friction dampers
Steering:	worm-and-wheel
Brakes:	rear drums, mechanically operated (handbrake) and transmission brake (footbrake); front drums (footbrake) from 1923, mechanically operated; hydraulic front and transmission brakes from 1926
Kerb weight:	24cwt (E-type tourer); 29cwt (OE tourer)

EVOLUTION

June 1913	Prototype 30/98 breaks record at Shelsley Walsh
Late 1913	Limited production authorised
December 1919	E-type deliveries begin
September 1922	Last E-type
Early 1923	First OE-series cars
September 1923	Front brakes introduced, initially as option
May 1924	Wensum introduced
Early 1925	Conterbalanced crankshaft
Late 1926	Hydraulic front and transmission brakes; new (close-ratio) gearbox
November 1926	Final batch of 30/98s laid down
Early 1927	Last car completed

BELOW Carrying the regular Velox body, this 30/98 still lacks front-wheel brakes, which only became available in late 1923. Even with four-wheel braking, though, stopping the 30-98 demands anticipation.

WOLSELEY HORNET SPECIAL

Max Speed 74mph*
0–60mph 21sec*
* 14hp EW Daytona

ABOVE Carrying one of the most popular body styles for the Wolseley, this is a 1934 Eustace Watkins International four-seat tourer.

BELOW Somewhat like a sports Balilla Fiat, this 'Continental' two-seater was offered in 1932 by Fox and Nicholl, better known for its racing Lagondas, and was bodied by Abbey Coachworks.

There will be more than a few old-stagers who will raise an eyebrow at the inclusion in these pages of the Wolseley Hornet Special. The Wolseley is not a real sports car, they will say, but a parody of one – a car for the 'Promenade Percy' of the 1930s who knew no better. With its bogus sporting paraphernalia it was the sort of car that drove such shuddering purists to form that defenders-of-the-faith union the Vintage Sports-Car Club: to one of its leading lights the Hornet from which it derived was 'technical pornography'.

Admittedly the car was a bit of a bastard. As launched in 1930 the original three-speed Hornet was little more than a Morris Minor with a skinny chassis long enough to take a six-cylinder version of the Minor's Wolseley-designed overhead-cam 'four': in engineering terms it wasn't very clever, but its torquey little 1271cc engine gave easy gearchange-free performance and the chassis provided an affordably tempting base for every coachbuilder in the land to ply his trade by giving the Wolseley bespoke bodywork.

In 1932 came the Hornet Special. Only available in chassis form, it could be as much or as little a sports car as the client wished, but the basic ingredients were certainly provided. There were twin SU carburettors on a special manifold, a raised compression ratio, double valve springs, an oil cooler, a remote-control change for the four-speed gearbox standardised in late 1931, larger ribbed drums for the hydraulic brakes, a generously-sized speedo and matching rev-counter, and the option of knock-off wire wheels.

Give such mechanicals a sports body, such as those offered

HORNET SPECIAL COACHWORK

The Hornet Special was almost certainly unique among run-of-the-mill models in being offered only in chassis form – traditionally such a practice was the preserve of upper-crust manufacturers such as – in particular – Rolls-Royce. Many of the styles offered were carried over from those available on the ordinary Hornet, or were offered additionally on the cheaper and less sporting chassis, and some were extremely attractive. The author has counted 33 different body designs, and happily accepts that there will be more he has missed. Most common were those offered by Swallow, the EWs sold by Wolseley distributor Eustace Watkins but generally made by Whittingham and Mitchel, and those by Abbey and by Kent coachbuilder Maltby's. Additionally Jensen offered various styles, including a coupé with unusual triangular rear side windows, and there were various oddities that probably remained one-offs, such as the slab-sided Parallite with its fitted suitcases in the front wings.

by Eustace Watkins or Swallow, and you had what the average punter would certainly regard as a sports car, even if it didn't have the crisp, well-honed nature of its MG blood-brothers. 'It is a most seductive motor car,' wrote *The Autocar* in its test of a Eustace Watkins Hornet. 'The car handles as lightly as a feather, runs as sweetly as a pleasant dream, and in every respect of roadworthiness is a pure delight'. That might have been a bit namby-pamby for the future guardians of the VSCC temple, but it hardly suggests a car of signal incompetence.

For 1934 the engine gained a crossflow head, and the gearbox was given synchromesh on third and top and a freewheel, while a new longer-wheelbase cruciform chassis was introduced – underslung at the rear. All this made the Hornet Special a better car, but the headlamp and grille stoneguards, twin exhaust pipes and quick-release filler-cap still part of the package smacked of over-egging the omelette. For its final few months the Hornet Special was given a 1604cc engine developing 50bhp, or 5bhp more than the 1934 model.

In all, something in the order of 3500 Hornet Specials were made, over three years, which compares with 1826 MG Magnas and 1110 roadgoing Magnettes in a period closer to five years. That suggests that the car struck a chord with the public – and they can't all have been idiots.

I DIDN'T KNOW THAT...

- At its launch the original Hornet was the UK's cheapest six-cylinder car. Its two-door fabric-covered or coachbuilt saloon body was virtually identical to that of the Morris Minor. For 1932 the engine was moved forward, allowing Wolseley to offer a four-door saloon body.
- The Hornet and Hornet Special always had hydraulic brakes – something of which contemporary MGs couldn't boast.
- Although the Hornet engine began life with shaft-and-bevel drive for its overhead camshaft, in the style of the Morris and MG units, for 1932 it went over to chain drive.
- The Wolseley Hornet Special was favoured by such respected lady racing drivers as Kay Petre and Margaret Allan. Male owners included none other than Lionel Martin, co-founder of Aston Martin.
- The Hornet Special was launched with the slogan 'Speed with Safety' – an interesting mirroring of MG's 'Safety Fast' motto.
- Among those offering bodies for the Hornet Special was Jensen, then starting out as a coachbuilder.
- Highly-developed racing specials based on the Wolseley have been successful in VSCC events – doubtless to the chagrin of the purists.
- The Hornet saloon outlived the Special, lasting until April 1936; from May 1935 it had a 1378cc engine. For 1934 it was joined by a four-cylinder variant, the Nine, latterly renamed the Wasp.
- The Hornet Special by no means disgraced itself in competition. One notable result was a team winning the July 1932 International Relay Race at Brooklands. That year 19 Hornets entered the MCC Lands End Trial, eight gaining Premier Awards.

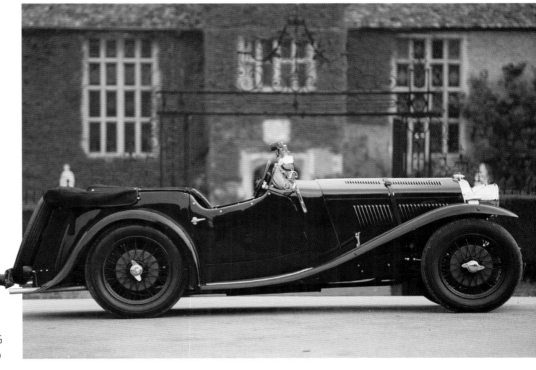

ABOVE A late Hornet Special, from 1934, with the 1604cc engine, this example has Eustace Watkins Daytona four-seater coachwork – in fact built by Whittingham and Mitchel.

SPECIFICATION

Engine:	1271cc/1604cc water-cooled in-line 6-cyl; ohc
Power:	45bhp at 4500rpm (1934 model)/50bhp at 4500rpm (1604cc)
Transmission:	four-speed gearbox; synchro on third and fourth and freewheel for 1934 only
Construction:	cruciform chassis, underslung from 1934 model year; body generally steel/ally over wood frame
Front suspension:	beam axle and semi-elliptic leaf springs; friction or hydraulic lever-arm dampers, depending on year
Rear suspension:	live back axle on leaf springs; friction or hydraulic lever-arm dampers, depending on year
Steering:	worm-and-segment
Brakes:	all-drum, hydraulic
Kerb weight:	17.25cwt (14hp EW Daytona)

EVOLUTION

April 1930	Wolseley Hornet announced
September 1930	Chassis available for coachbuilders; new factory two-door saloons
September 1931	New chassis; chain-drive camshaft; four-speed gearbox; four-door saloon, Morris-bodied coupé and chassis offered
April 1932	Hornet Special introduced – chassis only
August 1932	Improved steering and suspension
August 1933	Underslung cruciform chassis; part-synchro gearbox and freewheel; crossflow cylinder head; restyled saloon body for Hornet
August 1934	Three-speed pre-selector gearbox (not Hornet Special)
November 1934	14hp Hornet Special introduced
May 1935	New 1378cc model; Hornet Special discontinued
April 1936	Hornet discontinued

INDEX